TECHNOLOGY AND ENVIRONMENT
in North American History

Preliminary Edition

Jean-Louis Trudel
University of Ottawa

Kendall Hunt
publishing company

Cover image © Hulton-Deutsch Collection/CORBIS

Kendall Hunt
publishing company

www.kendallhunt.com
Send all inquiries to:
4050 Westmark Drive
Dubuque, IA 52004-1840

Copyright © 2014 by Jean-Louis Trudel

ISBN 978-1-4652-4266-2

Kendall Hunt Publishing Company has the exclusive rights to reproduce this work,
to prepare derivative works from this work, to publicly distribute this work,
to publicly perform this work and to publicly display this work.

All rights reserved. No part of this publication may be reproduced,
stored in a retrieval system, or transmitted, in any form or by any
means, electronic, mechanical, photocopying, recording, or otherwise,
without the prior written permission of the copyright owner.

Printed in Canada
10 9 8 7 6 5 4 3 2 1

CONTENTS

Preface v
Introduction ix

CHAPTER 1: Defining Technology 1

CHAPTER 2: The Environmental Human and the Human Environment . . . 17

CHAPTER 3: Launching a Revolution 33

CHAPTER 4: Canals, Raftsmen, and Snakeheads 53

CHAPTER 5: Railroads: An Iron and Steel Web 73

CHAPTER 6: The Age of Systems 99

CHAPTER 7: The One Best Way to Mass Production 127

CHAPTER 8: In the Year of Our Ford: The Automobile Era 141

CHAPTER 9: Mass Consumption and Technology in Daily Life 161

CHAPTER 10: The Atomic Age 177

CHAPTER 11: Remote Control: The Information Revolution 197

CHAPTER 12: Modern Technology and the Ecological Threshold 211

CHAPTER 13: Biotechnology: Old and New 243

PREFACE

The story of technology in North America cannot be disentangled from the evolution of society and the changing environment. For millennia, technology was one of the means with which human society coped with a hostile environment, beset by long winters and freezing cold in the north, parched landscapes and stormy weather in the south, and an abundance of untameable wildlife that was both bounty and menace. Before the arrival of Europeans, North American societies had achieved some measure of hard-won control over their immediate environment, though they remained at the mercy of shifting climates. One consequence of European settlement was the disappearance of crucial evidence of earlier occupation. What is certain is that the powerful new technologies brought to bear by European settlers on the natural landscape wrought a transformation that surpassed anything carried out previously and that they continue to affect the natural environment. Technology has been a pervasive presence in human affairs since prehistoric times, but the last couple of centuries have seen artifacts mediate more and more relationships within society.

The bulk of this book is devoted to the period during which technological change most affected social structures, human ties, and the broader environment. Since technology may be understood as any useful organization of existing resources, very little is off the table. Innovation changed the way North Americans eat, farm, work, travel, run their businesses, live at home, take care of their health, build houses and cities, make war, and have fun. Technology is not only electronic or mechanical; it extends to the manipulation of living organisms and to immaterial arrangements of productive activities in the workplace.

The causal relationships are often mutual and reciprocal. The evolution of technology cannot be understood without considering intellectual ideals, social mores, shared esthetics, and the power of mass opinion. Some technologies may not have the same significance outside of their original circumstances: a snowmobile is a utility vehicle in the Arctic, but an exotic curio in Arizona. The natural environment responds to human action, sometimes with utterly unintended consequences. The disappearance by the turn of the twentieth century of the Rocky Mountain grasshopper, which had once formed enormous locust swarms in the western Prairies, was probably caused by plowing and irrigation pursued by farmers who did not realize they were driving an insect species into extinction. While links are often clear, as between the invention of the birth control pill and changes in the status of women, the direction of the link is not always clear. The debate over technological determinism has abated as scholars have abandoned extreme positions, but the question of technology's autonomy is still worth pondering. On the one hand, the internet was not developed specifically to compete with the post office, and yet it is forcing the postal services in Canada and the United States to redefine their business operations. On the other hand, the triumph of certain technologies often depends on economic *lock-in*, independently of their technical merits, which happens when a sufficient number of investors or consumers commit early on to a brand or format and turn it into a default choice, as occurred with personal computers running Windows. In many cases, definitive answers are scarce, but understanding several sides of an issue is often the key to asking better questions.

The book's sections follow a roughly chronological path, but each is principally devoted to a given theme, so that overlap is to be expected. Conventional historical themes include key breakthroughs, the playing-out of so-called industrial revolutions, the transformation (with consequences) of transportation and communications, the rise of technological systems, the evolution of public attitudes about technological progress, the relationship between science and technology, and the role of public versus private funding in advancing technology. Some of these may be tracked from one section to the next. Environmental themes include the manifold impacts of the technologies wielded by industrializing societies, the evolving awareness of the environmental costs of everyday activities, and the ongoing debate about the stewardship humans should assume over the planet's fate.

During the last two centuries, the United States has been a fount of new technological developments. By the late nineteenth century, it rivalled the great powers of Europe with respect to the scope of mechanization and industrialization, though Europeans retained an edge in terms of sophistication and the partnering of science with technology. By the middle years of the twentieth century, the United States reigned supreme in most technical fields, with no true peers anywhere else in the world.

Canada didn't stand apart from these developments. Its inventors and entrepreneurs played key roles in the story of some ground-breaking technologies beyond the well-known example of insulin. Alexander Graham Bell tested and perfected the telephone in Ontario. A new process for distilling a key component of nineteenth-century oil lamps, kerosene, was patented by Abraham Gesner from Nova Scotia and it removed one economic rationale for hunting whales, which had been slaughtered to produce oil for lamps. In radio, amplitude modulation was invented by Quebec-born Reginald Fessenden. The use of quartz oscillators for timekeeping was pioneered by yet another Canadian, Warren Marrison. While Canada's proximity to the United States meant that its best talent often headed for the bright lights of a huge, open market offering more risk capital and better facilities, it also meant that Canada could often be an early adopter of technologies developed in the United States. Steamboats ran on the St. Lawrence within a couple of years of Fulton's demonstration on the Hudson. The completion of a Canadian transcontinental railroad in 1885, only sixteen years after the first in the United States, was a major feat for a much smaller and newer country. While the spread of electronic televisions was relatively slow in Canada due to political dithering, it was still fast enough to put Canada in the third rank of adopters worldwide by the mid-1950s. Such cases illustrate the complexities of technology transfer. Outside of the United States, most countries have faced within living memory the problem of playing catch-up when another country forges a technological lead in a given field.

As a result, the purpose of this book is broader than most. Not only does it attempt to tell the rich story of technology in North America since 1800, it will also strive to integrate a social and environmental dimension. Furthermore, it will try to indicate in what ways the Canadian experience of technology may have differed from the version in the United States. Some details may be sacrificed in order to gain a better understanding of outcomes at every point in time.

What is certain is that technology does not act for itself. Adopting or rejecting a technology is the result of human choices, responding to political forces, legal arguments, psychological factors, and so on. In most cases, there are winners and losers. One generation's celebrated, independent inventors may become the next generation's marginal loners while organized teamwork and research laboratories flourish—until innovation is outsourced to precarious start-ups or offshored to facilities outside North America. In almost every era, hard-won, specialized skills have become obsolete as a result of new technologies or the mechanization of human work to the detriment of the workers themselves. Gender, racial, and linguistic divides as well have been reflected in the degree of control individuals enjoyed over various technologies. To what extent were they able to shape them or resist the unwanted ones? While such differences were clearly a function of available wealth, social circumstances, and prevailing ideologies, they did not always happen without a struggle.

Indeed, the realization that those responsible for inventing and deploying new technologies could not be trusted blindly, not even when they invoked the authority of science, has become part of North American history. While optimism reigned about technology for much of the period covered here, the skeptical turn of recent decades may have become in and of itself a force to be reckoned with in the future development of technologies. Large technological undertakings for the collective good have become less popular than small, individualized technologies catering to the minutia of our everyday lives. The environmental and human costs of technological innovation have become part of the story, and this book will try to explore how a substantial minority of the North American population began to actively oppose certain technologies or at least favour alternatives.

INTRODUCTION

Why should technology interest us?
Technology separates us from the world and technology connects us to the world. Some of the most basic technologies, such as clothing and shelter, protect us from the environment by endowing us with the equivalent of another skin. They keep the elements at one further remove. Technologies like fire, tools, and weapons also come between us and the environment. They are easily seen as extensions of our natural abilities. The heat of fire, when applied to raw meat and vegetables, essentially begins the process of digestion by softening or breaking down cell walls, sparing the human gut from having to do the same or offering more easily assimilated calories. A stone used as a hammer makes it possible to apply greater force as a result of its added mass and insensibility to pain. Add a stick to create a stone hatchet and additional leverage is gained as well. A wooden spear makes it possible to strike from a greater distance and with greater force than with either teeth or nails.

Canadian theorist Marshall McLuhan classified many technologies as media because they mediate between our naked selves and the surrounding world. While they allow for a greater engagement with the environment, opening up new sources of food, of energy, and of building materials, such technologies also interpose new layers between us and the natural world. As our artifacts multiply, they become, in effect, another world with which we interact, more present than the weather or the shrinking pockets of true wilderness.

The world of human interactions has long earned the attention of historians, sociologists, psychologists, and economists. Similarly, the natural world is studied by natural scientists, including physicists, biologists, chemists, and ecologists. In turn, the world of technology deserves our attention as a result of its interactions with both the human world and the natural world.

The character of its interactions is often distinctive, marked by complexities that have sparked intense debate. Is technology just the application of science? Is it entirely subservient to the intentions of its makers and users? Is it a mere reflection of the priorities of political power?

What is clear is that technology now dominates nearly all aspect of our lives, from birth in the sterile surroundings of modern hospitals to the last moments of a body hooked up to sensors and communication devices. Understanding technology is, in the end, very much about understanding the North American way of life.

CHAPTER 1

Defining Technology

▶▶▶▶▶▶▶▶▶▶▶▶▶▶▶▶▶▶▶▶▶▶▶▶▶▶▶▶

One reason why technology seems like a hallmark of the modern world is that the word itself and its current sense are themselves modern. Before the latter half of the twentieth century, the word was not generally understood in the same way. A dizzying variety of expressions were used instead to talk about technology, from industrial arts to "technics" (distinct from techniques).

If the evolution of the word is instructive, so is the history of the concept of technology. Using a single word for such a complex human activity and its diverse results was not an obvious step. It is surely worth asking whether the unity presupposed by the use of the single word technology is more apparent than real.

THE HISTORY OF THE WORD

The concept of technology is surprisingly recent. The first clue comes from the very history of the word, which has two Greek roots. *Techne* is, perhaps surprisingly, the word for art. *Logos* has several meanings: word, discourse, or theory. When Aristotle speaks of technology, he actually means the "rules of the art (of speech)," what we might today call a rhetoric. So how did we go from a system of (rhetorical) knowledge to the study of technics, and then to the concrete apparatus of our modern technical societies?

Though the word's roots are ancient, it gained new meaning in modern times. In the sixteenth century, the word is still found to refer to the art of speaking about a subject, sometimes to a subject's terminology, or to any sort of general discourse about an art. It took a different reading of those Greek roots to turn *techno-logy* into the *theory* of the (productive) *arts*. This happened over a period of a century that, unsurprisingly, coincides more or less with the Industrial Revolution which started in the late eighteenth century.

In 1706, the *Phillips Dictionary* defines technology as "A Description of Arts, especially Mechanical." In 1728, German philosopher Christian Wolff defines it in Latin as the "*Scientia artis et operum artis*" (the knowledge of the arts and of their products). He adds that it must be understood as the science of things that men produce by the work of their body, especially their hands.

As the first engineering and technical schools were set up in France and Germany, it became necessary to define, at the very least, what would be taught. This led to the use of *technology* as a word describing the study and theory of the useful arts. The 1777 *Anleitung zur Technologie* by German professor Johann Beckmann defines technology as the science that teaches the processing of natural materials or the knowledge of crafts.

A final bit of slippage happened at this point, so that the word began to be applied no longer to the theory of the practical and useful arts, but to these arts themselves.

THE HISTORY OF THE CONCEPT

In Ancient Greece, the practical and useful arts were initially called *mechanical*. The Greek word *mechanè* was understood to be a solution to a problem, a quickly shaped plan, a scheme that could verge on outright deception. It could be a ruse, a trick, even a plot. In short, a *mechanè* was the embodiment of cunning, it was intelligence in action, it was the *praxis* of intelligence. And *praxis* is the Greek word most closely related to such words as *practice* and *practical*.

In essence, the mechanical arts demonstrated a combination of manual skill or dexterity (necessary to turn them to good use) and of a form of intelligence known as craftiness (necessary to come up with new objects and solutions). A potter required skill to handle the clay, shape it, and gauge the heat needed to fire it. The potter also needed to be crafty to come up with new shapes and solve problems that might arise in the making of an object.

The mechanical arts soon suffered from their association with slaves and tradesmen. The aristocratic Greek philosophers such as Plato and Xenophon came to consider them base and vulgar—*banausic* was the word—because the practitioners of such arts, who worked for a living, had to work all day and could not devote any time to philosophical discussions or democratic debates. Aristotle offered a more positive evaluation by talking of the "productive" arts, whose products sustained the life of the body (if not the life of the mind).

Throughout Antiquity, however, the divide endured between the banausic arts and the activities thought to be more praiseworthy. The Roman aristocrat Cicero contrasted the *liberal* trades, such as medicine, architecture, and agriculture which were practiced by free men (hence the adjective liberal, since these men enjoyed *liberty*), with the *sordid* trades which included usury, tax collecting, retailing, manual labour, and most mechanical arts. The liberal trades often entailed knowledge of the liberal arts, such as music, geometry, and history.

This opposition has come down to us in the form of a divide between the fine arts (music, poetry, painting, architecture, and sculpture) and the other productive arts, which are implicitly considered vulgar because they are not thought to demand the same refinements as the *beaux-arts*. These vulgar, banausic or productive arts comprise what were usually called in English the arts and crafts.

The medieval encyclopaedias grouped the different arts and crafts under similar headings. These subdivisions were basically defined by the arts and crafts they included. There was no general conception of what might be a common characteristic or unifying trait of such disparate activities. It was only when new arts and crafts started to develop that this became a problem. If the individual arts and crafts were not stable categories, forever limited in number, it meant that they were manifestations of a larger phenomenon. Once technology shifted from being an art of speaking about a subject to being a theory of the arts, it soon changed as well to mean the productive arts in general because a need for a general term was being felt more and more.

At the same time, as new arts and crafts multiplied, the need to master them led to a push for technical education as part of national agendas for economic development. In England and France, this included the development of patent systems to grant inventors short-term monopolies or other forms of encouragement. In France and the German states, schools were founded to train engineers, technicians, and technically-skilled managers. In the German states, this was part of the doctrine known as *cameralism*, which pushed the princely courts to intervene in the economy to improve the state's prosperity. The *cameral* schools taught civil servants the basics of financial management, but also touched on topics concerning the crafts and the associated guilds, factories, and economic growth.

The ideal of applying science to daily life, first articulated by Francis Bacon, drove many of these initiatives in the wake of what is sometimes known as the Scientific

Revolution in the seventeenth century. The enthusiasm for method, obvious in many fields such as the military, the sciences, and early statistics, led philosophers studying the arts and the scholars charged with teaching a broad knowledge of art to seek a theory, which came to be known as *technology* (a science of the arts) in the specialized circles dealing with technical education. In practice, this new "technology" encompassed writings on technics, technical treatises, and discussions of the practical arts.

Since there was no word for the productive arts in general, technology easily came to be applied to those arts themselves. In the United States or Canada, the word was seldom used in that sense before 1880. In 1861, the founding of the Massachusetts Institute of Technology reflected the beginning of a shift: earlier engineering schools had been called, for instance, "polytechnics," such as the Rensselaer Polytechnic Institute modelled on the École Polytechnique (1794) in Paris. In Canada, the precursor to the Faculty of Engineering at the University of Toronto was the School of Practical Science. The phrase "practical science" clearly reflected a need for a term that would be more general than engineering and that would also express the novelty of an increasing number of technical occupations. Another common phrase of the time, "applied science," reflected the same belief that the useful arts were the result of a common process: the application to practice of the systematic knowledge about the world gathered under the heading of science.

In effect, the word's further evolution in the nineteenth century to refer to the practical arts taken collectively reveals the realization that the individual arts and crafts of old were spawning new ways of doing things, all of which shared a common set of methods, goals, and outlooks in spite of their many differences.

TELLING THE HISTORY OF TECHNOLOGY

The earliest historians of technology, even before it was known as such, wished to chronicle the discovery or development of new arts and inventions. In Antiquity, Pliny the Elder wrote up the first listing of inventions and inventors as Book VII of his *Natural History*. Many of the inventors were semi-legendary figures or even minor gods. In medieval Europe, few scholars seemed to think their contemporaries might have come up with improvements on the technologies of Antiquity.

It wasn't until the fifteenth century that historians such as Giovanni Tortelli (1449) and Polydore Vergil (1499) began adding newer inventions to the ancient lists. Yet, they still mostly attempted to pin down the person responsible for a new piece of technology and the moment of its invention. Giving credit where credit was due was thought to be a good way to stimulate new inventors who would be assured of due recognition for their accomplishments. It was also clear to those early craftsmen and inventors that recognizing the efforts of their predecessors allowed them to make an even clearer and greater claim to originality and genius when they presented new technologies as their own inventions.

The modern patent system evolved out of this concern for priority of invention and for the associated recognition of inventors. The number of inventions recorded by the US patent system over the last two centuries (**Figure 1**) illustrates the continuing importance of inventions and explains why the history of technology remained for the most part a history of inventions until the late nineteenth century. Even today, we often tell the story of past technologies as a story of heroic inventors overcoming many obstacles in the course of perfecting a new and better mousetrap.

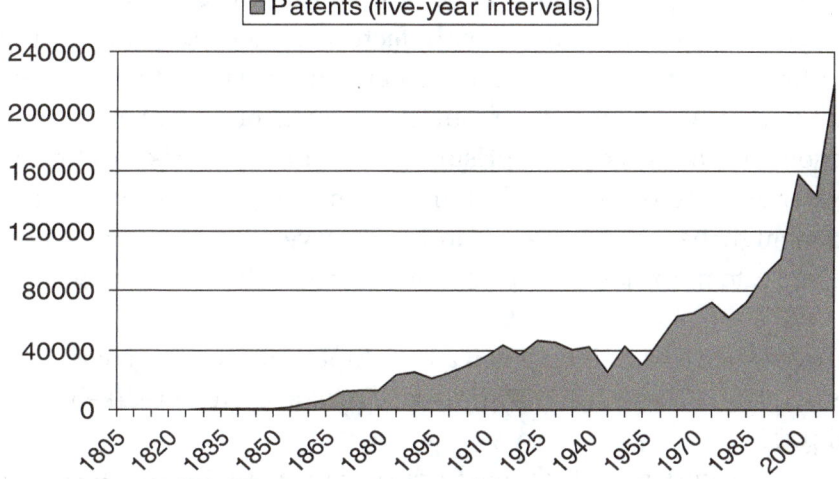

FIGURE 1 ▶ Over the course of two centuries, the number of patents awarded for useful inventions has increased to levels that reduce early totals to invisibility. *(Data source: United States Patent Office.)*

Nevertheless, as these new inventions affected the lives of more and more people and required more and more people to make them work, it became clear that any history of technology that focused only on the bright idea of the original inventor was incomplete. The pioneers of anthropology and archaeology were already showing that prehistoric cultures could be associated with distinctive sets of tools and studying the effect of a so-called primitive society's technical equipment on its culture. However, the values of the Western tradition were largely held to stand apart from the evolution of technology until historians such as Lewis Mumford (1934) began to tie together the social contexts of Western civilization with the achievements of inventors, engineers, and industrialists. The relationship between technical forces and social institutions was now presented as reciprocal and multi-faceted, which meant that technology might not only be shaped by technical specialists, but also by politicians, religious potentates, merchants, generals, and many other categories of users.

Furthermore, another realization of twentieth-century historians was that breakthrough inventions often needed to be nurtured, adapted, and turned into *technological systems* to be truly effective. A technological system incorporates a number of component parts required to work together to achieve a single, overarching purpose.

In some cases, a single invention or new design could be neatly slotted into the space occupied by its predecessor. The American axe was a specific design that did not really require new materials or manufacturing processes, though it made the work of cutting down trees easier. On the other hand, the invention of the locomotive did require large-scale changes in manufacturing and organization because it could only function within a system comprising specific railway tracks, rolling stock, supplies of water and firewood or coal, train stations, negotiations with the owners of animals that might be killed by trains, and a new level of engineering expertise. Such an extensive system cannot be implemented without the broader society's engagement.

While even such a basic innovation as the American axe may have profound ecological consequences, large technological systems are even more likely to impose an ecological price.

This is why historians of technology during the early twentieth century moved on to the consideration of a history of systems. The automobile system (comprising paved roads, divided highways, service stations, parking areas, garages) superseded the railroad system. The railroad system itself superseded, as we shall see, the canal system.

The systems approach was a good start to understanding the complexity of modern technologies, and the way they interact. Computer power may show up in the workstations that we usually associate with computers, but it can also be part of cars, planes, and many other machines.

However, to understand why a technology is adopted by the society at large, how it is shaped by the choices of its users, and how it influences the way society works, it is necessary to take another step back and look at technology in society.

Finally, during the past fifty years, it has become obvious that technologies affect directly and indirectly the natural environment. Older technologies changed the environment in grossly obvious ways: farming, mining, lumbering, large-scale construction projects, etc. Often, the point of these technologies was the resulting environmental modification: replacing an area's vegetation cover, moving ore from deep underground to the surface, cutting down trees . . . Later, we became sensitive to the environmental consequences of direct by-products of technological processes (industrial waste). Most recently, we have started to look for the secondary effects of technologies, often unintended and unforeseen.

THINKING ABOUT THE HISTORY OF TECHNOLOGY

For much of the nineteenth century, the nature of technology seemed obvious once it was settled that it matched and extended older categories formerly designated as the mechanical arts or applied science. Therefore, it included all the tools and machines, such as the shoemaker's implements or the weaver's loom, that were well-known in Europe by the eighteenth century. It also included the emblematic machines of the early Industrial Revolution, such as the steam engine and the power looms that could do the job of many individual workers.

For many, this was sufficient. A few thinkers argued that technology should be treated as an autonomous category, distinct from science or the arts, and proposed elaborate lists of basic mechanisms that could be combined and recombined at will. Others suggested seeing it not as a concrete phenomenon, but rather as a conceptual one.

So, while historians broadened the definition of technology by considering all of the people who helped to shape it or were touched by it, philosophers pondered its essential characteristics.

As we have seen, tools, and technology in general, are easily identified as an extension of the human body or mind. This nineteenth-century idea led Canadian theorist Marshall McLuhan to define any *medium* as such an extension, or an extension of an older medium. Clothing is an extension of skin, and a house is an extension of the body's heat mechanism. The stirrup, the bicycle, and the car extend the human feet. The computer extends the human nervous system. The telegraph is a medium extending the written word, and so on . . . A medium typically operates by "containing" another medium. This conception of technologies allows us to understand them as layers that *mediate* between us and reality. McLuhan's statements about media are basically true of technologies in general.

In addition to his definition of *media* as extensions, primarily seen in this guise as *enhancements*, McLuhan assigned to them the properties of *obsolescence, retrieval*, and *reversal*.

Every new medium makes older media and the forms of social organization around them obsolete in some respect. Email has superseded—for quick exchanges of information that do not require an interactive discussion—the use of the fax, the telephone, or the telegraph. That would be a case of *obsolescence* at work. Every medium also retrieves some features of older environments or older forms of action and human organization. This *retrieval* is clearly seen in the first passenger cars of European trains, which were modelled on the seating arrangements of stage coaches. On the other hand, every medium, when overextended, can either take on the opposite of its original features or create the opposite of its intended function. For instance, while email made it easier to respond quickly to a short query, the avalanche of email has often forced users to select the messages that will be answered first and its ease of storage allows them to think twice or procrastinate before answering. This *reversal* has cost email much of its original responsiveness.

A contemporary of McLuhan, German philosopher Martin Heidegger, answered the question concerning technology (1949) by defining it as a requisitioning process which treats the whole of nature as a standing reserve intended to fulfill human needs and wants. He emphasized the risk of extending this logic to the point where humans become either resources to be used up or mere elements of a larger technological system.

A theory of technology that would transcend its purely functional aspects and be neither purely philosophical nor entirely historical became imperative around the turn of the twentieth century. Most importantly, the problem of technological inequality and, consequently, *technology transfer* demanded a new analysis. Faced with the economic and political success of Western countries, attributable in large part to their technologies, many observers wondered which were the decisive factors. German sociologist Max Weber (1905) argued for a link between the Protestant virtues and the capitalist ethos. For others, European technological superiority was evidence for the intellectual and racial superiority of Europeans. For many, the key to Western technological superiority was Western science, even though the contribution of science to technological progress is arguable before the nineteenth century, but this only raised new questions about the origins of Western science.

The question of the origins of technological inequality over the long run—the last ten thousand years—has been addressed most recently by Jared Diamond in a synthesis (1997) that is less convincing for the shorter historical run. The issue of remedying technological inequality remains a complex one. Originally, some countries, whether newly independent or truly ancient, wished to gain the benefits of Western technology alone while ignoring everything else about Western countries (the rule of law, free inquiry, democracy, free speech, human rights).

Yet, "everything else" was part of the mix responsible for such fearsomely effective technics. Why did some technologies work so well in some contexts and not so well elsewhere? It was the fault of the human factor, one might say, but that only meant complex technologies did not operate in perfect isolation and that it might be necessary to include within them the people working with them and making decisions affecting them.

In that case, technologies may well have a political dimension. Ever since Plato, it has been claimed that, in certain circumstances dictated by technological constraints, there are no political options but authoritarianism. In a famous (and controversial) 1980 essay, Langdon Winner discusses the claim that modern machines and technological systems can be judged on their embodiment of specific forms of power and authority, which would make them not only political instruments but even political actors. It is easy enough to show that some technologies have been bent to overtly political ends, as in the case of the great boulevards and new streets opened throughout Paris by Haussmann in the nineteenth century, in part to facilitate the repression of popular uprisings. However, is it in the nature of certain specific technologies to compel social and political options?

Winner suggests that some technologies may be political because they determine winners and losers, by favouring holders of wealth or authority, for instance, or by discriminating against the poor and the handicapped. The problem lies in trying to attribute political choices to technological objects in and of themselves. Neither tools nor commodities seem to be bound to particular values; hence the temptation to blame rather the social or economic systems in which technology is embedded. As this tends to ignore the specific functions and constraints of technological objects, such an analysis would seem to have nothing definite to say about technology. In this view, all that counts are the social, political, and economical influences at play.

The solution probably lies in broadening the focus to look at *technological systems* instead of mere objects. For instance, the low overpasses built by Robert Moses above the parkways of Long Island are perfectly functional as long as cars are the only vehicles using those parkways—and perfectly neutral as long as other vehicles don't come into the picture. The exclusion of other vehicles has no meaning until one associates the buses that might have used those parkways with specific segments of the population (ethnic minorities, the poor). Thus, it is not enough to look at tools that can be turned to different political purposes (the way radio was used to broadcast both Hitler's Nazi propaganda and Franklin Delano Roosevelt's fireside chats proclaiming that "There is nothing to fear but fear itself."). The design of an object precedes its use and may determine its use (as in the case of North Korean radios preset to one and only one channel, the government's). Especially since a given design's consequences may be long-lasting: while the exclusion of commercial vehicles (buses, trucks, etc.) defined parkways when the Long Island parkways were built, the low overpasses enshrined that exclusion for as long as these structures would endure, even if the laws excluding commercial traffic were changed later.

Langdon Winner therefore argues attention must be paid to the meaning of the design and arrangements of our artifacts. The consequences of particular technical designs will not always be intentional (as it certainly is in the case of North Korean radios and may have been in the case of Long Island parkways); it was only realized recently how systematically the construction of everyday objects prevents the handicapped from moving about freely. (The realization that many technologies have quite unintended environmental costs is similarly recent.) Some technologies, furthermore, may be intrinsically *intractable*, that is to say that their very nature may require a particularly hierarchical or authoritarian form of management, while others allow the development of more varied forms of engagement with them. In the former case, the only possible way of dealing with such a technology may be at the outset, when it is still possible to choose whether or not to adopt it at all.

With respect to artifacts and politics, therefore, Winner asks two distinct questions: whether it is possible to not only use artifacts to political ends (something that is obviously possible since weapons have served the cause of terrorism, colonialism, imperialism, etc.) but to design artifacts to achieve certain political outcomes, and whether the intrinsic properties of certain technologies might, prior to any design choices, lead preferentially to specific political outcomes. Winner's concern is that some technologies might actually choose sides, by favouring authoritarianism over democracy, for example.

In his 1999 analysis of one part of this essay, Bernward Joerges demonstrates (convincingly though somewhat sloppily) that one of Winner's examples (the parkway bridges of Long Island) cannot be made to bear the argumentative weight that Winner placed upon them. As to the larger issue, Joerges retorts that, in most cases, the physical and technical properties of a technology matter less than its appropriation: who lays claim to it, who defines the rules for its use, and who gets to capture its benefits in the end? In the case of parkways, the rules governing them already excluded buses and commercial vehicles. In the case of Cyrus McCormick's manufacturing plant where new machines allowed the owners to undermine the bargaining power of workers, other union-busting tactics could have been used, though at perhaps a higher cost; the key was that McCormick made the rules and could force the adoption of the new machine. In the case of the boulevards of Paris, troops could be more easily deployed against a popular uprising as long as the government was ready to do so, but the boulevards could not and did not guarantee the survival of the Second Empire served by Haussmann. Ultimately, technologies may not be as politically important as the context of their use. Low overpasses on parkways may have excluded buses and other vehicles of a similar size, but the meaning of this exclusion also depended on public transit being associated with certain users: with car ownership becoming more general, buses might still be excluded, but drivers belonging to minorities and lower-income groups would not. This view may not differ so much from Winner's view of technologies such as the tomato harvester, which are not developed to further intentionally a political agenda, but whose very existence is subordinated to a given socio-political context.

Beyond politics alone, many social forces and factors can affect the design of a technology. Is technological change always synonymous with "progress"? Are new technologies necessarily better or more efficient? In what sense, for instance, were chemical pesticides better than the botanical pesticides or biologically-based methods they displaced? Were they superior in an environmental sense or in the economic sense only?

Even the idea that there might be "natural trajectories" or automatic successions of events is not always supported by the evidence (zeppelins might have lasted longer as a flying alternative without the *Hindenburg* disaster; the replacement of hydroplanes for long-distance air travel was accelerated by the development of land-based planes and airports during World War II). In fact, because of the phenomenon of increasing returns with adoption, a technology that gains a head start and is then adopted more and more widely may well overcome a "technically" better technology that was late getting off the ground.

Increasing returns with adoption depends on two self-reinforcing mechanisms. First, as a technology is adopted by more and more people, more resources are available for developing it further and experience in its use accumulate. As a result, increasing adoption leads to improvements in sheer, technical performance. (The "returns" take the form of improved performance and utility because the technology itself is improving.) Second, as certain technologies are adopted by more and more people, they either generate economies of scale (thus becoming more profitable: the "returns" being simply financial) or become more useful to their users because their utility depends largely on the size of the network (the "returns" do not result from technological change or from any change in the economics of the system, but from the use of the same technology by more people, as is often the case with communications technologies).

In the end, the history of technology needs to identify who gains from a technology and who decides the course of its development. One reason for this emphasis on people and groups is that technology cannot be divorced from human beliefs. Self-validating belief or self-fulfilling prophecy is a very real phenomenon in technological innovation. A sincere belief in a technology's future success may lead to the very investment that will make that technology a success.

Still, if we insist on asking whether technology is good or bad for humanity, the answer does not have to depend on personal belief or opinion. Much work has been done to research the effects of technology on economic growth and social well-being. In a sense, however, taking economic growth or social statistics as criteria of technology's benefits may be criticized for evading the core issue. Other researchers have been concentrating, for over fifty years, on the most fundamental question: whether or not people are happier with a given income, which may be easily related to a certain technological endowment in their own lives and in their own societies. The results of such polling (focused on happiness or "life satisfaction") have been somewhat paradoxical, according to Richard Easterlin.

In a nutshell, the Easterlin paradox may be summed up as follows. When comparing the average happiness of a country with a definite level of income (GDP) per capita with the average happiness of another country with a different level of income per capita, or when comparing average happiness within the same country at two different times, there was little significant evidence of a relationship between average happiness and income per capita. Two countries might differ widely in their GDP, or a country might have become significantly richer over time through sustained economic growth, but average happiness hardly budged or varied, as long as income was above a relatively low threshold. Yet, there is very solid evidence that, *within* a given country, people with more money are happier than those who make do with less, hence the paradox.

Easterlin's results have been criticized, but on the face of it, it would seem that more technology and more income do not always make people significantly happier over time. Therefore, asking whether the cost paid for technology is worth the material benefits if these do not improve our lives is a fair question. One answer may well be that Easterlin's data were deficient. Another answer is that, even if Easterlin was correct, he neglected the increase in longevity in most advanced societies. Thanks to this increase, which is definitely due in part to technological progress, even a constant level of average happiness will translate, on the individual level, into more years of life at the corresponding level of happiness, so that the individual sum of happiness throughout life becomes greater.

Finally, we come to the mutual shaping of technology and society. In some of his writings, French theorist Bruno Latour adduces three interrelated factors to explain the historical evolution of technological objects: nature, society, and discourse. Discourse may include art and myth, but it is primarily composed of the arguments, justifications, theories, and stories presented to make sense of things that are "real." Discourse comprises representations and other meaningful rhetorics produced by language games. A given discourse may reject or justify a certain technology. Society encompasses hierarchies, institutions, commercial enterprises, personal relationships, etc., all of which may be brought to bear on the development of a technology by providing support to inventors or hindering a technology's adoption. Technological facts are natural facts, up to a point, but this is even truer of environmental facts. Taken together, they are part of the realities that societies and discourses must deal with.

CONCLUSION: THE NATURE OF THE BEAST

Can we do what we want? One criticism of technology is that it curtails our freedom. The modern ideal of liberation is supposed to take the form of individuals gaining the freedom and the power to fashion their own destinies. The *bourgeoisie*, the poor, racial minorities, women, sexual minorities, and even children were successively emancipated in the name of modern liberal ideals. With respect to technology, the question arises as to whether technology grants us greater power to do as we will while constraining our freedom in subtle ways that effectively limit our autonomy. For instance, the internet is a great source of information and connectivity, but users must pay the price in equipment and, often, in greater access granted to others in order to benefit. Credit cards make it possible to spend money more freely, but our purchases become known to others. Surveillance cameras improve security, but at the expense of our privacy. Modern technologies have extended our control over many of life's circumstances, but we may have to yield some of our individual control to benefit. It is not a one-sided bargain in our favour, even if it may be the best deal we can make.

BASIC DEFINITIONS IN TECHNOLOGY STUDIES

Technology: those things that people have created so that they can manipulate or exploit the natural environment in which they are living, to useful ends.

Tools: instruments used to produce things or achieve various ends. Tools may produce other tools or commodities; *commodities* are products like bridges, houses, woollen cloth, clean laundry that serve an end and are directly useful, but are not used to *make*; both tools (wrenches, hammers, drills, looms, washing machines) and the things they produce (commodities, other tools, etc.) are included in the term technology.

Technology extends to domesticated animals and plants that provide humans with food and pharmaceuticals. It even extends to languages and the things that contain languages (such as books, letters, computer software, and student essays). All are things that people have created so as to better control and manipulate their environment, whether natural or social. Technology may refer to the concrete result of the application of existing knowledge (an artifact, whether it is a tool or commodity) and it may also refer to the capacity that results from an artifact, a method or recipe, or even a given organizational set-up (an army is one example of a special-purpose organization). Since technology deals with the fulfillment of human needs, it is often the product of a purposeful design process, starting with the identification of the desired end, continuing with the determination of possible characteristics, leading to the exploration of possible ideas, and the formulation of a preferred solution.

Technological Systems: arrays of coordinated technologies with a set of coherent purposes that may be reduced to one, overall purpose. Pure tools do exist: an axe used to chop down trees and a shovel used to dig out earth or sand are basic tools that require no other artifacts and no previous training of the users, but such tools are exceptions in modern, industrialized societies. A single tool is rarely self-sufficient; a hammer must be applied to something (a nail, a board) in order to function as a building instrument; a can opener needs a can; people appear as parts of technological systems; even a hammer needs somebody to pick it up before it can pound a nail. To use a hammer with a chisel to carve a work of art, furthermore, requires somebody trained to be a sculptor (by another sculptor or in a school). A technological system can be simple (like the combination of hammer, nails, and boards) or complex. Technological systems can become quite large and complex. The modern personal computer, for instance, requires an electrical network, a phone or cable network, software, memory media, printers . . . and also programmers, manufacturers, support personnel, etc. in order to come into existence and function properly. US historian Thomas P. Hughes has written extensively on systems and on how they are set in place

Networks: Bruno Latour uses the term to include not only concrete and tangible realities, such as those of the natural world or of technical artifacts, but also the social realities of values and power relationships as well as the discursive realities of texts (theories, stories, myths). Unlike a *technological system* that may be designed as such from the outset (Edison's electrical lighting system using direct current) or whose parts may be mutually adapted in order to work better together, Latour's network is more a description of the alliances forged to yield a given outcome. A network can be constructed from pre-existing parts (natural, technical, institutional) that are integrated or recruited on a piecemeal basis. Or it can result from the interaction of forces and factors quite unlooked-for.

Consider the 2004 tsunami in southeast Asia: it involved natural phenomena (plate tectonics, earthquakes, wave propagation, near shore underwater profiles) and various technologies or the lack thereof (wave sensors, full-time seismic monitoring, predictive software, the organisation of communications and early warning systems; the design of the buildings exposed to the surge; the logistics of relief efforts, the available disinfection products, the water purification equipment), but also the political choices made beforehand to concentrate on dealing with monsoons and typhoons (India), the political choices made afterwards to control the news (Myanmar), the complications introduced by potential hostilities, the conflict between the needs of tourists and the needs of locals, and the social arrangements resulting in shantytowns occupying some of the most exposed seafronts.

Beyond this, we observe the power of certain discourses: in Canada, the government was put under exceptional pressure to have its acts match its touted commitment to international governance. The United States reacted quickly when it felt targeted by the comments of one United Nations official about the stinginess of rich countries. And, in Canada, as a result of the outpouring of donations, public pronouncements proclaimed the generosity of ordinary Canadians, drawing the picture of a country that was what it wanted to be. Such storylines, whether or not they are demonstrably true, are considered to be *performative* to some extent. That is, these stories have an effect; they support certain actions and discourage others. Affirming Canadian generosity engendered shame or defensiveness among the stingy—who felt left out, even excluded—and exerted a form of peer pressure.

Thus, the *network* analysis emphasizes the interplay of profoundly different forces affecting each other reciprocally, so that technological developments are not considered in isolation.

FURTHER READINGS

Joerges, Bernward. 1999. "Do Politics Have Artefacts?", *Social Studies of Science 29*, 3 pp. 411–431.

Winner, Langdon. 1980. "Do Artifacts Have Politics?", *Daedalus 109*, 1, pp. 121–136.

CHAPTER 2

The Environmental Human and the Human Environment

▶▶▶▶▶▶▶▶▶▶▶▶▶▶▶▶▶▶▶▶▶▶▶▶▶▶▶▶▶▶▶

Humans are creatures of their environment. They draw sustenance from the vegetable and animal kingdoms. The very oxygen they breathe is the product of a biological process called photosynthesis that is an exclusive property of vegetation. They are at the mercy of natural phenomena such as earthquakes, hurricanes, and seasons. Their bodies harbour a myriad of other life forms, some of which they share with other species, some of which can kill them, and some without which they would die. Ultimately, they owe their existence to the narrow range of life-giving temperatures made possible by our planet's average distance from the Sun, the highly circular nature of Earth's orbit, the homeostatic boost provided by the biosphere, and the current state of the Sun's evolution towards ever greater brightness.

The human relationship with the environment is reciprocal. Like many other animal species, humans are neither mere observers nor passive components of the ecological forces at work. From the first, their lifestyle has affected the natural environment in ways that made it more congenial or actually reduced its ability to support them. In this, they are no different from top predators such as wolves that may exhaust their reservoir of prey to their own detriment, leading to opposite and complementary population booms and busts until the balance reverses again, or from animals such as beavers, attuned to the environmental cues that will lead them to convert a stream of running water into a pond of standing water with the potential of becoming a wetland or a bog.

While the earliest individuals of our subspecies, *Homo sapiens sapiens*, were limited in their power to shape their environment, they relied on a tool-set inherited from earlier hominins that quickly grew into an unmatched arsenal. Fire, stone tools, and some forms of adornment are all part of the paleontological record, but most experts agree that the surviving artifacts indicate as well an ability to shape wood, bone, animal skins, and plant fibres to fashion additional implements. Beginning about 100,000 years ago, *Homo sapiens sapiens* were not only anatomically modern, but also increasingly close in behaviour to contemporary humans.

The currently accepted view of human evolution posits that the ancestors of *Homo sapiens sapiens* evolved in Africa. Some stayed and some left. The great dispersal began between 100,000 and 40,000 years ago. The humans who left Africa encountered hominin cousins in Eurasia. Genetic analyses suggest some limited mixing of human populations with the Neandertalians and Denisovans whose ancestors had left Africa earlier. The extent of this genetic admixture is not presumed to exceed 5% in most modern humans and is comparable to the genetic variation found among human populations in Africa.

Humanity's expansion outside Africa remains obscure, in part because some of it occurred during glacial periods when sea levels were lower and human wanderings appear to have followed ancient coast lines now drowned by sea level rise. Yet, the very presence of humans on islands and continents, such as Australia and the Americas, which were impossible or nearly impossible to reach without some means of crossing stretches of open sea, reveals something of the skills and daring of early humans.

Humanity's great dispersal likely entailed physical changes linked to the new niches early humans occupied. For instance, a paler skin colour, whether inherited as a trait from older populations found outside Africa or developed anew, was favoured by the human body's need for vitamin D synthesized with the help of sunlight. Once humans left the tropic with their nearly constant solar illumination, they faced the highly variable nature of the Sun's illumination in regions with yearly changes in daytime length and simultaneous fluctuations in the intensity of sunlight. As these are the result of the axial tilt of the Earth, itself stabilized by the presence of the Moon according to astronomers, differences in skin colour may fairly be ascribed to astronomical factors older than life itself.

Some genetic modifications are presumed to have emerged in connection with new lifestyles or persistent diseases. Populations that relied on herding and on animal milk for a significant part of their diet favoured the development of adaptations for digesting lactose, a sugar derived from components of milk. Other societies exposed to malaria developed genetic mutations that helped mitigate the effects of the disease. However, a much quicker response to environmental challenges was eventually provided by technological innovation.

TECHNOLOGIES BEFORE THE HISTORICAL PERIOD

While several animal species (including beavers, birds, ants, and termites) manipulate their environment, only a few (primates, some birds) are able to use natural objects (mostly stones and sticks) as tools to gather food. These primitive forms of technology are far outstripped by the human ability to combine such objects into more complex ones and apply outside forces (such as fire) to their shaping, in order to create even more complex tools and devices.

Humanity's ability to adapt to new and extreme environments eventually depended on its technology. Clothing, shelter, and hunting implements such as weapons, nets, and traps, were keys to human survival in the wintry surroundings of ice age Europe, northern Asia, or North America. Beyond a certain point, technology may be said to transcend adaptation. Technology makes it possible to create enclosed environments able to sustain life quite independently of the conditions outside. Insulated shelters and heated buildings create micro-climates in the heart of winter. Accumulated food reserves may be consumed when no other fare is available. Breathable air can be stocked and regenerated to let small communities live under water for weeks and months aboard nuclear submarines, for instance. This phenomenon is most clearly seen in twentieth-century space exploration when the self-contained environments of the Apollo spaceships and spacesuits made it possible for humans to survive on the Moon. Even today, a relatively minor commitment of time, resources, and technology allows humanity to maintain a permanent presence in the absolutely desolate environment of Earth orbit.

As the latest glacial period ended about 12,000 years ago, humans moved on to even larger adaptations of the landscape. The origins and extent of agriculture remain uncertain, but the clearing of forests and the flooding of rice paddies by early farmers transformed natural habitats while changing the levels of greenhouse gases such as carbon dioxide and methane. The hunters of the Palaeolithic era may have contributed to the extinction of certain species, especially when they were isolated on islands reached by human seafarers, but the farmers of the Neolithic era brought about wholesale changes affecting the fauna and flora of entire regions, starting roughly 8,000 years ago.

ENVIRONMENTAL CONSEQUENCES BEFORE THE HISTORICAL PERIOD

Waste is a function of life. In order to grow and reproduce, a living organism must generate energy and organize matter. The laws of thermodynamics essentially dictate this cannot happen without at least some waste heat. In practice, most living organisms expel the by-products of respiration and digestion which provide them with usable energy and usable matter.

Humans are nearly unique because they resort to technology to create congenial environments and have developed machines with their own sources of power. Insofar as technology is subordinated to biological processes and often operates in similar fashion, its products will often entail the generation of waste. The amount of waste produced by humans is largely commensurate with the amount of energy mobilized by humans to serve their needs. This amount started rising when humans began domesticating animals (the dog, cat, horse, ox, and so on) that worked for them. Agriculture was in a sense a human takeover of the solar energy that once benefited forests, grasslands, and their inhabitants, but was appropriated to feed humans and their tame animal species. The amount rose again when humans began to draw upon inanimate sources of energy such as waterpower and wind power, using devices such as dams, channels, waterwheels, and windmills to turn the mechanical energy of wind and flowing water into useful work. Up to that point, humans had always worked within the solar energy budget of Earth: the ultimate source of the energy stored in plants, flowing water, and blowing wind is the Sun. However, once humans began to take advantage of fossil fuels, they tapped into the solar energy of the past so that they could increase their energy use without affecting their take of the Sun's current output. (Geothermal energy and nuclear technology are two sources of power that are independent of solar energy, either today or tomorrow.) Since then, the rise in energy consumption per capita has been nothing short of stunning.

As a result, humans generate more waste per capita than any other animal species. Large-scale pollution is as uniquely human as language, symbolic thought, and advanced tool-making. When humans first landed on the Moon, one of their first acts, even before Neil Armstrong stepped down the ladder, was actually to throw out a garbage bag (**Figure 1**) on the surface of our satellite to lighten the ascent stage and save fuel in case it needed to return to orbit. Looking at the night side of Earth, contemporary space travellers famously see wasted light outline the shapes of the continent. The sea lanes used by freighters and container ships crisscross much of the Northern hemisphere, spreading debris, machine exhaust, and other refuse. Cities and villages, highways and roads, railway tracks, power lines, fields, mines, and assorted resource extraction sites sprawl across the continents. Only Antarctica, various deserts, the Canadian and Russian tundra, the Tibetan plateau, the boreal forests of Canada and Russia, Greenland, and the Amazon remain more or less untouched.

FIGURE 1 ▶ The first picture taken by a human standing on the Moon focused, for safety reasons, on the landing strut. The shot happened to include the "jettison bag" thrown out from the lander about thirteen minutes earlier. (*Source: NASA Johnson. www.hq.nasa.gov /office/pao/History/alsj/a11/AS11-40-5850HR.jpg*)

CAUSES AND CONSEQUENCES

In *The Wizard of Oz* (Victor Fleming, 1939), Dorothy is famously heard to remark to her dog, "Toto, I don't think we're in Kansas anymore." Today, it may also be said that we do not live in North America anymore. At any rate, it no longer resembles the North America that existed for thousands of years after the last glacial period.

The modern North American landscape is the product of five hundred years of radical changes. European settlement and technological activity account for the most visible alterations, but a closer look also reveals a form of ecological imperialism not always deliberate or even noticed at the time. Europeans brought new animal and plant species, as well as new diseases that helped to cause a demographic collapse so large that it may have affected the global climate.

A flood of new species have carved out niches for themselves, and sometimes taken over large areas. The process is ongoing. In 2002 along the St. Lawrence River in Canada, between Cornwall and Trois-Pistoles, scientists counted a total of thirty-nine exotic plant species in the wild, including purple loosestrife. (Here, *exotics* are understood to mean plant species that were unknown before contact with Europe.) Most came by boat, their seeds probably mixed in with the sand and gravel loaded as ballast by ships coming from Europe. Marine species such as the zebra mussel or the Chinese mitten crab have also made the trip from elsewhere, taking advantage of the water ballast used by modern freighters. Ballast water commonly carries a wide variety of organisms, from single-celled diatoms and dinoflagellates to shrimp-like copepods, larval mollusks, and crustaceans. It has helped comb jellies from the North American East Coast make the trip to the Black Sea (where they devastated native life forms), brought Japanese sea stars to Australia, moved green crabs from Europe to San Francisco Bay, and introduced the zebra mussel, the round goby fish, and the Eurasian ruffle fish to the Great Lakes. It is also suspected to spread bacteria (such as the one responsible for cholera) and viruses.

Not all species are disruptive. It has been estimated that 90% of species transplanted to new surroundings have no significant effect on the species already present. (Making the life of existing species harder, by reducing the amount of food present and causing population numbers to fall, does not always count as significant.) European data indicate that a bit more than 10% of alien species have negative ecological or economic impacts.

Indeed, out of those thirty-nine intrusive plant species found along the St. Lawrence, only four to six are thought to threaten native species. When a new species has deleterious effects on existing species or the broader environment, it is termed invasive.

Several mechanisms are implicated: predation first and foremost, diseases, and ecosystem alterations. In some cases, a new predator will feast on vulnerable prey species, driving some to extinction. A new species may also bring new diseases capable of wiping out indigenous species. In other cases, a species may alter the environment to favour its own survival at the expense of others (the melaleuca, an Australian tree, has spread through the Florida Everglades by changing the frequency and intensity of fires; the Brazilian pepper tree has spread in the Everglades by exuding a poisonous sap that helps it clear space for itself). If an environment is physically small (such as an island or a wetland like the Everglades), species native to that environment may be more at risk of extinction because individual members are less numerous and have nowhere to move to if they are threatened.

A new species can also compete with an existing one, to the point of endangering the survival of the native species. (The Pontic rhododendron is an evergreen shrub that can grow up to 5–8 metres in height, shading many smaller plants so that they cannot thrive.) In other cases, an invasive species may instead hybridize with the local species, producing a new breed capable of replacing the original one. Some hybrids may become even more vigorous than the original invasive species. Hybridization may also reduce genetic variation and introduce maladaptive genes into a local population.

On the other hand, even if they don't threaten the survival of other species, intrusive species can have a grievous economic impact. Zebra mussels clog reservoirs and water-intake pipes in the Great Lakes, incurring a control and cleanup bill numbered in the billions of dollars annually. The Russian wheat aphid contributes to the yearly bite taken out of US crops by various pests, the total value of losses having been valued at more than ten billion dollars. Other introduced insects, diseases, and weeds damage lawns, gardens, and golf courses, costing a few billion dollars annually. Cumulatively, pet cats and feral cats kill an astounding number of birds. And rats cause losses also accounted in the billions.

Invasive species may also affect the general environment in ways that are broadly detrimental to its carrying capacity, so that fewer species (plant and animal) will be able to flourish to the same extent. Japanese knotweed has invaded much of Europe, where it produces large, dense stands of tightly spaced growths (several metres in height) that result in sites with lower plant and invertebrate species diversity, abundance, and (total) biomass. Japanese knotweed favours predator species at the expense of frogs and snails, while depriving herbivores of food since few indigenous species will browse on it. Its extensive root and rhizome system can also weaken building foundations, canal and river banks, and railway tracks. Such impacts of exotic species on an environment may also reduce the environment's general usefulness for humans (in terms of providing relatively clean fresh water and controlling run-off, supporting a population of pollinating insects, growing trees for logging or as a source of firewood, supporting sports hunting, or the operation of a fishery). In other words, such invasive species may reduce the filtering function of streams, increase run-off when it rains, reduce the number of pollinating insects, slow down the growth of trees, affect the number of game species, impoverish commercial fisheries, favour the spread of pests, and eradicate species with pharmaceutical potential.

Furthermore, when they find a niche, aliens can be hard to turn back. Though no more than 18% of all plant species along the St. Lawrence are exotics, exotics account for up to 40% of the plant cover in places like the Montreal area. Worldwide, the native species may be driven by intrusive species into niches much smaller than their original range; scientists now debate whether the limited size of these refuges necessarily means that their survival is threatened.

Across the continent, exotics, aliens, or intrusives include the lamprey eel, the Asian longhorn beetle, the gypsy moth (brought to North America in the 1830s to establish a silk industry) and the European rock dove (brought as a source of food), more commonly known as the urban pigeon. The scientific study of such species dates back to *The Ecology of Invasions by Animals and Plants* (1958), the work of British ecologist Charles Elton.

They are often found in the most diverse ecosystems, those that already support a number of animal and plant species because they are, by definition, able to support more species, being richer in water, light, and nutrients.

They are also found wherever humans are found, if only because many are domestic animals. Cattle have not only been spread far and wide by humans, they are also quite destructive. On the global scale, their grazing and trampling threatens about three times as many native plant species as are threatened by wild aliens. (Their impact merges with and amplifies the impact of habitat destruction to create their pastures.) The wild exotics are incriminated as the major culprits in only 6% of cases where native wildlife is threatened with extinction. Most of the other cases involve the combined impact of habitat destruction and domesticated species. Human hunting also plays a role in some cases, while climate change (global warning) is expected to put growing pressure on some species in this century.

For land-based species, some of the laws of biogeography are known. First, it is well established that the number of species in a given geographical area varies a lot depending on its location. Second, most species have small ranges; only a few have very large ranges. Most species with small ranges are locally scarce; they often are found in a few specific regions. Therefore, it should be no surprise that half of the world's species may live in about 25 tropical areas, mostly forested, where humans have already removed 70% of the original vegetation cover (these are known as "hot spots" of diversity).

THE EURASIAN SUCCESS STORY

Time and again, invasive species from Eurasia have displaced species native to the Americas. Most obviously, as Alfred Crosby pointed out in his pioneering work on the Columbian exchange, humans from Eurasia overran North America in the space of a few short centuries (five centuries in the Caribbean and in Central America, four centuries in the United States and Canada), crowding out the original human inhabitants of the land. The speed of this *swarming* was breathtaking.

When only a small fraction of intrusive plant species achieve such success, how is it that human invaders have proven so successful? It could be the biological luck of the draw, or it could be something else; but what?

Most clearly, technology played an immediate role in the overwhelming triumph of the European invasion. The native inhabitants had nothing to match the wheeled carts, the metal swords, the guns, and the cannons of the Europeans. Even European agriculture proved superior after some adaptations and borrowings, allowing European settlers to achieve higher population densities than the original population. Yet, the question then becomes: how did Europeans gain such technology?

Another proximate factor was more purely biological. Europeans profited from the deadly impact of their home-grown illnesses. Epidemics devastated North America's original human population, in part because the Native Americans were, biologically speaking, a "virgin soil" for pathogens brought by Europeans from the Old World and in part because Europeans settlers and traders introduced cascading disruptions of the existing societies, through territorial expansion, economic changes, war, and famine. Crowding, malnutrition, and poverty are factors known to accentuate the death rates of populations exposed to diseases.

Not all of the diseases that felled so many of the original inhabitants were necessarily introduced by the Europeans. In some cases, recent research suggests that they may have been opportunistic viruses that ran riot because the native population was "stressed:" displaced, impoverished, and hunger-stricken as a result of droughts, poor hunting, bad harvests, and deaths from warfare. Since European expansion overthrew existing societies, altered trading relationships, and caused a chain reaction of wars even when Europeans were not present themselves, the epidemics due to local pathogens could still be a consequence of European contact. Still, the collapse of the Mayan and Mound-Builder societies in Central and North America shows that stone-age civilizations did fail occasionally before any Europeans arrived.

Yet, the basic questions remain. Why did Europeans bring so many more new pathogens to the common pot than the North Americans? How did they come to be so "afflicted" by diseases?

Biogeography

The impact of biological newcomers is most clearly seen in the case of islands. In many historical cases, humans have caused the extinction of island-based vertebrate species (most often birds, but reptiles and mammals also) soon after setting foot for the first time on shore. The precise cause is rarely known, even in the case of the famous dodo bird of Mauritius Island, in the Indian Ocean. Excessive hunting has often played a role, but humans also modify existing habitats (burning or cutting down forests, creating fields or pastures) and introduce competitors or predators (such as cats and rats, but also including pathogens). Island populations are often small enough to be imperilled directly by such activities, but, in some cases, the human impact is not responsible for outright extermination. If the reduction in population numbers is such that the surviving population is so rare as to be no longer viable, it becomes susceptible to perturbations that may lead to its disappearance (through natural catastrophes, inbreeding, competition, or the extinction of an associated species) even without further human intervention.

The Americas are too large to be considered islands, but the effects of European colonization are reminiscent of the impact seen in the case of islands. It is plausibly argued by Jared Diamond in *Guns, Germs, and Steel* (1997) that the power of the European impact was in part a result of some favourable quirks of geography, geological history, and zoology.

When the last glacial period ended about 12,000 years ago, Eurasia held by chance a number of plants that could be bred for controlled farming in the temperate zone.

The Americas had fewer edible plants suitable for cross-breeding and, what is more, they were dispersed in a series of relatively narrow climate zones ranging from the Arctic to the Antarctic. With respect to cultivation, finally, Africa had relatively poor soil, in part a result of the accumulation of millions of years since the last glaciation to have affected it.

Thus, large-scale food production through agriculture began first in the Fertile Crescent and present-day China, rapidly spreading to Europe and other likely parts of Eurasia. The long east-west axis of Eurasia meant there were many places along the same latitudes that shared the same seasons and climates. In the Americas, there is some evidence that the spread of domesticated species was so difficult over the large north-south distances separating the same temperate zones that similar plant species were domesticated more than once in different areas.

Though it has been argued that the diet of the first farmers was less healthy than the diet of hunters-gatherers, agriculture made it possible for more people to live off a smaller territory. As a result, both absolute population and population density rose. Villages began to turn into small towns.

Agriculture generated both a food surplus and a surplus population that could live off that surplus without working: a ruling class made of kings, warriors, and priests. To manage the food surplus, accountants in the pay of urban rulers developed or improved both writing and numbering systems. Clay tokens found in the ruins of some early cities are thought to have served as counters to keep track of grain, livestock, and other products (bread, oil, perfume, rope, etc.), leading to the use of marks to symbolize the counters and so the items themselves. Later, many problems outlined on the clay tablets and papyri of Antiquity still dealt with the apportioning of land for cultivation or of bread for workers.

As cities grew, it became possible for craftsmen to specialize and earn a living with the practice of a single craft. As new products multiplied, merchants emerged to buy and sell them, joining an urban population of expert craftsmen, clerks, and religious functionaries to enlarge again the market for the arts and crafts. All of this fostered technological innovation in a continually accelerating manner that led Europeans, many centuries later, to enjoy a considerable advantage over Native Americans on three fronts: technology, commensal animals, and pathogens.

While agriculture led to civilization, and civilization to technological innovation, it depended not only on food crops but on a supply of suitable animals for consumption (poultry, hogs, cattle) or for work (oxen, horses, donkeys, camels, even elephants). Again, Eurasia was privileged to be home to several large mammals that could be domesticated. These animals were major sources of meat, milk, hides, horns, fertilizer, and even fuel in some cases, as well as work and transportation.

Though humans have tamed or learned to profit from several other species including the honeybee and the silkworm (among insects), chicken, ducks, geese, the guinea fowl, and the Muscovy duck (among birds), the wolf (in the canine family), the cat (in the feline family), as well as the rabbit, the guinea pig, and the giant rat (in the rodent family), most of these were small. Most only had a limited role to play: the silkworm provided silk, the cat killed mice, and the rabbit was a source of food (and of fur in a minor way). The wolf-descended dog and the poultry were undoubtedly more useful. Large mammals were even more useful.

Yet, if "large" is defined as massing over 50 kg, Diamond notes that only fourteen large terrestrial mammals (most of them herbivores) were truly domesticated before the twentieth century. (Here, truly domesticated animals are understood to be animals selectively bred in captivity and thereby modified in permanent fashion for the use of humans in control of their food supply and breeding.)

Of these, nine species became important livestock for people in only limited areas of the globe: the Arabian camel, the Bactrian camel, the llama and alpaca in the Andes (distinct breeds of the same ancestral species), the donkey, the Scandinavian reindeer, the water buffalo, the Himalayan yak, the banteng, and the gaur.

The remaining five species proved to be particularly useful, versatile, and adaptable in many areas of the globe: the cow, sheep, goat, pig, and horse. The wild ancestor of the cow was the now extinct aurochs, formerly found in Eurasia and North Africa. The wild ancestor of the sheep was the Asiatic mouflon sheep of West and Central Asia. The wild ancestor of the goat was the bezoar goat of West Asia. The wild ancestor of the pig (the only omnivore of the fourteen) was the wild boar, distributed over Eurasia and North Africa. And the wild ancestor of the horse was the wild horse of southern Russia, now extinct; a different subspecies of that ancestral species still survives as Przewalski's horse (out of Mongolia). Thus, the five most important domesticated species of large mammals all originated in Eurasia or North Africa. None originated in the Americas, Australia, or Africa south of the Sahara.

Why was this? It was not for lack of apparent candidate species, defined as large and herbivorous or omnivorous. (Carnivores have never been domesticated.)

Eurasia did have the most (72 candidate species, out of which 13 were eventually domesticated). Sub-Saharan Africa had the next greatest number (51), while the Americas only numbered 24 and Australia one. The low numbers of candidate species in the Americas and Australia are mainly due to the extinction of several species of large mammals after the last glacial period. Still, why were Africans and Americans unable to match the domestication batting average of the Eurasians? In the final analysis, the luck of the zoological draw appears to have been decisive. The candidate species outside Eurasia were simply not tractable enough to be bred in captivity.

The difficulty of domesticating large animals native to the Americas is graphically illustrated by the story of the bison that survived the massive population crash of the nineteenth century, when the large bison herds of the Prairies were reduced to as little as a thousand or so individual animals. One small herd of survivors that was brought from the United States to Canada in the early years of the twentieth century required a large expenditure of time, effort, and money to be rounded-up and moved to a park in Alberta. Modern-day ranchers still aver that buffalo raised on the farm remain less docile than domesticated cattle. And the hybrid bison that are the result of the interbreeding of Plains and wood bison are clearly no more tractable than their ancestors. They can be controlled (with fences, drugs, and trucks), but they are not judged as tame.

If twentieth-century ranching technology and breeding efforts have achieved so little, it seems reasonable that indigenous populations in the Americas would not have fared better. The pre-Columbian populations did not have horses, metal implements or anaesthetics. What is true of the wild and untameable bison may be taken to be true of the many American animals that have also resisted domestication at the hands of Europeans: that they have remained wild means that it was probably not for lack of trying by the early inhabitants of the Americas.

THE PERILS AND PROFITS OF SWAPPING GERMS

The abundance of plant and animal species domesticated by the inhabitants of Eurasia led to a snowballing process of urbanization that provided their descendants with a rich array of powerful technologies. It also plagued them with an unmatched diversity of diseases.

Urban living in the crowded cities of Antiquity implied frequent contact with other city-dwellers. While ancient cities developed running water and sewage drainage systems as early as 4,000 years ago in places like the Indus valleys (the Harappan civilization), houses were small and streets were narrow. Microorganisms causing diseases (pathogens) could spread easily and find many hosts. In evolutionary terms, this favoured the outbursts of virulent diseases that ravaged individual victims quickly because there were other potential hosts nearby. Cities were long reputed to be unhealthy places where babies and children died in droves, and epidemics struck regularly. Those who could afford to leave in times of danger found refuge in the healthier countryside.

Furthermore, as a result of animal domestication, Eurasians shared their lives with increasing numbers of other mammalian species, whether in farming hamlets or in towns where animals would still be present in the streets, in backyard coops, or in gardens. This was both unfortunate and fortunate for the populations of Eurasia, since domestic animals are major sources and/or reservoirs of diseases. Such animals contributed to the disease load that felled susceptible individuals. On the other hand, the survivors gained a hard-won immunity to many of those same diseases.

Diseases spread by animals have been known for ages, but not all are equally worrisome. Rabies, for instance, is lethal, but can only be communicated from an infected animal to a human. Humans do not spread rabies. On the other hand, the flu propagates freely in a human population even though the virus responsible may be derived ultimately from a bird or swine population, but the flu only kills a small percentage of the people it afflicts. Of more recent origin, the AIDS virus is thought to be of simian origin but can now spread from human to human, and is deadly if untreated. There are also many intermediate cases where a pathogen may be transmitted by animals to humans, but can only spread in a limited number of cases from human to human.

Since Eurasians often lived in close proximity with their domesticated animals (often kept in an adjoining yard or stable), there were many opportunities for a back-and-forth of pathogens that evolved to affect humans. Tuberculosis, for instance, is thought to have evolved into a human strain from a cattle strain about 8,000 years ago, though recent results have suggested that it had originated among humans before adapting to afflict cattle. In the same way, smallpox possibly came from camels, flu from pigs and ducks, and measles as well as various sleeping sicknesses from cattle too. As is well-known, rodents carry the pathogen for the plague.

The high population densities of Eurasian towns favoured the evolution of virulence, the appearance of additional opportunistic diseases, and the spread of animal-originated diseases. However, cities in the New World were much more recent when the first wave of European explorers reached them with their animals and associated pathogens. Furthermore, the much lower numbers of domesticated animals in the Americas meant that the human inhabitants of the New World bore a much smaller disease load. Their immune systems were unprepared to deal with the diseases unleashed by Europeans and the resulting pandemics, compounded by violent invasion, were a devastating demonstration of the role of non-human factors in human history.

CONCLUSION: THE COLUMBIAN EXCHANGE, A PREDETERMINED CATASTROPHE?

In 1492, Christopher Columbus opened a new era in the world's history, characterized by the markedly faster rate of species exchange between various parts of the world. When he reached the Americas, it should be understood that he was not only an explorer from Europe, but also the heir of the entire history of Eurasian civilization.

The Columbian exchange brought the products of this Eurasian history—such as wheat, guns, steel, the horse, the honeybee—to the Americas while the products of American civilization—such as maize, the potato, the tomato, chocolate, tobacco, the turkey—crossed the ocean in the other direction. What is now clear is that the exchange was not only limited to the items transported consciously and intentionally by voyagers. Exotic species including weeds, insects, and pathogens also stowed away on many of the same trips, and helped change human history.

The unequal nature of the Columbian exchange is evidenced by the sweeping transformation of the original ecosystems of North America. The Prairies ecosystem may be the one that has changed the most, at least in having become completely inhospitable to its former dominant species, the bison. Nevertheless, the conversion of the forests across a broad north-south swath of the eastern half of the continent into farmland and the large-scale irrigation of the arid terrains of the south, from modern-day California to Texas, have also contributed to creating what may now be called truly a New World.

FURTHER READINGS

Diamond, Jared. 1997. *Guns, Germs, and Steel: The Fates of Human Societies.*

CHAPTER 3

Launching a Revolution

▶▶▶▶▶▶▶▶▶▶▶▶▶▶▶▶▶▶▶▶▶▶▶▶▶▶▶▶

Technological change becomes a major social factor during the Industrial Revolution which came to North America after 1800. By harnessing a new source of inanimate energy (steam) and increasing the use of old ones (water and wind power), technology multiplied the productive capacity of Western economies by relying on new processes revealed by scientific inquiry. The result altered the world's power balance and drove the transformation of North American societies in a single century, even more radically than Europe's simultaneous progress. While the nineteenth century turned as a result into a period of stupendous economic growth and rapid settlement of the North American continent by newcomers, the stage had been set earlier.

The exploration of the North American eastern seaboard by Europeans began a millennium ago with the voyages of Icelandic seafarers who settled hardscrabble farms near the tip of Greenland and traded with the aboriginal peoples of the Canadian Arctic. Their hunting and logging ventures extended much farther south, though the archaeological site of L'Anse-aux-Meadows in Newfoundland is the southernmost evidence for their presence in temperate latitudes. European exploration resumed as early as the late fifteenth century, when Giovanni Caboto sailed across the Atlantic to Newfoundland in the employ of British merchants. Europeans began to cross the Atlantic regularly during the sixteenth century. Seasonal cod fishing and whaling drew many to the seas off modern-day Canada. A number of attempts to establish permanent settlements by the French (in Canada, South Carolina, and Florida), the Spanish (in Florida and South Carolina), and the British (in North

Carolina) proved ill-fated and abortive. Long supply lines as well as the hostility of both the native population and Spanish forces postponed the beginnings of colonization to the seventeenth century. By then, native populations had been much reduced by epidemics and Spanish power humbled. Various European countries began to convert seasonal trading posts or relationships into the footholds for long-term colonies. The British founded Jamestown in Virginia in 1607 and Cuper's Cove in Newfoundland in 1610, while the French occupied the future site of Quebec City in 1608.

Over the next two centuries, European settlers adapted to new conditions in a variety of ways. They brought with them the technologies they knew, but they also needed to adapt the skills and know-how of the original inhabitants. However, the resulting society remained largely pre-industrial until the beginning of the nineteenth century.

FROM LANDSCAPE TO CITYSCAPE

The Industrial Revolution started in England. That much is sure. The rest is debated.

First and foremost, it was marked by a break in economic growth rates leading to the overall enrichment of the population. Before 1780, the yearly growth of the English economy had rarely exceeded 0.5–0.6%. Afterwards, an average growth rate of over 2% per annum was sustained for decades. While the population increased by about 1.25% per annum, the upshot was that, by 1850, the per capita income of a much larger population was multiplied by 2.5 and the English economy was increasingly dominated by industrial activity. A once largely agrarian society turned capitalist, with much of the workforce paid a salary by the owners of the means of production.

The Industrial Revolution was preceded in England by the start of an agricultural revolution. An ongoing process, the transformation of English agriculture was still underway when the British economy began to industrialize. This earlier revolution was characterized by the use of new tools, the development of new animal breeds, the move to enclosed fields, and a general interest for a more rational, even scientific, pursuit of farming. Between 1500 and 1850, the adoption of new crop rotations in the late 17th century (shifting from triennial rotations to a four-year rotation, such as the "Norfolk cycle" of wheat-turnips-barley-clover) and intensive manuring produced a doubling of average wheat yields. (Both techniques improved the replenishment of the soil's nitrogen content.) Indeed, by 1850, the best Dutch and English wheat yields were triple the average medieval yields, but this did not mean farms could support three times as many people, as a significant share of the improved harvests was diverted to animals. Nevertheless, food production increased sufficiently for the English population to increase as well.

The typical large grain-and-dairy farms of the agricultural revolution seen in the Netherlands and England could support 3–4 people per hectare, a relatively low number, though the resulting diet was rich in meat and dairy products. In comparison, the complex agricultural system in southern China (under admittedly better climatic conditions) could support 7–8 people per hectare on average around 1900. Before industrially produced fertilizers, only a few localized areas did much better. In the Zhujiang delta of Guangdong province, for instance, the dike-and-pond farms combining animal husbandry (pigs, ducks, carps, and cattle), multiple cropping (rice, sugarcane, mulberries, etc.), and massive manuring would have produced enough to support 17–25 people per hectare . . . if most of the harvests had not been intended for sale. Around nineteenth-century Paris, suburban growers took in massive quantities of stable manure from the city's horses pulling carriages, cabs, omnibuses, etc., and cultivated various vegetables (a quarter of them under glass). The theoretical productivity reached levels that would have supported 15 people per hectare, though few people might actually choose to survive on a pure salad and vegetables diet if given an alternative.

In the Netherlands, China, and England, high agricultural productivity drove higher levels of urbanization, but this did not lead to an industrial revolution in China or the Netherlands. And yet, China was tremendously active in commerce and manufacturing, while the Netherlands even developed the beginnings of a capitalist economy around its shipbuilding, fisheries, and overseas trade. The new urban population in England was a low-cost labour force as well as a potential market for any nearby industries.

Causes and Factors

Many factors may help to explain the shift to an industrial economy in England between the eighteenth and nineteenth centuries. Deciding which ones were paramount has occasioned no little controversy.

Dating the Industrial Revolution is often enough to set the terms of the debate. Expansive definitions of the Industrial Revolution take in all of the eighteenth and nineteenth centuries in order to consider the entire course of social, economic, and technological changes. Narrower definitions focus on the period between 1800 and 1850 when all of these changes are at work simultaneously for the first time.

From the viewpoint of industrial activity, England did not become a predominantly industrial nation until the 1820s. While that may be economic fact, it understates the novelty of the transformations rooted in the achievements of the previous century.[1]

From the viewpoint of the history of technology, it makes sense to concentrate on an intermediate period extending from 1759 to 1859, coinciding with the accelerating rise in patenting activity (**Figure 1**) and the emergence of new technical systems—canal networks, innovative metallurgical facilities, steam-driven machinery, mechanized textile mills—even though these would only gain country-wide economic significance during the first half of the nineteenth century. By the second half of the nineteenth century, however, those very same technical systems were being replaced by a new set of technologies based on the electrical generator, the internal combustion engine, and industrial chemistry. Obviously, the dates for such broad transformations cannot be precise, but 1759 and 1859 are also milestones in the history of science which may serve to point to the complex relationship between science and technology during this period.

English Patents, to the End of the 18th Century

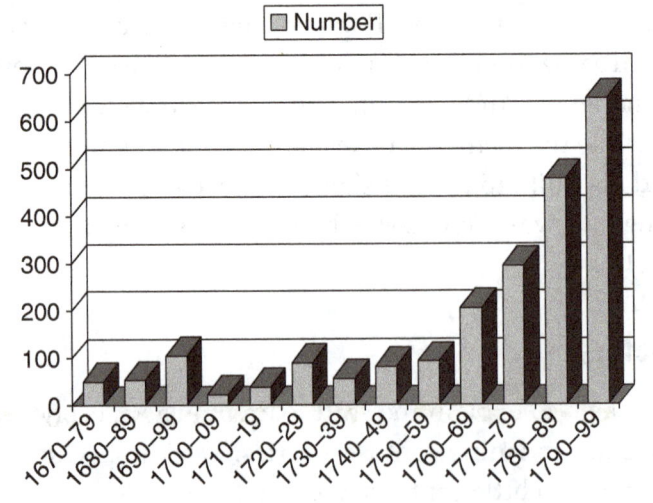

FIGURE 1 ▶ Starting around 1760, the number of British patents taken out by inventors rises rapidly. *(Data source: Christine McLeod,* Inventing the Industrial Revolution: The English patent system, 1660–1800, *1988.)*

---

[1] Jeff Horn, ed., *Reconceptualizing the Industrial Revolution* (2010).

In Europe, natural philosophers of the 17th century such as Galileo, Kepler, and Newton overturned many venerable scientific dogmas. The Catholic Church long opposed the heliocentric theory positing that the Earth revolved around the Sun. While it could not prevent Catholic astronomers from using the theory, it held on to the position that it was only a theory until the early nineteenth century. However, in 1758, it quietly dropped its general prohibition against works on heliocentrism. By then, the scientific method expounded by such philosophers as Francis Bacon and René Descartes was largely recognized as the best way of gaining new knowledge about the world. Beyond physics and mechanics, other philosophers applied the same methods to life itself. In 1758, the Swedish botanist Carl Linnæus published the tenth edition of his *Systema Naturae*, which extended to animals the nomenclature system the author had already established for plants. The systematic study of living beings would lead to the publication by Charles Darwin of the founding work of evolution, *On the Origin of Species*, in 1859.

In the 17th century, scientific societies, including the Royal Society in London and the Académie royale des Sciences in Paris, also expressed the belief that the same rational approach could improve the arts and crafts. If England hosted the Industrial Revolution, it may have been due in part to the expansion of the cult of mechanical rationality launched by Newton's works and fame. Laymen could attend lectures on Newtonian mechanics and mechanical experiments delivered in the coffee-houses of London during the first decades of the 18th century. Gazettes and books propagated the new discoveries and theories of scientists.

When Thomas Newcomen developed an atmospheric steam engine, he benefited from the results of scientific experiments conducted before his time. The very concept of atmospheric pressure had been a highly-publicized result of the Scientific Revolution, demonstrated by the dramatic experiments of Otto von Guericke using metal hemispheres held together by air pressure. Denis Papin's attempts to measure atmospheric pressure had relied on steam-filled cylinders capped with a movable piston. But steam technology would have gone nowhere if England hadn't had plentiful supplies of cheap coal that made it possible to operate Newcomen engines in a profitable way. Neither might British inventions have enjoyed the same success without the partial protection of a patent system.

Indeed, beyond the role of the Scientific Revolution and of technological innovation, other factors had to come into play for England to convert these contributions into the groundwork for an Industrial Revolution. The Scientific Revolution was in no way a monopoly of Great Britain. Philosophers from what is now Italy, Germany, France, the Netherlands, Sweden, Belgium, or Switzerland all shared in the effort to subject the natural world to fresh scrutiny. Nor was technological innovation exclusively confined to Great Britain in the 18th century. Steam-driven pumps, for instance, have a long and shadowy history, showing up as early as the 16th century in mining texts relating to locations as far apart as Germany and Spanish South America.

Beyond urbanization and the new sciences, England was set apart from many other European countries by a number of characteristics. As noted above, it was generously endowed with coal and iron reserves; furthermore, the specific types of coal and iron ore found in England would prove to be crucial for the first wave of new metallurgical techniques. While it imported cotton (first from Asia, later from North America), it was a major wool producer thanks to the large-scale raising of sheep.

Compared to the kingdom of France or the constellation of German principalities, England proper was also relatively compact, its modest territorial expanse already crisscrossed by navigable rivers, canals, roads, and toll roads by 1750. Its terrain was relatively flat, with only a few hilly areas (mainly in the north) or marshes to hamper travel. This only compounded the transportation advantage of being an island, dotted with ports easily reached or linked by sea. By the 18th century, colliers sailed by sea from Newcastle in the north to London in the south to supply the growing city with coal for heating.

Indeed, England became a sea power of the first rank in the course of the 18th century. It outclassed the Netherlands, Spain, and France to begin acquiring a vast colonial empire. By 1763, this empire included colonies settled in North America, holdings in the Caribbean, and trade access to vast parts of India. Though the independence of the United States markedly reduced the size of this first British Empire, the development of trade with India, of sugar plantations in the West Indies, and of the colonial North American population meant that Britain's colonial market was a steadily growing one.

Scholars have pointed to the attraction of such constantly growing returns as an incentive to invest capital in more productive machinery. Did capitalism drive innovation or did innovation drive capitalism? The clearest role of innovation was probably to magnify the rewards of capitalism and colonialism.

Governance is sometimes neglected in such listings and yet it was one of England's clearest comparative advantages. In an age of absolute monarchs, England enjoyed by the middle of the 18th century, a stable limited democracy bequeathed by the Glorious Revolution of 1688, the rule of law, and great respect for property rights, extending to the intellectual property rights embodied in the patent and copyright systems. This meant that entrepreneurs could create new businesses without needing to worry that an arbitrary act of state power might deprive them of the fruits of their labour, while inventors could market a patented invention and know that they were guaranteed a monopoly over its exploitation. Of course, technological innovation might not have been as present or as fast in a society less open to free enterprise. The regulatory burden of 18th-century England may have been lighter than in the better organized Continental states, but it seems certain that, for much of this period at least, existing regulations were not enforced as rigorously as elsewhere.

Religious dissenters also enjoyed some degree of protection from persecution in England. In European countries subject to Catholic rule, Protestants might be marginalized or wholly ostracized. After 1688, Catholics were barred from most official positions in England, as were other religious minorities such as Jews, Quakers, and other Protestant denominations standing apart from the official Anglican creed. Barred from seeking success through government careers, members of such minorities may have sought it from business endeavours and found fewer barriers to such success than in the Continental states. Protestant dissenters and Jews did play a disproportionate role in some fields, but most of the innovative activity was carried out by members of the majority, Anglo-Saxon and Anglican.

Others have pointed to a broader atmosphere of intellectual ferment arising out of the age of geographical discoveries opened by Columbus, the Protestant Reformation of the 16th and 17th centuries, and of the Scientific Revolution. If so many certainties could be overturned, as English poet John Donne noted in 1611, what else might be called into doubt and wholly altered by new insights?

The use of metallic movable type for printing combined with the small number of letters required by Western alphabets led to a printing explosion in Europe. By the end of the 15th century, editions of the books on architecture by Roman builder and engineer Vitruvius were among the first technical books to be printed. During the 16th century, printers began to offer theatres of machines featuring images of technical devices both realistic and fantastical. While such albums were too expensive for the majority of craftsmen, other printing products increasingly catered to a more popular audience. By the 17th century, science journals included reports of a technical nature. In the 18th century, the first gazettes and newspapers devoted increasing space to novel devices and other inventions.

Indeed, Great Britain enjoyed a broad freedom of the press. Combined with the greater possibilities for interpersonal contacts in growing cities, it favoured the circulation of many ideas, some of which could find fertile ground in the English business environment. At the very least, the habits of public discussion associated with the existence of a free press made it easier to put forward new possibilities, including in the business and technical fields.

In the 18th century, the French monarchy controlled closely what was published in Paris and other French institutions (the Church, the regional Parliaments, professional corporations) also played the role of gatekeepers. The power of censorship was intended to protect legitimate publishers, printers, and booksellers from pirate editions, but it acted in practice to discourage the free circulation of ideas. In England, the Parliamentary licensing system used in the same way collapsed by the end of the 17th century, which had also seen the eclipse of episcopal censorship and the wane of corporate influence over publishing choices. Libel, obscenity, and blasphemy laws were the main tool left to the English government to control the press in the eighteenth century. Since they required active intervention, the practical result was much greater freedom of the press in England than in the Continental states.[2]

However, one needed to know how to read to access this growing literature. Literacy rates were rising across much of northern Europe in fact, as a result of the slow rise of living standards and of the spread of Protestantism which encouraged believers to read the Bible for themselves. They rose higher and faster in England, though. For instance, literacy in France rose from 29% to 47% for men and from 14% to 27% for women, between 1686–1690 and 1786–1790. However, in England literacy is estimated to stand at 45% for men and 25% for women around 1714, close to the levels achieved in France three quarters of a century later. During the second half of the century, English literacy levels reached 60% for men and 40% for women, clearly outstripping the French. In New England, however, perhaps as a result of its settlement by Puritans, literacy rose from 61% to 84% for men and from 31% to 46% for women between 1660 and 1760.

National averages hide significant variations. In 1786–179, the average literacy rate for France is estimated to have been 37%, but male literacy rates in northern parts of the country reached 80% while the same rate in the south was 29% or less. While female literacy rates were on the increase, they remained lower than male rates. There was also a clear dichotomy, not only between the sexes or between regions, but also between cities and the countryside. In Paris, 66% of men and 62% of women were able to read in the time of Louis XVI (1774–1792). Similarly, average literacy rates for major cities such as Lyons, Marseille, and Toulouse were also

---

[2] Anastasia Castillo, *Banned Books: Censorship in Eighteenth-Century England* (GRIN Verlag, 2010), pp. 66–68.

significantly higher than the national average, so that rates in the countryside needed to be even lower. The same was true for a city like Amsterdam in the Netherlands.

While literacy was not a prerequisite for a technical career, even in England, there is no doubt it was nearly essential for an entrepreneur wishing to function within the legal framework of patents and contracts. An inventor also needed to be able to find out what the state of the art was for a given technology to avoid covering old ground. Modern research suggests that greater idea flow (as measured by physical mobility, communications, or purchasing behaviour) correlates with higher productivity and creative output from small groups. Greater engagement within groups as well as a willingness to import ideas from outside the group often yield positive outcomes.

The innovation-minded did find other ways to facilitate the flow of new ideas. Specialized clubs and societies were created to share and disseminate knowledge, quite apart from existing universities concerned with traditional education. Though certainly one of the oldest, the Royal Society founded in London in 1666 was only the best known. One of the most influential of the 18th century was the Lunar Society of Birmingham, gathering luminaries of the Industrial Revolution such as James Watt, Matthew Boulton, and Josiah Wedgwood, as well as noted philosophers. Many lecturers travelled and took advantage of the multiplication of coffee-houses since the 17th century to deliver talks or public courses on the new discoveries of the day in fields like mechanics, electricity, and chemistry. By 1750, as a result of the availability of such lectures and the ease of publishing, the relatively literate English population enjoyed unparalleled access to the new scientific and technical ideas of the day.

In short, while no single English advantage may suffice to explain why the Industrial Revolution was launched in Britain, the accumulation of so many English advantages would certainly leave scholars at a loss to explain, if the Industrial Revolution had in fact begun elsewhere, why it would have failed to take root in England first.

By the second half of the 18th century, a transportation revolution described in the next chapter created additional opportunities for the entrepreneurs who invested in the breakthrough technologies of the age. While toll roads reduced travel times in England, canals would float coal to the new forges that would turn it into coke for use, supply engine boilers with coal or wood, or bring mechanically-woven cloth to customers.

DEFINING TECHNOLOGIES OF THE INDUSTRIAL REVOLUTION

The Industrial Revolution was built upon a set of interrelated innovations. Three categories of technological transformations—in power generation, metallurgy, and mechanization—may be identified as hallmarks of the early Industrial Revolution as long as it is remembered there were other significant inventions in the 18th century. Though better known today for his automata, French mechanic Jacques Vaucanson pioneered not only the automation of silk weaving but the improvement of machine tools. The ideal of standardized, interchangeable parts for complex devices was first pursued in earnest by artillerist Jean-Baptiste Vaquette de Gribeauval and gunsmith Honoré Blanc in France shortly before the French Revolution of 1789. Liquid bleach was discovered in 1789 by French chemist Claude Louis Berthollet as an outgrowth of contemporary chemical investigations. Gas lighting was pioneered in 1792 by Scottish engineer William Murdoch, a then employee of Boulton and Watt.

Many of the era's innovations were incremental improvements, while others were only implemented on an industrial scale in the nineteenth century. On the other hand, the defining technologies of the Industrial Revolution achieved concrete results almost immediately and proved to be fruitful beyond the applications first envisioned for them. The steam engine was quickly applied to navigation and land transportation. Mechanization benefited weaving and spinning, but also flour-milling in North America. As for the cheaper forms of cast and wrought iron, they found a range of uses in manufacturing and infrastructure.

What was singular about England was that it not only led in a single sector. Besides steam engines, its lead in metallurgical improvements was unmatched elsewhere. And the mechanization of the cotton industry resulted in significant labour savings for manufacturers while creating a mass market for cheap consumer goods.

Furthermore, these defining technologies generated definite synergies. In the area of power generation, a series of inventors including Thomas Newcomen, John Smeaton, and James Watt created an increasingly versatile prime mover able to compete with the age-old machinery turning water or wind power into motion. First created as a mere water pump, the steam engine converted the thermal energy of coal into mechanical energy.

By the end of the 18th century, the manufacture of Watt's steam engine was cost-effective in part because of another series of innovation in the area of metallurgy. Coke replaced charcoal in the production of cast iron, driving down its cost, while assorted improvements also decreased the cost of wrought iron and even steel.

The mechanization of spinning and weaving advanced by leaps and bounds in the space of 40 years. By 1779, the spinning mule jenny of Crompton could be driven by the improved steam engines of Smeaton or Watt. The fact that machinery could now be tended by a handful of women and children heralded a change in the organization of labour that would yield its full effects during the following century.

Steam Engines

Power technology was certainly important. French prosperity in the Middle Ages had owed much to the application of water power to gristmills, sawmills, foundries, breweries, etc. Starting in the 16th century, the Netherlands developed wind power to compensate for its lack of water power. Windmills were used for pumping water and draining new fields, but they also helped saw wood, grind flour, etc. When Europeans began settling North America, they brought over both watermills and windmills **(Figure 2)**.

FIGURE 2 ▶ A rare case of the two main types of mills on the same nineteenth-century site: on the right, a windmill of the tower type; on the left, a watermill supplied with water by a wooden conduit. *(Picture by author at Isle-aux-Coudres, Québec, 1992.)*

Throughout Europe, scientists began to analyze the performance of waterwheels by the turn of the 18th century, relying on the laws of mechanics developed by an earlier generation of physicists. In France, members of the Royal Academy of the Sciences like Antoine Parent, Henri Pitot, and Charles Bossut were in the forefront of this effort. In England, engineer John Smeaton studied both waterwheels and the Newcomen steam engine in order to optimize their design. What the French academicians and Smeaton helped to establish was the apparently unimprovable efficiency of the overshot vertical waterwheel.

By then, though, a new and quite different machine held out promise as a prime mover.

England had been burning coal since the Middle Ages (for heat) and coal was used as a source of heat in foundries, glass-making workshops, etc. It was only in the 18th century however, that coal became the key to a power source more versatile than water power or wind power, and one that became more powerful too in time.

The origins of the steam engine are obscure. By the end of the 17th century, a long tradition of crude devices intended to raise water with the help of steam pressure had led to a pump patented in 1698 by Thomas Savery. In 1699, this savvy and well-connected inventor obtained an act of Parliament extending the validity of his patent for any use of the driving power of fire so that he enjoyed thereafter a legally-mandated monopoly over steam-driven machinery in England for a period of over 30 years.

When the French experimenter Denis Papin came to England in the early 18th century with the design for a steam pump based on his scientific work involving atmospheric pressure, he was naturally treated as an unwelcome interloper by Savery and his entourage. On the other hand, Savery was apparently able to come to an agreement with the inventor of a truly effective steam pump. In 1712, English ironmonger Thomas Newcomen completed a machine made possible by the fortuitous discovery of the rapid condensation of steam by water injection. In the Newcomen engine, atmospheric pressure did most of the work and steam merely served to restore the machine to its starting position with the help of a counterweight.

The Newcomen machine used up prodigious quantities of fuel to perform its work, but if the uniquely powerful pumping motion that it generated was absolutely required or if the fuel was no object, it could provide an irreplaceable service. Within less than 20 years, it was replicated throughout Europe. Venice had one built in 1717–1718, the Belgian city of Liège in 1720, France in 1726 and 1732, Sweden in 1728, and so on. The Newcomen engine was sufficiently expensive to run that it was only imported to North America in 1753, when Philip Schuyler wished to drain his copper mine in New Jersey. It was adapted to land transportation by French military engineer Nicolas-Joseph Cugnot in 1769, while French machinist Jacques-Constantin Périer attempted to drive a small boat on a river with an underpowered version in 1775 and the French inventor Jouffroy d'Abbans managed to get a much larger craft to steam upstream in Lyon eight years later, for about fifteen minutes.

In spite of its inefficiency, the Newcomen engine showed the way for further progress. While Smeaton tinkered with its design, James Watt took a more radical approach. In 1776, he added a separate condenser to the basic cylinder. Instead of having to cool and reheat the cylinder, the steam was evacuated into a separate vessel where it would condense apart from the cylinder, which would stay hot. Other innovations followed.

Newcomen engines were hulking beasts: the larger they were, the more efficient they were. The fittings tended to be crude since a few leaks counted for little in the general energy budget. In comparison, Watt's design was high-precision engineering taking advantage of a series of improvements in the art of boring metal cylinders and achieving tighter tolerances. Unlike the Newcomen pump, the engine offered by Boulton and Watt was manufactured in their own workshops instead of being assembled on the site where it was to operate. It was sold on the basis of its superior fuel efficiency and Watt kept improving its performance. Tighter fittings and the back-and-forth action introduced by later models allowed the engine to become more compact and open new vistas for the applications of steam power.

Producing Wrought Iron

The oldest iron furnaces were mere pits dug into the ground so that the resulting metal had to be lifted out of the hole. Efficiency was low, with less than 20% of the metal in the raw ore being converted into usable form. Later furnaces might be dug into a hillside, topped with a masonry chimney, and pierced with openings to blow air onto the mixture of burning charcoal and iron ore. These were known as *bloomeries*. In medieval Europe, a new type of low furnace developed, sometimes called a Catalan forge. It was provided with an opening near the base so that the iron *bloom* could be taken out more easily leading to larger models. Bellows driven by a waterwheel produced the required airflow.

Such a furnace produced nearly pure iron. It was delicate work as the amount of raw materials—charcoal, iron ore, limestone, or a similar material used to stick together the ore residues—needed to be closely matched so that the molten iron didn't absorb any carbon from the charcoal used as fuel. Air circulation was key, to take away the carbon, and leave in the end a metal mass crusted with slag. The bloom could then be hammered by a smith or a forge worker to get rid of the slag.

The product of this direct process was known as bar iron or *wrought* iron (because it had been *worked*). It included less than 1% carbon as well as various other impurities in vanishingly small proportions: manganese, sulfur, phosphorus, and silicon. Wrought iron could also be worked afterwards because it was relatively malleable and ductile if it was heated. It could stretch or bend without breaking as readily as other forms of iron. It also stood up better to sudden shocks. Tools or other implements were made from it in villages remote from larger installations.

By the 15th century, these bloomeries competed with blast furnaces, loaded from above and heated to produce a continuous flow of molten iron. Besides slag, blast furnaces produced cast iron (or pig iron): a mix of iron, carbon (up to 4%), and various impurities. Hard but relatively brittle, cast iron could be poured into a mould, either immediately or after a second heating. To convert cast iron into a form suitable for use in tools, the carbon content needed to be reduced and the metal recrystallized. In the 18th century, this was done by reheating the pig iron in the presence of an air flow to oxidize the carbon (thereby removing it from the iron). This produced something resembling bloom iron in the form of wrought iron bars that could be turned into tools, weapons, and other products requiring the specific toughness of wrought iron.

Blast furnaces were taller, more expensive masonry structures, but they quickly demonstrated a level of productivity the bloomeries could not match. By the 18th century, they could produce a tonne of cast iron a day, but they had run into size limitations. Past a certain height, the weight of iron ore simply crushed the fragile charcoal and ground it into dust, which did not burn as well.

To use a terminology popularized by Thomas Hughes, fuel was the reverse salient that prevented iron production from progressing. The blast furnace was perfectly adequate to the task, but charcoal wasn't. Coal was an obvious substitute, at first glance, but the sulphur content of most coal seams led to contamination of the resulting metal, which was prone to fissuring or flaking. To eliminate the sulphur and other volatiles, coal was eventually transformed into coke, either through simple heating or a more complex distillation. More resilient than charcoal, coke could be piled into a larger furnace without being flattened, producing more heat and making it possible to process more ore at one go.

Since coal was abundantly available in England, the limited stock of wood no longer mattered as long as coal could be extracted and moved cheaply. Steam engines used to pump water from mines increasingly helped to control extraction costs, while the exploding canal network of the later 18th century helped with transportation costs. By the end of the 1780s, 80% of English cast iron was produced with coke. By 1810, the proportion reached 90%.

Since the Darbys had demonstrated the advantages of using coke as early as 1709, uptake was not that fast. In fact, the adoption of coke was slowed by one drawback: the increased presence of silicon in the pig iron produced with it. The development of puddling by Peter Onions and Henry Cort in the early 1780s, followed by the invention of the rolling mill by Cort, made it possible to produce a better grade of iron using coke.

The key invention was the reverberatory furnace. It made it possible to reheat the cast iron in the presence of oxygen while separating it from the sulphur- and phosphorus-rich fuel. This was achieved by the construction of a reverberation vaulting that channeled the hot gases produced by combustion so that the heat generated by the burning fuel was both radiated by the flowing gases and also reflected from above onto the ore bed. A small aperture cut into the side of the furnace allowed workers known as puddlers to stir the molten cast iron. Only the toughest men, renowned for their endurance of heat, were up to the job that required them to stir the molten iron with a pole held at arm's length for up to an hour. When the impurities were oxidized, the purer iron began to solidify as its melting point increased. The puddlers would then break the metal crust to expose the liquid underneath to the air.

Since the reverberatory furnace could use coal instead of the costlier charcoal, cast iron could be turned into wrought iron at a lower cost. The wrought iron removed from the reverberatory furnace was forged with a shingle or shingling hammer, and then transferred to a rolling mill, where the metal was given its final shape using rollers introduced by Cort. By the middle of the nineteenth century, the largest ironworks supplied the railways with massive quantities of wrought iron for rails.

While coke unlocked the iron-making potential of 18th-century England, it was not a sine qua non. In the United States, almost all iron production still relied on charcoal as late as 1840 due to the still abundant reserves of wood throughout eastern North America. The move away from charcoal happened quickly, though. By the middle of the 1850s, less than half of the US output of cast iron relied on charcoal. By the end of the US Civil War, it was about a quarter.

In the United States, anthracite coal (characterized by its nearly pure carbon composition) was the most common substitute for charcoal as it was more abundant east of the Alleghenies. It wasn't until railroads crossed the mountains and Pittsburgh centralized iron production that coke-produced iron prevailed.

Coke came even later to Canada. It wasn't until the 1870s that it fuelled a blast furnace on a large scale, in Londonderry (Nova Scotia), and it only came into general use in the early twentieth century. However, by then, coke had been used extensively for puddling for many years. Indeed, countries including the United States, Sweden, Russia, and Austria continued to use charcoal for cast iron production down to the Second World War. The reasons included the abundance of forests, coal grades that could not easily be converted into coke, transportation costs, and tariffs. Charcoal also yielded a better grade of iron, with less phosphorus and sulphur, all else being equal.

Down to the early twentieth century, iron produced with charcoal continued to find niche uses where reliability was paramount: locomotive axles, gears, and drive shafts, high-end cutlery, and surgical implements. Cart wheels absorbed most of this production. In 1894, 90 of 94 North American blast furnaces still using charcoal named them as one of their main products.

Producing Steel

Steel did not play a crucial part in the early Industrial Revolution, though it played a much larger role in the transformations of the late nineteenth century, sometimes dubbed a Second Industrial Revolution. In 18th-century England, though, steel was something of a specialty metal.

If desired, smiths would reheat wrought iron in the presence of charcoal (pulverized in some cases) in order to endow the iron with a surface slightly enriched in carbon. The blisters that formed on the surface of the original wrought iron bars contained the best steel, naturally called blister or cementation steel, characterized by intermediate carbon content (approximately 2%). Once worked by a smith to give it greater homogeneity, cementation steel combined the advantages of cast iron (hardness) and of wrought iron (springiness).

By 1740, an English clockmaker, Benjamin Huntsman, perfected the melting of cementation steel in small crucibles. The process only yielded about 30 kilograms of steel at a time, but crucible steel became the new standard for the ultimate in steel quality. As such, it could be used in clocks, where springs needed to be reliably wound and unwound thousands of time. It could also be used to make medical instruments that needed to retain an edge while avoiding untimely breaks that would leave fragments inside a wound or incision.

MECHANIZING HUMAN WORK

The mechanization of human labour took different courses in Great Britain and North America, especially with respect to the activities transformed by key breakthroughs. Inventors took advantage of relatively simple mechanical devices, sometimes known since Antiquity, to mechanize work that had previously been done by hand, often in home workshops.

Mechanization does not always imply new sources of power. Until the twentieth century, water power (using waterwheels down to the first half of the nineteenth century, and highly efficient turbines later) proved sufficient for many mechanized processes. Starting with Watt's double-acting steam engine, it became feasible for such engines to drive the rotation of a power shaft. As a consequence, any machinery designed to be driven by the rotary motion of a waterwheel or turbine could henceforth be driven by a properly designed steam engine. In practice, however, the cost of the machinery and fuel was high enough that water power remained competitive for decades.

To justify the expense of mechanization, entrepreneurs targeted commercial staples: cloth in England and flour in the United States. Such basic necessities are always needed, however dire the overall economic situation. Though it was possible to produce clothes at home, people will spend money on clothing before they will spend it on many other items. At the right price point, store-bought clothing could save householders much time and effort. Even basic textile products required a number of distinct processing steps to get from the raw material to the final product. Cotton, for instance, needed to be cleaned and sorted; carded; stretched and straightened into "rovings;" spun to form thread; woven; bleached, and often dyed or printed before it could be sold. The process was similarly involved, though with some differences, for linen and wool.

This could be done on a small scale at home, in the worker's own "cottage" or in an adjoining shed or outbuilding. If an individual contracted with a cloth merchant to perform this work, taking in bundles of raw fiber to be turned into cloth, the entire process of making cloth for sale (carding, spinning, weaving, bleaching, dyeing, printing) was designated a *cottage industry*. Some equipment was needed, such as a spinning wheel or a loom, but it was mechanically simple and easily maintained. For the contract workers in the countryside, the associated income was rarely their sole livelihood. The merchants could pay them less, but what they saved by not having to deal with the city guilds of workers, they would spend in part on travel costs. It was only one example of the "putting out" system applied to a number of trades for which entrepreneurs would distribute work to rural men or women working out of their homes.

Mechanization first took hold early in the textile industry, though North American entrepreneurs were less innovative and mostly followed the technological lead of the British industry. By 1750, to reduce their travel costs, British cloth merchants had turned to concentrating the workers responsible for manufacturing on a single site, and often within a single building, the "factory" (or mill). The new "factory" made it easier for the merchants to supervise and control their workers. But the mechanization of textile production reinforced the trend towards concentration. The capital investment needed to acquire and operate more complex machines became so great it started to take manufacturing out of the hands of small businessmen. To ensure maximum return on their investment, the new industrialists gathered all the machinery under one roof, close to the source of power (a watercourse or steam engine), so that both the machines and the workers could be kept under close watch.

Devised in the 1730s, John Kay's flying shuttle made weaving easier and it became widespread in both cotton and wool production in the 1760s. Around 1764, James Hargreaves invented the *spinning jenny* to stretch, straighten, and then twist together the raw fibers to produce thread; it could handle more yarn than the traditional spinning wheel and deal with even the finest fibers. A single woman could turn the handle of the wheel putting a number of spindles in motion.

In 1769, Richard Arkwright patented a spinning machine that he only sold to factories using water power (the "water frame" machine); as a result, it was suited only for the strongest cotton fibers. By 1779, Samuel Crompton had combined the two in a *spinning mule* that became the basis for the British cotton industry's success for most of the nineteenth century.

Eventually, these machines were driven by steam power. As there were economies of scale to be gained from operating larger waterwheels (or turbines) or larger steam engines, it was more profitable to gather several machines (operated by one prime mover) under one roof. As a consequence, the mechanized factory became synonymous with the changeover from the cottage era to the industrial age.

As early as 1785, however, the lead of the British textile industry became obvious to outside observers. One British expatriate employed by the French government warned that, compared to French facilities, the British enjoyed a cost advantage of up to 30% in cotton spinning, due to greater mechanization (facilitated by a lower cost of capital), easier water transportation (on canals and navigable rivers), and a better supply of coal. While France was estimated to have about 900 spinning jennies by 1790, the British industry could rely on 20,000 spinning jennies and up to another 8,000 mule jennies.

By 1811, the British textile industry had accumulated between five and six million spindles, while France trailed with a million spindles. The German state of Saxony was ahead of the rest with about 250,000 spindles, which was more than Switzerland (150,000) or the United States (100,000). Furthermore, British industrialists relied more and more on steam power while other manufacturers made do with water power. Therefore, British mills or factories were more often found in cities and small towns, since they relied on coal brought by canals or railways, while their North American counterparts were often rural, since they depended on water power.

The new methods of the textile industry were slow to cross over to North America. In 1790, the United States had 2,000 spindles while Great Britain had 2.41 million. Successfully transferring textile technology depended not so much on bringing over machines as it did on attracting skilled workers who understood the machines.

English-born Samuel Slater (1768–1835) came to the United States in 1789. By 1793, he'd founded his own spinning mill, mostly employing children. While Slater's practices were widely copied, the United States textile industry only progressed slowly before 1812, when the leap to 100,000 spindles in the United States paled when compared to the 6 million spindles of British industry. The competition from British-made cloth was fierce, and manufacturers stuck with waterwheels while English manufacturers converted to steam power.

In the early United States, gristmills were one of the first places to develop a substantial level of mechanization. Around 1785, Oliver Evans, a millwright and mechanic, invented the grain elevator and the hopper boy. The grain elevator applied to grain a well-known mechanism for raising water, strapping small buckets to a leather belt running up and over the drive shaft of a waterwheel. The elevator could raise up to 300 bushels of grain an hour, taking over the work done previously by strong men.

The hopper boy was a large revolving rake attached to a vertical drive shaft, spreading the ground meal on a surface to help it dry and then guiding it to a chute. As its name implied, the invention replaced the boy who used to do the work. In combination with several other devices, these inventions largely mechanized the operations of a large mill. Evans obtained patents in 1791. Teaming up with his brothers, he designed and built a mechanized flour mill as a showpiece, describing an idealized version of it in a pivotal book, *The Young Mill-Wright and Miller's Guide* (1795). The savings of time and labour, as well as the improvements in flour quality, eventually convinced a generation of US millwrights to consider mechanization.

These inventions helped boost merchant milling, already one of the principal revenue generators in the early United States. Though adoption was slow, most mills built or refurbished during the early nineteenth century were mechanized. By 1860, flour milling was the leading industry of the United States by dollar value, but it employed far fewer people (27,000) than those employed in the manufacture of cotton cloth (114,000) or of boots and shoes (123,000).

Evans also perfected a high-pressure steam engine that he tried to use in land vehicles before applying it to flour mills. Though Evans was definitely a pioneer, an increasing number of machine shops in both Canada and the United States were able, by 1810, to turn out such complex machines as steam engines. Many employed native-born draftsmen, metalworkers, founders, fitters, and machine builders, though a number of firms depended on experts brought in from abroad, usually Great Britain.

The last word in mechanical competence was still British. In 1830, when Robert Stevens wanted to build the first steam railroad in North America, he travelled to England to select and purchase a locomotive. A decade later, however, American-built locomotives had become available.

By then, the price of flour had been lowered by the reduction in production costs brought about by mechanization, and also by the decrease in transportation costs resulting from the availability of canals, steamboats, and railroads.

CHAPTER 4

Canals, Raftsmen, and Snakeheads

▶▶▶▶▶▶▶▶▶▶▶▶▶▶▶▶▶▶▶▶▶▶▶▶▶▶▶▶▶▶

After the opening of land for cultivation which led to rapid deforestation in the eastern half of North America, the next great transformation of the landscape was wrought by canal fever. The success of the Erie Canal stimulated the building of many more and led to the generalized management of waterways (through dams, levees, and channels) to control flooding, generate power, and facilitate commerce. The linking of once separate hydrographic basins and the access of inland waters granted to sea-going ships have had powerful effects on the natural environment, biodiversity, and the exploitation of natural resources. The combination of cultivation and river management led to the draining of many wetlands. The opening of new waterways allowed exotic species to reach inland lakes and rivers, either as stowaways or as invaders using canals to bypass natural obstacles. By boosting commerce, canals fostered greater exploitation of natural resources, including forests.

BASIC TECHNOLOGIES OF EUROPEAN SETTLEMENT

The spread of European settlers depended on the mastery of a number of different technologies. The firearm is often held to be a distinctively European advantage. However, by the time European powers such as France, Great Britain, or the Netherlands began to lay claim in earnest to North American lands, traders were already offering guns to the aboriginal populations who were even more dependent than settlers on hunting for their subsistence and correspondingly willing to offer more for appropriate firearms. Towards the end of the 17th century, native hunters and warriors of the Eastern seaboard often owned flintlock muskets that were more advanced than the older matchlock muskets brought over by English settlers or provided to them out of military stocks. The French colonists mostly relied on hunting guns using flintlocks made in France and widely shared with aboriginal allies or fur trading partners.

During the 18th century, marked by nearly 50 years of intermittent military conflict, flintlock use became common. New types of guns, such as the long rifle, became available for hunters and pioneers on the frontier. The overall firearm ownership rate may have declined somewhat by the turn of the nineteenth century as peace returned, cities grew larger, hunting became less of a necessity, and the risk of armed clashes with native populations more remote. Nevertheless, firearms remained crucial for the subsistence of both settler and aboriginal populations well into the nineteenth century.

The oldest metal axes were made in Europe, following ancient patterns, and brought over to North America for use or trade. By the end of the 18th century, though, North American blacksmiths increasingly opted to make what became known as the felling axe or poll axe. It was characterized by an iron blade that was short and wide, provided with a steel edge, and counterbalanced by a heavy poll (or butt) on the other side of the (hickory or maple) handle so that it moved steadily through the air and struck true, with increased hitting power. Greater accuracy made it easier to cut down trees to clear fields or to be sold as lumber.

By the second half of the nineteenth century, such axes were made of a solid piece of steel as the cost of steel plummeted. US manufacturers found a sizable market abroad for their best axe heads and British makers sometimes copied them, right down to the identifying marks. Other types of axes continued to be made and sold for purposes besides tree-felling, featuring broader blades for hewing, for example.

By then, though, the twin-bladed (or double-bitted) axe was becoming popular throughout the northern part of the continent. One bit was kept finely honed and used for felling and lopping branches off fallen trees. The other was left rougher and used in circumstances where it could be damaged: carving stumps and roots, or clearing out brush. By the turn of the twentieth century, the crosscut saw began replacing axes for most professional lumbering and the rise of the chainsaw wrote their epitaph during the second half of the twentieth century.

While the axe answered the needs of both individual users and commercial concerns, the watermill was an industrial operation from the start, whether it turned out flour, paper, wool, or sawn timber. The use of the waterwheel for milling goes back to Antiquity and European settlers wasted little time in establishing both watermills and windmills in North America. While the windmill was rarely used for anything but milling grain and pumping water in North America, the watermill was turned to a number of industrial uses. As the Industrial Revolution spread to North America, the watermill underpinned many early industrial enterprises and gained a new lease on life as the more efficient turbine replaced the older waterwheel. Indeed, steam power didn't start displacing water power in US manufacturing establishments until the 1860s.

The development of canals for transportation in North America mainly occurred during the first half of the nineteenth century, in the age of the felling axe, the musket and rifle, and the watermill. Canals were a lynchpin of the era's transportation system, assisting both settlement west of the Appalachians and industrialization.

COMMERCE AND TRANSPORTATION IN A LAND OF MOVING PATHS

Rivers were the first highways of North America. As the 17th-century French philosopher Blaise Pascal noted, they are "moving paths that take you where you want to go." The European settlers adopted, especially in Canada, the Indian canoe in order to travel faster by water, but they also used boats modeled on the ones they had used in Europe.

Though Europe was covered with roads, rivers were even there the first choice for the transportation of many goods. Transportation costs by water were usually about 25–50% of transportation costs overland. Towns and villages were sited by rivers which provided the power for flour mills, saw mills, and the trip-hammers of forges, as well as water for the tanneries and breweries. Major towns often grew where roads intersected rivers so that goods brought overland could be transferred to boats or ships.

Rivers carried not only ships, boats, barks, and rafts, but also logs floated down from the forests upstream. In North America, the logs might be gathered to make large rafts steered by raftsmen. Such rafts were known as *"cages"* in French-speaking Canada. The last timber raft was floated down the Ottawa River past Canada's federal Parliament on June 18, 1904, though logs continued to be floated downstream for several more decades, using tugs and log booms.

In the absence of a motor, travelling upstream on most rivers is hard work. It can be done with oars or poles, with sails, or with the help of men or horses pulling a barge by sheer strength. Most rivers are not wide enough to let sailboats tack upstream, and very few rivers run in the right direction relative to the prevailing winds. One exception was the Loire in France, which runs almost due west over a long stretch before reaching the sea. This helped river traffic immensely since it was possible to go downstream with the current, perhaps rowing to go faster, and then to use the prevailing winds from the west to go back upstream. This was one of the main factors that made the Loire a major commercial artery of its day.

Even on rivers characterized by a fast and powerful flow, such as the Rhône in France, the cost of goods hauled upstream was still 25% cheaper than goods carried overland. Going downstream, which was both easier and faster, the cost of goods carried by water was as much as 80% less than the cost of cartage. Often, the main use of roads, with respect to commerce, was to provide travellers with the shortest path between two rivers. In Europe, roads became bottlenecks as trade volume rose and both England and France spent more and more money on the improvement of roads.

To make rivers easier to navigate, the merchant guilds in Europe financed towpaths and levees, erected signposts, and financed regular dredging. Dams and weirs were built to regulate the flow of the rivers (**Figure 1**). This created stretches of calmer flow, and the addition of portals or doors to these dams or weirs turned them into flash locks that simplified navigating up and down stream. Unfortunately, these had drawbacks: first, when the gate was opened, a boat had to wait for the water levels to equalize before proceeding upstream; then, once it entered the upper

FIGURE 1 ▶ A weir used to control the water level of a reservoir behind a hydroelectric dam. *(Picture by author near Montreal, Québec, 2007.)*

part of a river sectioned by a dam or a weir, it might have to wait a long time before the water level in the upper section rose sufficiently to let it enter the following section. These waits made the process a long one. Furthermore, if the weir stocked water for a mill, the boatmen had to come to an agreement with the miller, and doubly so if the way through was up or down a mill race.

In some places, boats and barges were winched, either upstream between the piles of a bridge or up a dry or wet ramp that substituted for a lock. Some of the earliest canals, especially in China, used such ramps, if only to reduce the water lost through the use of locks. Canals, as they were perfected, became the gold standard of water transportation. On a properly (i.e., minimally) graded canal, running straight with packed towpaths alongside, a horse could haul in excess of 30 tonnes, depending on speed and distance travelled.

At the same time, major rivers were increasingly provided with towpaths (**Figure 2**), so that horses or men could pull upstream barges carrying various goods. This was easier than poling a barge upstream. One horse pulling a river barge could move a 25-tonne payload (excluding the weight of the boat) while one horse pulling a cart would not move much more than 2 tonnes over the best macadam roads available in the 18th century. (In 1698, Thomas Savery asserts he's seen a horse haul as much as 100 tonnes in a barge, going about three miles an hour—though he doesn't say for how long.) Once canals started to be built, the comparison between transport by water and transport by road became particularly stark.

FIGURE 2 ▶ A towpath running by the side of the Canal du Midi, wide enough to be used by men or horses hauling a barge on the canal. *(Picture by author near Argeliers, France, 2007.)*

Still, towpaths cannot be built securely alongside mighty rivers like the Rhône, with annual floods and a strong current continuously undercutting the banks. Even less impetuous rivers have obstacles: shoals, sand banks, snags, rapids, falls ... Floods and droughts make it harder to navigate a river with any regularity. In Europe, the cutting down of forests was responsible for the greater vagaries of rivers, aggravating both floods and droughts.

In North America too, rivers were major highways. The fur trade depended on canoes, characterized by their shallow draft, light weight, and easily repaired hulls.

The lumber industry used rafts or just floated down logs individually. Until the middle of the nineteenth century, North American rivers hosted four other types of boats: keelboats, flatboats, steamboats, and horseboats, though motorboats eventually overcame all their competitors for productive uses.

The keelboats were distinguished by their keels. They relied on oars or sails or pole setters or some combination thereof for propulsion. In Canada, the famous York boats were keelboats; they came into general use around 1820 and served well into the twentieth century. They managed to keep a toehold for several decades in the face of competition by steamboats because they were cheaper and could venture into rivers too narrow for early steamboats.

The flatboats were barges built to carry bulk goods such as harvests, raw materials, or construction goods downstream. Often, they took advantage of the spring or fall floods. Once they were unloaded, they were often dismantled and sold for scrap to spare the crew from having to navigate them upstream. As their name indicates, they were flat-bottomed. Their lack of a keel made them poor sailers, but it helped them negotiate rapids and shallows. In a pinch, they could easily be dragged on a riverbank out of trouble without risking structural damage. In Canada, the smaller breed of flatboat was originally called the *batteau plat* by the French. Measuring about 10–12 metres in length and 1.5–2.4 metres in width, such flatboats became known as *batteaux* or *battoes*. They could carry a load of three to five tonnes. Sometimes equipped with a single mast and square sail, the Canadian batteau was usually rowed by men pulling oars about 5 m in length. The first recorded batteaux were built in 1665.

The horseboats (also known as teamboats) used teams of horses to propel a ferry or a similar craft over a relatively short distance and heavily-travelled route. The horses did not pull the boat from a towpath; instead, they were on the boat, powering a horse whim, treadwheel, or treadmill that drove paddlewheels to propel the boat. In effect, the horses replaced the steam engine. At first, such teamboats rivalled the reliability of steamboats at a lesser cost; however, they could not match the steadily improving performance of steamboats in spite of their own technical improvements. Never numerous, they were pushed out of their role as ferries by the spread of steam propulsion and the construction of new bridges.

The steamboats came into their own gradually, but they ended up sweeping all before them by the end of the nineteenth century.

TRANSPORTATION AND INDUSTRIALIZATION

Before the Industrial Revolution, there was a transportation revolution that created new markets by making it easier to reach new parts of countries like Great Britain, France, and the United States. This transportation revolution drove down the cost of various resources of use to manufactures while also driving down the cost of getting the finished products in the hands of customers. In the United States and Great Britain, the first step was the creation of toll roads, also known as turnpikes in the United States. Between 1740 and 1760, the total length of toll roads in Great Britain more than tripled, reaching about 15,000 kilometres. By 1800, it would reach an extent of nearly 30,000 kilometres. In France, a new corps of engineers entrusted with the building and upkeep of roads and bridges was set to work on the improvement of major roads. At the same time, coaches were improved so much that, by the end of the 18th century, travel times were cut down.

Though this increase in speed clearly benefited travellers, the transportation of goods overland remained slow and expensive. The movement of goods was transformed by the spread of canals. The benefits of even a small, winding canal were demonstrated by the one built by the Duke of Bridgewater in 1759–1761, that enabled the Duke to sell his coal in Manchester at a profit. The example set by this canal was soon followed and 3,500 kilometres of canals were built in Britain by 1850. In most cases, the canal barges were hauled by horses using the towpaths alongside the canals and aqueducts, as can be seen in several pictures. Inside tunnels, often too narrow to include a towpath, it was necessary to "walk" barges.

However, Britain stopped investing in its canals in the second half of the nineteenth century, whereas France, for instance, continued to extend its network, and to widen the major canals in order to let motorized barges use them. As a result, there was a clear limit in England to the size of the boats able to use many of its canals.

Canals

Navigation canals come in two main types. The lateral or side canal usually links two parts of the same river, sometimes just to go around rapids or a dam, sometimes to cut through a meandering river course which does not require a separate reservoir of water. The summit canal connects different rivers, or even different watersheds, which usually involves going over a rise of land and which does require its own supply of water (often from a reservoir created by a dam). There are also irrigation canals whose purpose is to carry water needed by fields and canals that supply cities and towns with drinking water.

In Antiquity, a small number of navigation canals are recorded, dug by the Persians (to go around Mount Athos during the second invasion of Greece), by the Egyptians (to connect the Nile with the Red Sea), and by the Romans (to do the same). Irrigation canals are much more numerous and far older.

In China, canals were also built over two thousand years ago, but the greatest achievements in canal-building are dated to the seventh and eighth centuries, in the time of the Sui and Tang dynasties; most noteworthy was the Grand Canal, at the heart of a network of linked canals extending over 2,000 kilometres.

In Europe, the Netherlands (13th–14th c.) and Italy (15th c.) pioneered the construction of new canals and artificial waterways, including the canal from Milan to Lake Como (97 km). The modern pound lock got its start in Europe at this time.

In Europe, the pace of construction picked up after the Renaissance, generally speaking. England invested in various waterway improvements during the 17th century, adding 400 kilometres to its water transportation network, including some side canals. In France, major canals were dug in the 17th century, such as the Briare canal (1604–1642) connecting the Seine to the Loire and the great (240 km) canal "des Deux Mers." Also known as the "canal du Midi," the latter was built by Pierre-Paul Riquet (1604–1680) and François Andréossy between 1665 and 1681. It featured a number of stone-lined pound locks still visible today (**Figure 3**). Since the "canal du Midi" didn't start paying a profit on Riquet's investment until 1724, it hardly inspired imitation before then, but it showed that it was possible to dig very long canals and operate

FIGURE 3 ▶ One of the 17th-century pound locks of the Canal du Midi. *(Picture by author near Béziers, France, 2007.)*

them over the long term. One of its technical innovations was a tunnel large enough for the canal to go through it, with a narrow ledge usable by a man or a (small) horse (**Figure 4**).

In Europe, the canal boom of the Industrial Revolution truly begins with the Duke of Bridgewater, Francis Egerton, who visited the "canal du Midi" in 1753 and had the Bridgewater canal built on his lands between 1759 and 1765 by James Brindley and John Gilbert in order to carry coal from his mines to Manchester. Financially, this small winding canal was a huge success and had many imitators. Such engineers as Thomas Telford became known for their canal-building feats. Most British canals were dug within the central part of the island, an area the approximate shape of a square about 300 kilometres on its side. Distances were modest and nowhere did any of these canals exceed 200 metres in altitude, but they improved communications immensely within this area.

FIGURE 4 ▶ The world's first canal tunnel, dug to serve the 17th-century Canal du Midi, known as the Malpas tunnel. *(Picture by author near Nissan-lez-Enserune, France, 2007.)*

Before 1750, France had built about 600 kilometres of canals and river improvements (including the "canal du Midi"). During the second half of the 18th century, another 400 kilometres of canals were accumulated, yielding a total of about 1,000 kilometres of canals and 7,000 kilometres of navigable rivers, versus 40,000 kilometres of roads in various states of repair and disrepair, just before the French Revolution in 1789.

In Canada, the first canal-building efforts anticipated all other in North America. The Lachine canal in modern-day Montréal, created to avoid the rapids on the St. Lawrence, goes back to some initial cuttings during the French régime. The first lock canal, at Coteau-du-Lac, Quebec, was built in 1779–1781 along the St. Lawrence upstream from the island of Montreal, replacing an earlier *"rigolet"* canal. The Lachine canal was finally planned as a complete waterway starting in 1819 and was completed in 1824. That early Lachine canal included seven locks, testifying to the difference in level that would allow later industrialists to take advantage of the water's force. Geographically, the Lachine canal turned the Great Lakes into a hinterland for the St. Lawrence valley. Until the middle of the century, Quebec City was Canada's major seaport since the St. Lawrence River upstream to Montreal was essentially impassable for sea-going ships until a channel was dug in the middle of the riverbed. In combination with the Welland Canal, the Lachine Canal also threatened to turn the St. Lawrence into a major transportation artery connecting the Ohio basin and the entire upper American Midwest to the sea, to the detriment of the US port cities on the Eastern seaboard.

In the United States, the distances involved and the sparsely settled land did not justify initially the same sort of investment in canals as in Europe. However, the 1783 Treaty of Versailles granted the United States sovereignty over vast territories west of the Appalachians, all the way to the Mississippi. Yet, the pioneers settling these territories were cut off by the mountains from the Eastern seaboard. If they wished to trade the commodities they produced, geography forced them to head downstream for Spanish Louisiana, whose capital city was New Orleans. It was therefore vital for the United States to improve navigation upstream over the Appalachians in order to trade with its western offshoot. If the new country was to survive, it also needed to make it easier for the western settlers to sail upstream on the western rivers so that their goods did not only benefit a foreign power.

Thus, in 1785 George Washington launched a program of improvements to the Potomac and James rivers in order to help navigation in the direction of the Ohio. The modest means available for the project limited the construction of canals to the shortest possible side canals avoiding rapids, falls, or other impediments to navigation. The most successful 18th-century canal was actually the Middlesex canal (44 km), dug between Boston and Lowell (1794–1803), though the Santee Canal (1793–1800) in South Caroline came slightly earlier. In 1807–1808, Jesse Hawley drew inspiration from the "canal du Midi" to advocate a canal between Lake Erie and the Mohawk River. A similar canal was finally built between 1817 and 1825, linking the Hudson River to Lake Erie over a distance of 584 km—the Erie Canal. It would prove to be as pivotal and influential for canal-building in the United States as the Duke of Bridgewater's canal had been for the British canal boom.

In Canada, the war of 1812 persuaded the British government to improve communications between Lower and Upper Canada since the St. Lawrence River, sitting between Montreal and Kingston on the border with the United States, was too exposed to enemy action. After work started in 1826–1827, the Rideau Canal was completed in 1832 under the supervision of Colonel John By at a cost of 822,000 British pounds. Not counting turnover (and about a thousand deaths, many due to unhealthy working conditions in mosquito-ridden swamplands), the work force numbered up to 2,000 workers a year. The entire canal system linked Ottawa to Kingston, spanning 202 kilometres, dug to a depth of 1.5 metres and a breadth of 10 metres, and including 24 dams as well as 46 locks (measuring 40.8 metres by 10 metres). As a consequence of the strategic rationale for its construction, it was never commercially vital and never rebuilt to a newer standard so that it may well be North America's oldest operating canal in its original conditions. It was built as a "slackwater" system using (dammed) reservoirs to hold back water and flood parts of the system to navigable depths. The work was done by hand with the aid of some draft animals. The excavating was carried out by men with shovels, pickaxes, and wheelbarrows. Rock was laboriously hand-drilled and blown up with blasting powder.

CANALS AND THEIR IMPACTS: THE INVENTION OF STEAMBOATS

In Great Britain, canals flourished until the 1840s when railway companies acquired several canal companies. In the United States and Canada, the great spate of canal-building was definitely a phenomenon of the early nineteenth century. In North America, many rivers were already navigable over long stretches and a few side canals could multiply those lengths. As other canals were dug to connect such rivers, the network took on a size that allowed it to cover much of southern Canada and the northern United States. Once canals were undertaken or completed where it was economical to do so, encouraging navigation and water-borne commerce, it became all the more imperative to improve inland navigation where the canals didn't go.

In some cases, this led to the development of horse-powered paddlewheel boats, which enjoyed greater success in North America than in Europe. Geography and history were both factors. Horse-powered paddlewheelers mostly served as ferries in North America. However, Europe's great rivers either did not compare to North America's mighty watercourses or were already spanned by bridges, thus obviating the need for ferries. Labour costs were higher in North America, which made the use of horses more attractive. The early designs had horses turning capstans for hours and days on end, which led to the animals becoming dizzy when they no longer needed to go in circles. Yet, the need was sufficiently acute for American horseboat owners to persist even though horses were often good for no other work after a prolonged stint on horseboats. As the technology improved, horseboats increasingly served as unobtrusive ferries on rivers, on lakes, and inside large harbours such as the one at Toronto, Canada.

Mostly, the quest for improvement stimulated the adoption of steamboats in order to master river basins or networks too extensive to be served by canals. While steamboats had been discussed for years in Europe as a potential solution to upstream haulage. French inventors were hampered by the crude steam engines known to them while English inventors faced the opposition of canal owners who were afraid that faster boats would degrade canal banks and increase maintenance costs. In the young United States, however, inventors were free to focus on the potential of river navigation with steamboats.

US artist and inventor Robert Fulton (1765–1815) was initially caught up in the canal fever of the late 18th century and thought up schemes for new canals in Europe. Indeed, he was something of a utopian. He believed that the improvement of inland navigation would boost trade as well as helping to spread knowledge, eliminate local prejudice, enrich the poor, and abolish war.

However, he was an American first and foremost. Knowing that canals were difficult to justify in the United States, Fulton transformed navigation in his homeland by building an effective steamboat. Though he is sometimes called the inventor of steamboats, he was not the first to come up with the idea. However, Fulton himself believed that an invention could be the latest in a series of improvements on an original idea, especially if the inventor combined, in a new way, components that were already familiar individually.

Before him, John Fitch (1743–1798) had also seen the opportunity open to steamboats. All summer long in 1790, he operated a steamer known as the *Steamboat* on the Delaware River between Philadelphia and Trenton. It used a home-built steam engine to move mechanical paddles. It was actually a bit faster than Fulton's *[North River] Steamboat* launched in 1807 and it covered up to 130 kilometres a day, faster than the barges and cheaper than the stagecoaches. However, a single steamer could not really compete with the stagecoaches, which offered more frequent service. That summer, Fitch and his company lost money. As a result, no more funds were invested in the project. The final blow came when a United States patent office decision stripped Fitch of almost all protection, forcing steamboat inventors to await the expiry of the patents in the time of Fulton.

Another inventor, James Rumsey (1741–1792), worked on a water jet propulsion system, but the resulting boat never achieved any significant speed.

Fulton succeeded on the Hudson River with a boat that did not achieve initially greater speeds than Fitch's. His steamer used side paddlewheels and a Watt-type engine with a separate condenser.

Compared to Fitch's, Fulton's steamboat enjoyed some crucial advantages. First, it was larger, which made it able to carry more paying passengers. Second, it had no serious competition on the run between New York and Albany. The road running alongside the river was rough and the terrain rougher; stagecoaches could not compete. The winds were too gusty and unreliable to let sailing barges compete either, and Fulton's partner, Robert R. Livingston, a rich and influent New York politician, had obtained a steam navigation monopoly from the state government. Fulton was not the first to patent a steamboat, so the joke goes that he patented the Hudson instead.

It's worth noting that Fitch had to design and build all by himself the parts of his 1790 steamboat. On the other hand, by 1807, Fulton was able to simply order a ready-made Boulton and Watt steam engine and have it shipped over from Great Britain. Fulton also opted for the simplest propulsion system: paddlewheels. Screw propellers were not unknown, but they were largely untried and in the shallow waters of inland rivers, paddlewheels were the better choice because they did not plunge as deeply into the water.

On the other hand, once steam-powered ships attempted sea crossings, it was soon observed that paddlewheels, whether side-mounted or stern-mounted, were particularly exposed to the smashing action of waves. Their superior efficiency aside, propellers were adopted because they were less prone to suffering wave damage.

Fulton's success on the Hudson led his company, as well as competitors, to aim for the opportunities offered by Western rivers flowing into the Mississippi. West of the Appalachians, the population was increasing and there were few means of transportation. Twenty years earlier, Fitch had been very much aware of the same opportunities, writing:

> "And where streams constantly tend one way, great advantages will accrue to inland navigation, and in particular to the Mississippi and Ohio Rivers, where the God of Nature knew their Banks could never be traversed with Horses, and [He] has laid in a store of fuel on their Head Waters, sufficient to last for the latest ages [. . .] But the Grand and Principle object must be on the Atlantick, which would soon overspread the wild forests of America with people, and make us the most opulent Empire on Earth, and at all times carry on a trade on the coasts of Barbary with impunity, and Chastize them at pleasure. Pardon me generous public for suggesting Ideas that cannot be digested at this day, what opinion future ages will have of them time only will make manifest."[1]

---

[1] John Fitch, *The Autobiography of John Fitch*, John Prager, ed. (Philadelphia: The American Philosophical Society, 1976), p. 176.

Fitch was prescient in identifying the forests of the Mississippi watershed as a crucial source of fuel. As long as early steamboats (and later trains) ran on wood, they were able to go anywhere forests could be cut down, without having to worry about coal.

Fulton also envisioned steamboat commerce in the West as an opportunity to be developed. He argued that steam navigation "will give a cheap and quick conveyance to merchants on the Mississippi, the Missouri, and other great rivers."[2] Unlike Fitch, he was able to turn his schemes into reality. This was partly a consequence of the greater reliability and increasing performance of his steamboats equipped with better engines and serviced by trained mechanics, some of whom had emigrated from Great Britain. It also partly happened because the United States now controlled most of the West since they had discreetly purchased Louisiana (which included a much vaster area than the modern-day State of Louisiana, mostly west of the Mississippi) in 1803. By 1804, US sovereignty extended almost all the way to the Rockies.

Finally, since the time of Fitch, the settlement of the western slope of the Appalachians had progressed. In 20 years, the population had steadily increased, thereby increasing the size of the market for goods shipped by river. Soon, Fulton and his competitors launched a number of steamboats to fight over the opportunities they afforded. Fulton's company was awarded a monopoly in 1811 and its first steamboat, launched in Pittsburgh, reached New Orleans in January 1812.

By 1818, however, Fulton's monopoly was annulled and several other steamboat builders jumped in. While Fulton's use of low-pressure Boulton and Watt engines (sometimes called atmospheric because the steam pressure only exceeded a little atmospheric pressure) was not imitated, his other technical choices proved well suited to Western rivers.

Paddlewheels, for instance, were not as efficient as screw propellers, but they better withstood collisions with floating debris, submerged logs, ice, and other snags found along the untamed reaches of Western rivers. If the paddles were damaged, they were easily repaired since they were made of wood and easily brought up, outside of the water. A paddlewheeler was also able to maneuver and back up more easily than a boat with one propeller, which was a definite advantage on rivers where a landing was often a matter of just driving the ship into the river bank.

At sea, the large housing of the paddlewheels bore the brunt of the wind and waves. The tossing of a ship might not allow the paddles to plunge into the water

---

[2]James T. Flexner, *Steamboats Come True: American Inventors in Action* (New York: The Viking Press, 1944), p. 326.

with equal effectiveness every time, thereby wasting some of the steam engine's power. Propellers soon replaced paddlewheels aboard steamships going to sea, but rivers were more forgiving and paddlewheels better adapted to the frontier environment. As a result, steam-powered paddlewheelers continued in use on some rivers and lakes well into the twentieth century. For much of the nineteenth century, they ruled. The best known type was flat-bottomed, multi-decked, and equipped with a single rear-mounted paddlewheel. The high-pressure steam engine developed around 1804 by Oliver Evans in the United States and Richard Trevithick in Great Britain provided the needed power. Such steamboats greatly increased the pace of western settlement; they provided a vital lifeline between the river towns.

The various steamboat operators enjoyed such success on the Mississippi that, as late as 1840, the aggregate tonnage of steamers using Western rivers (83,592) was still approximately equal to the total tonnage of commercial steamships flying the flag of the British Empire (86,731). US steamboats were exported abroad.

Long before this, Fulton's example inspired the Montreal beer maker John Molson to launch a wholly-Canadian built steamboat on the St. Lawrence in the fall of 1809. The *Accommodation* travelled from Montreal to Quebec City in 66 hours (included 30 hours spent at anchor during the nights). Though it was faster than any other means of travel (competitors might take a week), it was far from efficient and Molson installed a British-made Boulton and Watt engine the next year.

In Canada, steamboats benefited from the input of both British and US engineers. The low pressure engines endorsed by Fulton as well as Boulton and Watt were used longer. However, in Canada as in the United States, the development of steamboats did not preclude that of canals. In many cases, the combination of canals and steamboats was in fact synergistic. Whereas British canal owners initially refused access to steamboats, other canal systems eventually grew to accommodate them.

NORTH AMERICAN CANALS DOWN TO THE TWENTIETH CENTURY

Though some canals were built for strategic and military reasons (the Rideau Canal or the "canal du Midi" in its original conception), most were built to facilitate haulage and so assist commerce. The Erie Canal was spectacularly successful as a commercial highway. This helped the US corps of Army engineers win funding from the United States Congress—a total of 43 million (contemporary) dollars before 1861—to improve navigation via dredging, the part-financing of canals, and the construction of ports, lighthouses, jetties, buoys, and beacons. Many more canals were started by the private sector, with the assistance of individual states and British capital.

In the United States, the bursting in 1836–1837 of the land speculation bubble that allowed individual states to raise the funds necessary to finance canal construction led to a depression, caused numerous bankruptcies, and placed enormous pressure on British investors, both private and corporate (banks). In 1841–1842, nine states stopped paying the interests on their debts, while Indiana and Michigan repudiated part of their debts. The crash erased millions of (contemporary) dollars in value. Upper Canada had been part of the same bubble, borrowing heavily to dig the Cornwall and Welland canals, and it was only saved by its amalgamation with much less indebted Lower Canada, which made British banks (especially Baring's) happy since they held most of the bonds issued by Upper Canada.

In 1851, the failure of the canal designed to link Chesapeake Bay to the Ohio, already threatened by the rise of the new railways, essentially ended the era of grand canal projects in the United States.

Until the first major railways started operating, in the late 1830s and in the 1840s, the canals carried both passengers and commercial goods. In Great Britain, the railways superseded most of the canals' functions, even though operating costs were sometimes cut to the bone. France continued to invest in the improvement of its canal network and chose to connect it to its new rail network.

In the United States, the canals started in the first half of the nineteenth century were eventually completed, though the original investors rarely recouped their investments. Work by the US Army Corps of Engineers maintained the navigability of the network of waterways by widening canals and river channels, with much of the work happening during the late nineteenth century and early twentieth century.

The end result was a freight-bearing network of US waterways totalling 19,000 kilometres. Today's freight barges carry everything from grain, coal, and salt to jet fuel, butadiene, and the wax for coating milk cartons. Overall, US waterways still carry about 13% of intercity freight annually, compared to 33% and 45% for truck and rail freight. They remain the cheapest alternative for bulk transport. The cost of moving goods by barge is about a tenth of the cost by truck and two-thirds the cost of rail freight.

In Canada, the St. Lawrence River and the Great Lakes have long remained the almost exclusive focus of canal builders. While the Ottawa-Rideau canal system had been designed to by-pass the St. Lawrence, almost all other Canadian canal projects down to the present day have been intended to improve navigation within the Great

Lakes and the St. Lawrence valley, or to facilitate the movement of sea-going ships in and out of the North American heartland.

The greatest single effort to open the Great Lakes to seagoing ships was the construction of the St. Lawrence Seaway between Montreal and Lake Ontario, completed in 1959. The 306-km stretch of river was dammed, deepened, widened, and provided with new locks so as to allow sea-going freighters free access. Including other navigational improvements (the St. Lawrence channel, the Welland canal, etc.), the entire seaway spans nearly 3,700 km from Sept-Îles (Québec) in the Gulf of St. Lawrence to Duluth (Minnesota) at the farthest tip of Lake Superior. Canada paid about 70% of the construction costs of the St. Lawrence Seaway proper and reaps the equivalent share of the revenue. However, the increasing size of today's container ships prevents 95% of them (as of 2005) from fitting through the 50-year-old locks of the original Seaway, and the seaway is increasingly used for internal shipping.

CANALS AND THEIR IMPACTS: ECOLOGICAL INVASIONS

There were ecological consequences to the existence of canals. They allowed fish (such as snakeheads) and other marine animals (such as zebra mussels) to move into new watersheds or reach new lakes and river networks.

An early invader was the sea lamprey, a primitive fish that once spawned in freshwater but spent the rest of its adult life in the Atlantic Ocean. However, it has also proven capable of living in freshwater rivers and lakes where it does not face any predators. It is itself a voracious predator, larger and hungrier than native freshwater lamprey species found in North America. Lacking jaws, the sea lamprey uses its mouth as a large sucking disk by fastening itself to a fish with its sharp teeth and piercing through the scales with its file-like tongue in order to feed on body fluids. Six out of seven fish attacked by a lamprey die. The disappearance of three whitefish species in the Great Lakes is blamed on the sea lamprey invasion.

After the 1824 completion of the Lachine Canal and following other improvements along the St. Lawrence, the sea lamprey was first spotted in Lake Ontario in the 1830s. After the 1919 improvements to the Welland Canal, it was able to move into Lake Erie, where it was first seen in 1921. Afterwards, its spread to the rest of the Great Lakes was unhindered and it reached Lake Michigan by 1936, Lake Huron by 1937, and Lake Superior by 1938. Controlling the sea lamprey population in order to protect commercial and sports fishing, costs about $21 million annually.

In all, 185 invasive species are thought to have moved into the Great Lakes with the help of canal works, including 57 that have benefited from the opening of the

St. Lawrence Seaway. The impact of the sea lamprey pales compared to that of the zebra mussel. Originally an Eurasian species, zebra mussels are believed to have been introduced around 1985–1986, being first discovered in Lake St. Clair in Ontario in 1988, before spreading to all of the Great Lakes, and plaguing lakes Erie and Ontario most of all. While in the larval stage, they are virtually undetectable and they can be transported accidentally to new water bodies by fishermen. Zebra mussels are detrimental to native freshwater mussels because mussels past the larval stage swim freely for a few weeks in a juvenile stage and then attach themselves to rocks or other hard surfaces—such as boat hulls, water intake valves—and mature native mussels.

The local clams were virtually wiped out; some insect species disappeared. Other native species of mollusks, fish, and insects survive in streams and rivers. Zebra mussels were later joined by a cousin from the same part of the Caspian Sea, the quagga mussel. Both are *Dreissena* mussels and are such voracious feeders that they've depleted much of the algae population of the lakes they've colonized. This has been good for water clarity and removing pollutants now fixed into the sediments, but it has decimated lake life, deprived fish of their usual food, and promoted the growth of toxic blue-green algae that the *Dreissena* mussels themselves often reject instead of eating.

Weedy algae known as Cladophora also profit, but their death and decomposition processes absorb oxygen from the surrounding water. This oxygen-poor environment favours the growth of botulism bacteria that are then taken up by the quagga and zebra mussels. When the mussels are consumed by another invasive species, the goby fish, the botulism bacteria contaminate the fish. If the fish are preyed upon by loons, the end result may be poisoned loons.

BASIC DEFINITIONS OF CANAL TECHNOLOGY

Mill Race: the narrow trench or cutting used to lead water from a reservoir to a mill in order to turn its waterwheel (also known in Great Britain as a "mill leat.")

Pound Lock: another name for the modern canal lock furnished with two sets of doors opening outwards; the pound lock connects two waterways sitting at different levels, or a waterway and another lock, or even two locks in a series.

Rigolet: a narrow, navigable channel created along a riverbank by a parallel structure (dam, levee, or stone wall) at a place where the river's course is interrupted by rapids.

Towpath: the path running along the water's edge that is used by men or horses pulling barges.

Weir: a dam, usually submerged, that raises the level of a stream or river.

FURTHER READINGS

James Thomas Flexner, *Steamboats Come True: American Inventors in Action*, 1944.

CHAPTER 5

Railroads: An Iron and Steel Web

▶▶▶▶▶▶▶▶▶▶▶▶▶▶▶▶▶▶▶▶▶▶▶▶▶▶▶▶▶▶▶

Railways took over where canals had left off. They were faster and they could operate in a greater range of climates and weather conditions, crossing deserts or facing winter blizzards. Freed from some of their geographical constraints of canals, they were able to go up mountains and link more towns and villages. Within a few years, they could also move significant loads. In North America, they fostered the growth of industry, accelerated the settlement of the frontier, and became a dominant force in the workings of the agricultural sector. They also transformed the landscape in new ways. Steam locomotives required water and fuel (wood, then coal). Railway bridges had to be stronger and bigger. New types of bridges emerged: suspended bridges, girder plate bridges, truss bridges, and cantilever bridges (as at Quebec City). Cuttings, embankments, and viaducts multiplied to control the grade of railway tracks. They facilitated the spread of new species while helping bring about the near destruction of some, such as the Plains bison.

AN ECONOMIC TRANSFORMATION

In 1820, moving a ton of grain or salt or ore overland from Buffalo to New York might cost about $100 as a result of the cost of human labour, fodder for the horses, and equipment. Even using the available rivers, such as the Hudson, the labour costs of transferring such a load from barge to cart, and vice-versa, added a lot to the final bill. Five years later, after the opening of the Erie Canal, the same load could be *shipped* via canal and river barges between the same two cities for $9. Ton mile rates for wagon transport varied between 30 and 70 cents at the time; ton mile rates on the canals varied between 2.70 and 4.5 cents.

The same advantages of water transportation were extended beyond canals by steamboats. In their heyday, before rail could compete, they were faster than any other mode of transport. Flatboats and keelboats had once taken a month to six weeks to float downriver from Pittsburgh to New Orleans (and four months or more to go back up, if they went back up at all). On the Hudson, sailing packets transporting passengers between New York and Albany had spent anywhere between two days and two weeks making the trip. By the 1830s, much improved steamers took only ten hours. Railways shortened most travel times even more wherever they ran (**Table 1**).

Canals were efficient, but canal navigation was painfully slow before the use of steam, and even after if canal owners feared for the sides of the narrower canals. Canal boats and barges could hardly go faster than the combined speed of the water's flow and of the horses (or men) pulling them. Even the advent of steam engines did not change things right away. Steam propulsion took a while to produce significantly greater speeds.

From the very first, the railways were fast, and they soon got even faster. Within a few years, trains reached speeds that outstripped all but the most exceptional performances by other modes of transportation (clipper ships, ice yachts). And trains achieved these speeds routinely. For the overland transportation of goods, they reduced rates enormously since their speed made it possible to move several loads from

TABLE 1 ▶ The Evolution of the Cincinnati to New York Run

Year	Route	Means of Transportation	Typical Duration
1817	overland (turnpikes), up and down rivers	horse-drawn wagon, keelboat	50 days
c. 1820	down the Mississippi, across the Gulf and up the Atlantic coast	Mississippi steamboat, sailing packet	28 days
c. 1830	Ohio Canal, Erie Canal, and Hudson River	canal boat	18 days
1850	overland	railroad	6–8 days

(Source: Ruth Schwartz Cowan, *A Social History of American Technology,* 1997, pp. 115–116.)

point A to point B in the time it might take carts or barges to make a single trip. Passengers also benefited.

Nowadays, it is hard to recapture the heady sensation produced by the speed of the new railways, though the testimony of Fanny Kemble in 1830 illustrates the wonderment of the first passengers (**Box 1**). Some were afraid that the quick passage of trains through tunnels would produce suffocation. (Though this concern was exaggerated, the smoke thrown back into open carriages or compartments with open windows was not particularly pleasant to breathe.) After several days' hiking, something of the rush produced by that first experience of great speed may be rediscovered by simply getting into a car. Some drivers may also remember their first time at the wheel of a car and how fast it seemed to go.

BOX 1 ▶ Witnesses: Fanny Kemble (1830)

"You can't imagine how strange it seemed to be journeying on thus, without any visible cause of progress other than the magical machine, with its flying white breath and rhythmical, unvarying pace, between these rocky walls, which are already clothed with moss and ferns and grass; and when I reflected that these great masses of stone had been cut asunder to allow our passage thus far below the surface of the earth, I felt that no fairy tale was ever half so wonderful as what I saw."

(Fanny Kemble was a young actress at the time, describing her trip beside George Stephenson during a pre-inaugural trial of the Liverpool and Manchester Railway.)

(Source: L. T. C. Rolt, *George and Robert Stephenson. The Railway Revolution*, 1960, p. 191.)

The enthusiasm aroused by these new, intoxicating velocities helps us to understand the railway fever that gripped countries at several points throughout the nineteenth century. More than any other innovation until then, perhaps, railways symbolized speed, progress, and improvement. As early as 1837, British historian Thomas Macaulay referred to the ability to "traverse the land in cars which whirl along without horses" as one of the more obvious signs of human progress (**Box 2**). Builders were increasingly able to push through new lines and projects, to "railroad" them through the countryside, through villages and cities. The railroad companies were often able to overlook or to get the public to overlook major accidents as being either acts of God or the fault of human error.

This enthusiasm had in no way abated by the last years of the nineteenth century when railway builders tackled some of their grandest projects. In the United States, a transcontinental railroad link was completed in 1869, while Canada finished its own

BOX 2 ▶ Witnesses: Thomas B. Macaulay (1837)

On progress:

"It has lengthened life; it has mitigated pain; it has extinguished diseases; it has increased the fertility of the soil; it has given new securities to the mariner; it has furnished new arms to the warrior; it has spanned great rivers and estuaries with bridges of form unknown to our fathers; it has guided the thunderbolt innocuously from heaven to earth; it has lighted up the night with the splendour of the days; it has extended the range of the human vision; it has multiplied the power of the human muscles; it has accelerated motion; it has annihilated distance; it has facilitated intercourse, correspondence, all friendly offices, all despatch of business; it has enabled man to descend to the depths of the sea, to soar into the air, to penetrate securely into the noxious recesses of the earth, to traverse the land in cars which whirl along without horses, and the ocean in ships which run ten knots against the wind. These are but a part of its fruits, and of its first fruits. For it is a philosophy which never rests, which has never attained, which is never perfect. Its law is progress. A point which yesterday was invisible is its goal today, and will be its starting-post tomorrow."

(Source: Macaulay, Essay on Bacon)

BOX 3 ▶ Witnesses: Miles G. Bixby and Frank S. Bixby, publishers (1888)

On railways and the Grand Trunk Railway of Canada:

"Railways are the wonder of the world. Nothing during the last half century has created so marvellous a change as the great iron revolution of science. Beneath it the features of old Christendom have become changed, and its wealth and physical grandeur augmented. Other revolutions have scattered luminous influences over the world, but it remains for the new generation of railways to bring about one of the mightiest moral and social revolutions that ever hallowed the annals of any age. Omnipresence is one of the principles of their progress. Content with no limits, they have thrown a girdle round the world itself. Far off India woos them over its waters. China listens to the voice of the charmer. The Atlantic and Pacific are connected, and the American Continent is pierced by a net-work of roads.

"Prominent among the railways of this continent is the Grand Trunk Railway of Canada, which by its establishment and subsequent development has done so much to open up and increase the wealth and commerce of the Dominion. It was originally chartered in 1851, and by constantly adding to its mileage and developing new territory, has grown to its present extensive system. By consolidation, in 1882, with the Great Western, about 1,000 miles were added; and now with the Northern & North-Western Chicago and Grand Trunk and Detroit, Grand Haven and Milwaukee Railways, over 4,000 miles are controlled. It was the first great system in order of time; being originally designed as a trunk line running from Montreal to Sarnia, with a branch to Portland as a winter port. It was built by English capital, under English management, although the Government of Canada contributed fifteen millions of dollars to it, and it has proved of enormous advantage to the Dominion. It owns or controls three of the most remarkable bridges in the world—the Victoria Bridge across the St. Lawrence at Montreal, the Suspension Bridge at Niagara Falls, and the International Bridge across the Niagara River."

(Source: Commercial Industries of Canada: Historical and commercial sketches of Quebec, Point Levi, Three Rivers, Richmond, Sherbrooke, St. Johns, and environs, 1888, pp. 32–33.)

transcontinental railway in 1885. Russia later completed the Trans-Siberian railway to help span all of Eurasia in 1905, while Australia built its own transcontinental link in 1917. Railways dominated everyday life in most advanced countries by the end of the nineteenth century, but they arguably played an even greater role in North America where the very evolution of Canada and the United States as they exist today would have been markedly different in their absence. The pride of railway promoters is obvious in the 1888 pronouncement on Canada's Grand Trunk Railway in a commercial prospectus (**Box 3**).

HISTORICAL BACKGROUND

Railroads may have been the first complex, large-scale *technological systems*. In addition to the locomotives (the result of an intricate adaptation of the basic steam engine to locomotion), trains could not roll without a large quantity of other material equipment (tracks, rolling stock, stations, yards, signalling devices, fuel supplies, water supplies). Furthermore, a railroad was made possible by a corporate organization, a large capital investment, and a great number of specially trained managers, engineers, conductors, and mechanics (in addition to less specialized employees such as porters, stewards, cooks, ticket agents, etc.). Because railroads operated over a large geographical area, 24 hours a day, every day of the year, in all kinds of weather (unlike canals), they demanded a new breed of professional managers. The methods of the older family-owned-and-operated firms could not fill the bill. Such a complex technological system required an organized, hierarchic bureaucracy.

Steam vehicles go back to the eighteenth century. Aside from a toy exhibited in front of the Chinese emperor in 1670, the first steam-driven vehicles were built in France by 1770 by Joseph Cugnot. (They worked, but they were too slow and inefficient to be of much use.) The dawn of the nineteenth century saw new attempts in Great Britain and the steam coaches of Trevithick and Gurney enjoyed some success until they were forced from the roads by laws favouring horse-drawn coaches. Steam locomotives were used on the private railways of collieries by 1812, but George Stephenson's experiments with locomotives on railways available for both freight and passenger transport met with greater success, unhindered by public or political opposition since he ran his steam trains over privately-owned tracks.

The world's first fully commercial steam trains were developed in England in 1825, running on the Stockton and Darlington railway, which operated like a turnpike or canal of the day insofar as it was open to anyone who paid tolls or used vehicles in conformity with the way's charter. Initially, the locomotive-drawn carriages were pitted against horse-drawn carts, but the locomotive won a decisive victory by 1833.

By then, the first major steam railway line (52 km) had opened in 1830. In 1827, a French railway started operating out of Saint-Étienne, though locomotives didn't run on railways in France until 1829–1830. Also in 1830, the first regular steam railroad (10 km) opened in the United States (Charleston and Hamburg). Other countries followed suit: Belgium, Germany, and then both Canada and Russia in 1836. Canada's first railway ran between Saint-Jean and La Prairie over 40 kilometres, completing a major commercial route between New York and Montréal.

The working conditions of the *navvies* (short for "navigators," a name given to those workers because they'd first been hired to work on canals) who built the first British railways were harsh. They were housed in shantytowns. Drinking and fighting were common pastimes. Yet, the workers who built North American railroads faced the same strenuous labour, but often in the middle of the wilderness. In Canada, the freezing gales of winter could be avoided by stopping work or hunkering down in heated shacks, but not the mosquito swarms of summer. For decades, the digging equipment of the navvies remained primitive, reliant on pickaxes and shovels, with only exceptional use of gunpowder for blasting. In fact, the tools of the navvies were probably not much different from those used in medieval and even Roman mines.

The first railways did not always use metal rails. Stone was tried, for instance. In North America, some early railroads tried hardwood rails (much cheaper than metal). In spite of the low speeds and limited weight the first locomotives were able to pull, the hardwood rails did not last long. The next step was to produce wooden rails plated with metal, but the thin metal strips sometimes detached from the wood and caused accidents. Wholly metallic rails were more expensive, but their benefits outweighed the costs and they were increasingly adopted. Cast iron was used at first, and then puddled wrought iron until new production methods lowered the cost of steel to the point where rails could be made of it.

The conservatism of the Industrial Revolution should not be underestimated. Engineers had no real way of finding out the effectiveness of new designs, except by trial and error. The mathematical methods of contemporary engineering theory were rarely up to the task of calculating or modeling the stresses at work. Hence, the first generation of engineers erred on the side of safety, often by sticking to tried and true shapes, such as that of the round, Roman arches used on early viaducts, even though many cathedrals and medieval buildings had experimented with pointed arches. In Great Britain, Isambard K. Brunel, the son of Franco-British engineer Marc I. Brunel, may have been familiar with the work of Rodolphe Perronet and the French Corps des Ponts et Chaussées when he resorted to flattened arches for the Maidenhead

Railway Bridge, but he was criticized for the apparent foolhardiness of his design, as Perronet had been in his day for the shallow arches of the bridge at Neuilly.

This conservatism is seen in other areas: when iron became a cheap and robust building material, engineers such as Thomas Telford applied it to old stone templates they had learned as part of an apprenticeship in architecture or stone masonry. Thus, the late 18th-century cast iron bridge erected in Shropshire replicated the classical arch of a stone bridge. Later, Telford replicated Chinese and South American suspension bridges with iron chains, in particular over Menai Straits. Innovation only came later, with Stephenson using a squared iron tube to span the same distance since the choice of the tube made for greater stiffness.

The influence of older technologies is also seen in the design of train carriages. The individual compartments of early passenger carriages essentially replicated the central body of the older horse-drawn stagecoaches. Originally, the compartments opened directly onto the track, but a running board was added to one side to let ticket controllers visit each compartment. Eventually, the running board was enclosed to protect railway employees from the weather, allowing for communication between the compartments.

Railway expansion was feverish in Great Britain. In 1854, British railways carried 111 million travellers an average distance of 19 kilometres. The entire network required by then a yearly total of 20,000 tonnes of iron for rail-laying or replacement. By 1856, there were over 12,500 kilometres of railway tracks crisscrossing Great Britain. The railroad companies employed about 90,000 people, consumed two million tonnes of coal, and ran trains that covered about 120 million kilometres all told.

The pace of expansion was even faster in the United States. By 1840, the total length of railroads in the United States was double that for all of Europe. This was due in part to the absence of national boundaries and to the significantly lower price of land. What was spent on land and construction in the United States might be spent on land alone in Great Britain. By 1860, on the eve of the Civil War, the United States had hundreds of railroad companies and 49,000 kilometres of tracks, the most in the world.

On the other hand, North American companies were forced to import British locomotives during the first decade of railway operations. British engines were better, but other aspects of locomotives needed to be adapted to North American conditions. Because the tracks were often more winding, a bogie truck of independently mounted wheels was designed to keep the locomotives from derailing. As railroads were rarely fenced off, cowcatchers were added to the front to keep dead cattle from jamming the wheels and derailing trains. To avoid collisions, bells and whistles were used to warn off trespassers, human or otherwise. Smokestacks were made larger or included meshing to reduce the sparks produced by burning wood, or at least keep them from exiting, in order to prevent fires along the route. As US manufacturers took over, they also built more powerful engines, able to tackle the steeper grades of North American railroads.

In Canada, the first railway line connected La Prairie on the St. Lawrence River near Montreal with Saint-Jean-sur-le-Richelieu, a small town bordering the Richelieu River. It opened in 1836 as a vital shortcut between two river routes linking New York to Montreal, taking over the role played for the previous decade by Canada's first macadam road between the same two locales. After investing in the first Canadian steamboats, the Molson family of Montreal was also among the backers of the first train.

While trading volumes between Montreal and New York justified the expense and risk of a railway line, Canadian governments gradually realized that railways could further economic development elsewhere. To compete with the US railway boom, the 1849 Guarantee Act spurred the building of longer lines by providing government support for new initiatives and sparked a railway boom which created a market for manufacturers and a demand for engineers. By the end of the nineteenth century, Canadian investment in railway lines would create such an extensive network that figures for the length of railway tracks per capita in Canada outstripped those for the United States or Mexico (**Figure 1**).

Railroad Networks
(Tracks in km per Thousand Inhabitants, 1880–1950)

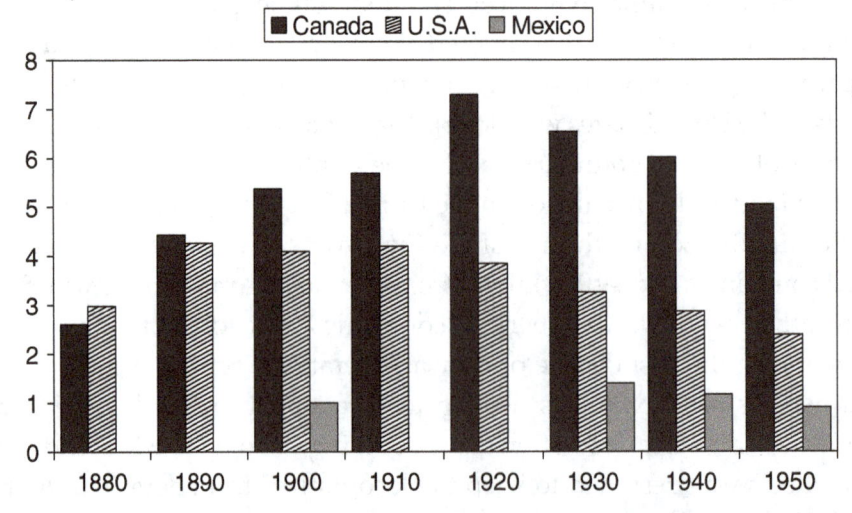

FIGURE 1 ▶ Railroad tracks (in km per thousand inhabitants) for Canada, Mexico, and the United States. (The data for Mexico are fragmentary due to the absence of a national census before 1900 and the disorganization of the government during the civil war that began in 1910.)

SOCIAL AND ECONOMIC CONSEQUENCES

In Canada, trains became part of the wood-based economy of the nineteenth century. Wood was a source of building materials (as lumber), of fuel (as firewood for locomotives and steam engines, as charcoal for smelters and ironworks), and of fertilizer (as the raw material for the manufacture of potash). The clearing of forests in Southern Ontario left only 20% of the original forest cover standing by 1880, but it made possible the rise of wheat farming for export. Railways played a part by helping move both raw timber and the products of the wood-based economy; they also needed wood to burn before the switch to coal and as a construction material for bridges, train sheds, and train stations outside of large population centres.

However, railways transformed not only the economy but much of nineteenth-century society. While the great canal construction projects of the early nineteenth century had served as a training ground for many young engineers, railways created a demand for engineers that outran the possibilities of on-the-job training. Until then, would-be engineers in the English-speaking world had usually learned their trade by serving apprenticeships under more experienced professionals. The sheer scale of railroad-building in North America by the middle of the nineteenth century led to the development of new facilities for engineering education.

In Canada, the first engineering classes were probably taught in 1854 at King's College in Fredericton, New Brunswick, though the first complete program wasn't offered until 1859. In 1858, the first engineering degree was awarded to a McGill University student in Montreal. In Toronto, the first civil engineering courses were taught as early as 1857. However, it took decades for engineering to become a recognized part of university education. In 1874, an École Polytechnique opened in Montreal. Though it bore the same name as its famous French predecessor founded in 1794, it operated on a much smaller scale for several decades before growing into a solid institution in the course of the twentieth century. Many of its early graduates went to careers in surveying and consulting. In 1877, a School of Practical Science opened in Toronto to offer students the opportunity to gain a solid grounding in a number of engineering fields; it was annexed by the University of Toronto in 1889 and became its Faculty of Applied Science and Engineering. In Kingston, Ontario, Queen's University also began developing engineering courses in 1887. Other universities followed suit by the turn of the twentieth century, emulating the rise of engineering education in the United States as a consequence of the 1862 Morrill Act.

While the railway boom clearly affected the engineering profession, the railways transformed to some degree almost every aspect of daily life by the end of the nineteenth century once the newly-built networks of tracks connected nearly every significant city and many towns as well. Urban centres deprived of a rail connection often lobbied and fought for one.

Time itself was reformed as a result of the growing extent of railway networks. In Canada as in the United States, railway companies faced increasing challenges associated to their operations and inter-operations over great distances. In a single trip, trains could encounter as many as 58 different time zones, occasionally governed by a clockmaker or jeweller's determination of local time. Scottish-Canadian railway engineer Sandford Fleming claimed in 1876 that a traveller who took the train from Halifax to Toronto would find "the railways employing no less than five different standards of time." Indeed, he went on to insist that every "existing Canadian city has its own time." Railway guide books for the United States and Canada were said to still include in 1881 at least 75 irregularly chosen standards of time.

In smaller countries such as Great Britain and France, it was feasible to adopt a single standard time for all train stations and this happened by mid-century. The situation could not be solved so easily in North America.

In Canada, Fleming is often credited with the inception of both standard time and a worldwide system of time zones. However, the idea of standardizing time for railways in the United States was put forth as early as 1869 by Charles Dowd, it was supported by Benjamin Pierce, and US railwayman William F. Allen oversaw its implementation on 18 November 1883 as railway time zones throughout the United States and Canada. Fleming did play a major part in mobilizing international concern over timekeeping, working through institutions and associations, but also through his developing ties to astronomers and geographers, and through British official channels. His 1879 proposals were forwarded to 18 countries by Canada's Governor-General, a significant number considering that only 25 countries were invited to the International Conference on the Prime Meridian and Universal Day in 1884 in Washington.

While Fleming has a credible claim to advocacy of a global time zone scheme, several features of the final system that came out of the 1884 conference in Washington (including the international date-line on the Greenwich anti-meridian) contradicted some of Fleming's most cherished ideas. The Washington conference endorsed standard time, but did not reach a consensus over the prime meridian. However, enough countries adopted the principle for the change to take effect over the next decades, starting on New Year's Day, 1885. While Fleming was rebuffed on several issues, what he called "Universal" time was now accepted, though it wouldn't become an international reality until 1925.

While trains served the needs of commerce by moving goods, supplies, and raw materials, they also answered other needs. In North America, immigrants and pioneers used trains to reach the destinations that would become their new homes. A growing number of workers took the train to commute between work and home. Small suburbs developed around such train service.

Businessmen began spending part of their week aboard trains to negotiate deals in other cities, supervise the operation of distant branches, or attend to other elements of their enterprises. In some cases, the wealthier class of businessmen would own an entire private car, complete with offices and living quarters, that could be hooked up to a train for a regularly scheduled run. At the very highest levels, the use of an entire train might be reserved to heads of state and government officials. During the First World War, the general staff of the German army ran its side of the war out of a specially appointed train.

Indeed, trains became increasingly important assets in military conflicts. Their primary role was to move large numbers of troops as close as possible to the front lines or the battlefield. They also transported ammunition and other supplies. By the time of the First World War, heavy artillery could be mounted on train cars and fully armoured trains were deployed in a few conflicts in an attempt to create mobile fortresses. However, trains were too vulnerable for this to work unless the enemy was weak or extremely disorganized. By the end of the First World War, tanks became the motorized, armoured spearhead of modern warfare sought by military reformers. War trains continued to be used to shuttle troops, ammunitions, and supplies.

Trains also played more benign roles. In Canada, during the middle part of the twentieth century, train cars were transformed into mobile classrooms catering to logging camps and other remote locations deprived of regular schools.

However, one of the first roles played by steam trains was to facilitate organized travel. In France, some of the first passenger trains were set up to carry visitors to a famous fair in the city of Givors, in part to generate positive publicity for the new means of transportation. By the second half of the nineteenth century, the tourism industry had grown by leaps and bounds thanks to the new railway lines. New destinations opened up. Seaside resorts flourished in Europe as a broader class of tourists experimented with short stays and trips to the beach. A more adventurous breed dreamed of truly exotic destinations. Only the nobility and the very rich had been able to afford grand tours of Europe. For the inhabitants of the British Isles, all of Europe now became accessible by train. The Swiss Alps, the French castles of the Loire Valley, the sunny coasts of the Riviera, and the historical monuments of Rome could all be reached by train. The famed Orient-Express carried travellers to Istanbul, from which they could go on to Egypt, India, and the Far East by steamship.

Elsewhere, the partnership of railway companies and shipping lines also made it possible to offer trips to distant locales. By the end of the nineteenth century, the Canadian Pacific Railway (CPR) advertised fares to destinations as remote as Alaska, Hawaii, Japan, China, and Australia to travellers wishing to depart from Toronto. Other companies, such as Cunard, catered to North Americans voyaging to Europe.

Infrastructure developed to accommodate railway travellers. Great railway hotels were built in Britain, Canada, and elsewhere near the busy train stations of major cities. In some cases, a railway hotel might be a destination in itself. In Canada's Banff national park, the CPR built a hotel that promised every conceivable comfort to travellers attracted by the prospect of untrammeled nature.

In most cases, however, train travel for leisure was more modest in scope. In North America as in Europe, upper middle class families ventured on trips to riverside, lakeside, or seaside resorts. Pleasure might be combined with health when the destination offered mineral springs or baths renowned for their salubrious effect on the human constitution. The pleasures of travel could also be combined with piety if the purpose of the trip was a religious pilgrimage or retreat. Shorter trips might take the form of outings to the nearest big city, for a taste of culture and high-end shopping, or to the countryside, for a stay among relatives or a bit of hunting.

As train travel became familiar, if not quite an everyday experience, the geography of cities was redesigned in a sense by the construction of train stations and the laying down of tracks. In some cases, the neighbourhoods beyond the train tracks were seen as cut off from the finer parts of the town. There was a right and a wrong side of the tracks. Train stations defined the downtown core, especially when railway companies began to collaborate by building central stations where several lines converged. Such union stations made it easier for travellers to change trains, without having to leave the building.

TECHNOLOGICAL RISKS AND FEATS

Accidents were nonetheless common. The great speed of trains meant that accidents were bound to be deadlier if cars left the tracks. The number of people each train carried also increased the risk of injuries and deaths. Some of the earliest accidents were the deadliest and the most dramatic. Even after the catastrophic explosion of a series of tanker cars wiped out the downtown of Lac-Mégantic, Quebec, and killed over

40 people in 2013, the crash of a train into Quebec's Richelieu River in 1864 still ranks as Canada's most lethal railway accident as it killed nearly 100 passengers, many of them immigrants. As train traffic increased, so did the yearly human toll. Between 1875 and 1960, the greatest number of deaths associated with train mishaps was recorded in 1913 when 710 people were killed throughout Canada. Taking into account the rising distance covered by trains in Canada, however, the relative death toll was approximately constant between 1886 and 1906 (**Figure 2**).

Canada: Killed and Injured per Million Miles Travelled (1886–1906)

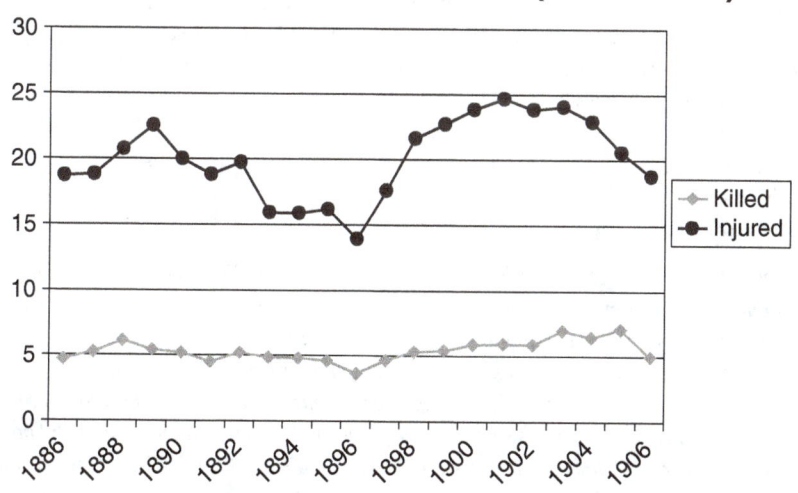

FIGURE 2 ▶ Numbers of people killed and injured in railway mishaps per million miles travelled, 1886–1906. (*Data source:* Historical Statistics of Canada, *1983.*)

It took accidents, tragic ones sometimes, to foster new attention to safety. The first train accidents horrified bystanders, if only because of the novelty of such events. In 1865, English writer Charles Dickens was involved in the Staplehurst train derailment caused by the removal of tracks for maintenance and a signalling error, though he narrowly escaped being one of the ten victims (**Box 4**). The following year, he wrote a fantastical tale where ghostly apparitions warn a signal-man of imminent train accidents. In Great Britain, the Tay Bridge disaster of 1879 killed over 60 people when a bridge was overthrown by a storm and an entire train sank beneath the waves as a result of the collapse. It was something of a turning point since the inquiry called to investigate the accident concluded that human negligence had played a role. Failures in design and quality control were implicated.

BOX 4 ▶ Witnesses: Charles Dickens (1865)

"Gad's Hill Place, Higham by Rochester, Kent
Tuesday, Thirteenth June, 1865

My dear Mitton,

I should have written to you yesterday or the day before, if I had been quite up to writing.

*I was in the only carriage that did not go over into the stream. It was caught upon the turn by some of the ruin of the bridge, and hung suspended and balanced in an apparently impossible manner. Two ladies were my fellow-passengers, an old one and a young one. This is exactly what passed. You may judge from it the precise length of the suspense. Suddenly we were off the rail, and beating the ground as the car of a half-emptied balloon might. The old lady cried out "My God!" and the young one screamed. I caught hold of them both (the old lady sat opposite and the young one on my left) and said: "We can't help ourselves, but we can be quiet and composed. Pray don't cry out." The old lady immediately answered: "Thank you. Rely upon me. Upon my soul I will be quiet." We were then all tilted down together in a corner of the carriage, and stopped. I said to them thereupon, "You may be sure nothing worse can happen. Our danger **must** be over. Will you remain here without stirring, while I get out of the window?" They both answered quite collectedly "Yes" and I got out without the least notion what had happened.*

Fortunately I got out with great caution and stood upon the step. Looking down I saw the bridge gone, and nothing below me but the line of rail. Some people in the two other compartments were madly trying to plunge out of the window, and had no idea that there was an open swampy field fifteen feet down below them, and nothing else! The two guards (one with his face cut) were running up and down on the down side of the bridge (which was not torn up) quite wildly. I called out to them: "Look at me. Do stop an instant and look at me, and tell me whether you don't know me." One of them answered, "We know you very well, Mr Dickens." "Then," I said, "my good fellow, for God's sake give me your key, and send one of those labourers here, and I'll empty this carriage." We did it quite safely, by means of a plank or two, and when it was done I saw all the rest of the train, except the two baggage vans, down in the stream. I got into the carriage again for my brandy flask, took off my travelling hat for a basin, climbed down the brickwork, and filled my hat with water.

Suddenly I came upon a staggering man covered with blood (I think he must have been flung clean out of his carriage), with such a frightful cut across the skull that I couldn't bear to look at him. I poured some water over his face and gave him some drink, then gave him some brandy, and laid him down on the grass, and he said: "I am gone," and died afterwards. Then I stumbled over a lady lying on her back against a little pollard-tree, with the blood streaming over her face (which was lead colour) in a number of distinct little streams from the head. I asked her if she could swallow a little brandy and she just nodded, and I gave her some and left her for somebody else. The next time I passed her she was dead. Then a man, examined at the inquest yesterday (who evidently had not the least remembrance of what really passed), came running up to me and implored me to help him find his wife, who was afterwards found dead. No imagination can conceive the ruin of the carriages, or the extraordinary weights under which the people were lying, or the complications into which they were twisted up among iron and wood, and mud and water.

> *I don't want to be examined at the inquest and I don't want to write about it. I could do no good either way, and I could only seem to speak about myself, which of course I would rather not do. I am keeping very quiet here. I have a—I don't know what to call it—constitutional (I suppose) presence of mind, and was not in the least fluttered at the time. I instantly remembered that I had the MS. of a number with me and clambered back into the carriage for it. But in writing these scanty words of recollection I feel the shake and am obliged to stop.*
>
> *Ever faithfully,*
>
> *Charles Dickens"*

In Canada, the Quebec City Bridge disaster of 1907 was equally pivotal. The collapse of a bridge under construction as a result of an engineering miscalculation killed about 75 workers and triggered a thorough inquiry, pointing to design errors. When it was finally completed, the bridge relied on a much more massive structure, still standing today (**Figure 3**).

FIGURE 3 ▶ Originally built to carry railways, the Quebec City bridge today still boasts the world's longest central span for a cantilever design. *(Picture by author in Quebec City, Québec, 2006.)*

The exceedingly ambitious feats of railway bridge engineers were called into question by such disasters. The conservatism of early builders had given way to a willingness to experiment on a grander and grander scale. Suspension bridges using chains of cast iron links were replaced by bridges using metal cables. When bridge builder Charles A. Roebling was commissioned in 1851 by the Grand Trunk Railway to complete a suspension bridge over the Niagara River, he demonstrated the superiority of cables over chains by delivering an impressive double-decker bridge with an upper deck for the railway and a lower deck for road traffic. The Grand Trunk Railway went on to commission the Victoria Bridge connecting the city of Montreal (set on a large island in the St. Lawrence River) to the mainland. The bridge, designed by British engineer Robert Stephenson (the son of George Stephenson) stood as the longest railway bridge in the world when it opened to regular traffic in 1860. Its construction as an enclosed metal tube replicated on a larger scale the earlier Britannia Tubular Bridge over Menai Straits in Great Britain.

As long as locomotives used firewood as fuel, travelling through an artificial tunnel almost three kilometres in length filled with wood smoke and soot seems to have remained a barely tolerable experience, but the replacement of wood by coal generated such noxious gases that an opening was eventually cut into the roof of the tube. By 1899, the whole bridge had been rebuilt with metal trusses.

Designs using metal latticework prevailed for many railway bridges during the second half of the nineteenth century. When the Tay Bridge was finished in 1878, outdoing the Victoria Bridge in total length, the time of using stone arches like Roman aqueducts was long past, but the bridge's reliance on lattice girders perilously underestimated the loads they might be subjected to. New cantilever designs were adopted by bridge engineers in the following decades because they made for greater resistance to various loadings. However, the original Quebec City Bridge extended its central span too far for the strength of the support spans.

In the twentieth century, railway technology was rarely in the forefront of engineering challenges, though major tunnels (such as the one under the English Channel) and high-speed trains were significant achievements. Less heralded but no less significant, by the early twenty-first century rail became a safer mode of transport for passengers (for equivalent travel distances) than any other save airlines.

ENVIRONMENTAL CONSEQUENCES

The amazing speed of trains lent a new impetus both to North American settlement and to the spread of intrusive species. While canals had made it possible for aquatic species to reach previously inaccessible bodies of water, trains made it possible for species to move accidentally or to be moved deliberately over great distances in short time spans. New infrastructures created for railways (bridges, tunnels, embankments, cuttings) sometimes divided habitats, erected physical barriers to movement, or offered new paths for migratory animals.

According to biologist Edward O. Wilson, the top three causes of species extinction in the United States today are, in order, habitat destruction, biological pollution (the influx of alien species that outcompete native ones), and chemical pollution. In their heyday, railways, along with axes and guns, facilitated habitat destruction as well as species replacement. Throughout the North American prairies, the Plains bison was replaced with various cattle species preferred by ranchers and farmers.

Changing the Landscape

The ancestors of the modern bison (*Bison bison*) reached North America from Eurasia between 600,000 and 300,000 years ago. The original species (*Bison priscus*) gave rise to several offshoots (*Bison latifrons, Bison antiquus, Bison occidentalis*), which were generally larger in body than the modern bison. The current species emerged about 10,000 to 12,000 years ago, just as many other large mammalian species were dying out in North America. The horses, camels, mammoths, and mastodons then present vanished with surprising rapidity, as well as their predators such as the giant short-faced bear, the American lion, the dire wolf, and several species of saber-toothed cats.

The cause of this massive species loss remains undetermined. Some, such as archaeologist Paul Martin, have blamed early humans of the Clovis culture for hunting some of these species to extinction. Climate and habitat changes coinciding with the end of the last ice age are also incriminated. Another theory blames it on an impact by a large meteorite. The latest thinking points to the impact of the gradual disappearance of the largest herbivores (mammoths and mastodons) on the entire balance of fauna and flora, leading to the rise of a wooded environment that was less hospitable to some existing species. Whether pressure exerted by human hunting played a role in this progressive extinction of mammoths and mastodons is unclear, but the beginnings of the decline predate the Clovis culture.

In any event, the modern bison survived, perhaps because it was faster on its feet than either human hunters or the wolf packs that emerged as the principal predators of large North American herbivores. Left to dominate almost alone the central grasslands, the bison thrived.

However, in the nineteenth century, the conjunction of a small number of technologies transformed the heart of the North American continent. New transportation technologies—canals, steamboats, and railroads—facilitated the spread of settlers and their companion species from Europe or elsewhere. Guns allowed them to hunt and defend themselves. New agricultural implements (all-metal plows, mechanical harvesters, and barbed wire) facilitated farming on the Prairies.

It was part of a larger pattern of migrations that began with the European discovery of the Americas (1492) and remade natural habitats in both North and South America in the context of the Columbian exchange. Crops with even more distant origins were also part of the transfer: rice, coffee, and cotton were transplanted to the tropical zones of the Americas. This could be termed ecological imperialism, but the exchange was not all one-way; American plants and crops (maize, tobacco, potatoes, and tomatoes) and some animals (the turkey) did spread around the world, sometimes with such astonishing speed their American origins became doubted; a comparative handful of diseases with purely American origins (including venereal syphilis, and Chagas') spread to Europe and elsewhere.

Horses reached the Prairies first, competing with the bison for grass, and enabling hunters (aboriginal or European) to bring down many more bison than before. As guns spread westward, they provided horse-mounted hunters with a formidable new weapon that far outstripped the older methods of aboriginal populations. For some, such as the Canadian Métis, this was a boon that made life easier and turned the bison into an economic resource (a source of meat and pelts) at first for the Hudson's Bay Company and then for buyers south of the border.

Neither the native nor Métis hunters were ever numerous enough to really affect the bison population. Before the arrival of horses and guns, the bison population may have numbered as many as 30 million animals found mostly in the Western Prairies, but also east of the Mississippi and as far north as the boreal forest. During most of the nineteenth century, even the Métis were limited to such transportation means as the horse, the Red River cart, and the canoe. All were slow and could only carry a limited load. To reduce the bulk of the bison meat, the Métis would transform it into pemmican, a somewhat labour-intensive and time-intensive process that was ill-suited to the handling of large numbers of dead animals.

However, canals and railroads followed the guns, bringing more and more hunters to the central plains. Both brought in settlers who were unable to domesticate the bison and who could not tolerate it near their fields and pastures. These settlers, who were also equipped with firearms, exerted a double pressure on the bison population by encroaching on its habitat, and killing more of them. Guns were also improving. Samuel Colt invented the revolver and it became possible to turn out mechanically-produced rifles after 1855. Rifling involves cutting spiral grooves inside a gun barrel. When a gun is fired, the grooves impart a spin to the bullet that stabilizes its trajectory and improves the shooter's chances of hitting whatever he or she was aiming at.

The speed of the railways also made it possible to ship fresh meat in bulk, as well as pelts, back to the densely populated regions of the eastern continent. New markets for bison meat and hides soon developed. As guns improved, especially after the US Civil War flooded the continent with cheap breach-loaders and repeater rifles, the hunters coming to the Prairies on trains could afford to shoot bison indiscriminately, as well as other animals. This—and other measures (grass fires) taken to control the movements of the bison herd or restrict their food supply—was encouraged both by the settlers and by the military who found it an effective way to undermine the independence of the native peoples of the Plains (Sioux, Métis, etc.) who often depended on the bison for food and other necessities. Once tanners back east found a way to treat bison hides, the lure of easy profits led to a final spate of mass slaughter that virtually eliminated in a few years the Plains bison population.

As the huge bison herds of previous decades vanished by 1880, systematic farming became possible and farmers raised crops for export. The old bison stamping grounds became the home of more and more settlers. During the lean years, when the crops failed, they would hunt to put meat on the table or eliminate animals considered to be nuisances or worse, and this steady pressure helped finish off species such as the passenger pigeon within a couple of decades (**Box 5**). These extinctions and near extinctions happened almost in living memory, stranding even such recent cultures as that of the Métis who were forced to either adapt to a farming economy or retreat northwards to eke out a living from a combination of trapping, subsistence farming, and odd jobs. In Canada and the United States, the aboriginal populations faced a similar transition, hampered by paternalistic policies

BOX 5 ▶ Document: The Passenger Pigeon

Response of a committee of the Ohio State legislature in 1857 when asked to protect the passenger pigeon:

"The passenger pigeon needs no protection. Wonderfully prolific, having the vast forests of the North, as its breeding grounds, travelling hundreds of miles in search of food, it is here to-day, and elsewhere to-morrow, and no ordinary destruction can lessen them or be missed from the myriads that are yearly produced."

The last passenger pigeon died in 1914.
(Source: David Quammen, The Song of the Dodo, 1996.)

Modern ranching and farming became possible in the newly-vacated lands of the central Prairies. The settlers may have farmed for themselves at first, but they soon farmed for customers far and wide, subject to the whims of distant markets served by the railway companies. This was a more systematic type of farming, subservient to the demands of an increasingly integrated and industrialized economy. Ranching evolved as well. Cattle herds initially grazed the open range, overseen by cowboys who also took on the job of shepherding the herds to market. Cattle drives became shorter in 1867 when a Chicago livestock dealer, J. G. McCoy, brought a railway line to Abilene, Kansas. Once barbed wire was introduced by Joseph Glidden in 1874, the open range could be divided into private parcels. The use of silos, starting around

1875 in Illinois, to accumulate feed made it possible for cattle owners to function with smaller lots of land.

Fencing affected another large Prairie mammal, the pronghorn antelope found from Alberta and Saskatchewan down to northern Mexico. Like the bison, its population in the early 1800s may have numbered as high as 30 or 35 million individuals throughout its range. By 1924, only about 20,000 remained. The pronghorn is one of the world's fleetest runners, attaining speeds of nearly 100 km/h, but it is unable to jump fences. Modern roads, railways, and fences have curtailed pronghorn migrations, and sometimes barred it from needed access to food and water. Recent initiatives have modified fences to lift the bottom wire high enough for the animals to scurry under it, as well as substitute smooth wire for the barbed wire of standard fences.

As the railroads started to move livestock (cattle on the hoof) supplied by ranchers, they extended the process whereby consumers grew ever more distanced from the source of even the most basic products. When the citizens of large cities like New York ate meat from animals slaughtered on the outskirts of town but transported all the way from the Midwest, they abandoned the close, traditional relationship between location and subsistence.

By the second half of the nineteenth century, this relationship grew ever more distant. The progress of canning, refrigeration, and food processing created a diet rooted in a multiplicity of remote locations. In North America, the historical origins of this estrangement may be traced to bacon and ham from Cincinnati. During the first decades of the nineteenth century, the city of Cincinnati developed at a nexus point of the navigable rivers and canals of the Ohio basin west of the Appalachians. Fattened with the corn, grain, and scraps of farms along the Ohio Valley, hogs were increasingly brought in for slaughter to Cincinnati by the 1830s. The farmers took advantage of a narrow seasonal window when the weather wasn't so hot that the freshly-killed meat would spoil rapidly and so cold that the rivers would freeze, preventing the packed meat from leaving.

Since refrigeration was minimal and the number of animals kept growing, the riverfront slaughter houses of Cincinnati developed new efficiencies. The hogs ascended to the top of a building from which each one would be cast down a chute to be stunned and bled in turn. Around 1850, a "disassembly line" had developed to accelerate the butchering and processing of the animals. Early on, the hogs had been suspended from an overhead wheel that could be turned by steps to let specialized workers perform a single operation on the carcass before passing it on to the next stage. The wheel was then replaced with an overhead conveyor carrying the carcass from one station to the next. The final product was salted pork, which travelled well, especially once the railways took over from steamboats and canal boats. In essence, the hog was a means of reducing the bulk of the crops grown west of the Appalachians into an item compact enough to be transported economically to urban markets. Distillation was another means to the same end. The improvement of the column still by Irish inventor Aeneas Coffey in 1830 made it possible to produce grain whiskey as another high-value, low-volume item that could be exported east of the Appalachians.

While the major US railway companies profited from the shipping of livestock from the trailheads of the West to the cities of the East, Chicago businessmen invested in a centralized facility starting around 1865 to take advantage of Chicago's location at a nexus point of a railroad network covering much of the upper Mississippi basin. The Chicago Union Stock Yards covered half a square kilometre with a complex of pens, alleys, and sheds where thousands of pigs, cattle, and sheep could be processed every day. For some animals, the Chicago yards were mere waystations on the road to their final destination. For others, it was the end of the road. The packing plants produced meat—cured, salted, or dressed—that could be sent by railway to every part of North America. By 1875, they added corned beef to their menu as J. A. Wilson patented a process for its canning.

The volumes involved, as the railways leading to Chicago drained an increasing fraction of all animals raised by US farmers and ranchers, drove Chicago meatpackers to be innovative and to take full advantage of the sheer number of animals passing through their abattoirs. What would have been a waste product in a village slaughterhouse could become commercially valuable if it was available in quantities that justified processing it in turn. The result was an additional margin of profit that allowed the Chicago meatpackers to take on the local butchers.

While they replicated the disassembly line pioneered in Cincinnati, the Chicago meatpackers broke new ground in using refrigeration. Ever since the colonial period, dwellers in northern climes had built ice houses that could be used to store ice cut in mid-winter from a nearby river or lake well into the summer months. By the 1820s, standardized designs using straw or sawdust as an insulator allowed for a generalization of the practice.

Since railways, unlike rivers and canals, were able to operate year-round, trains could ship bulk ice from the Northeast in order to refrigerate the packing plants and let them operate even in high summer, using the ice to cure hog carcasses before preserving them with salt. Ice was then applied to the refrigeration of railroad cars, the first experiments happening in 1867–1868. Gustavus Swift came up with the cooling of meat suspended on hooks using ice packed in a compartment above the storage area. Initially, much of that business involved the Grand Trunk Railway of Canada, less reliant on livestock shipping than other companies and the owner of northern routes favoured with lower temperatures. By 1880, however, the first practical ice-making machines were turning out artificial ice on a commercial scale.

Thanks to the margin provided by the sale of other animal products and to the other economies of scale inherent in their operations, the Chicago meatpackers were able to undersell local butchers, even in New York. By 1883–1884, more beef was packed for export than was shipped live to Eastern plants. The Chicago Union Stock Yards became a wonder of the age. Nowhere else were the resources of half a continent drawn and concentrated into a single facility. Their dominance lasted until the continued expansion of the railway network allowed other centres to take advantage of shorter lines of communication.

For decades, the gory spectacle inside the Chicago meatpacking plants amazed visitors, but the pressure placed on workers to attack and dismember each passing carcass as speedily as possible led to shortcuts at the expense of hygiene and cleanliness. The great meat-packing operations in Chicago and the small-scale slaughterhouses found in towns across North America shared a common disregard for sanitation.

By the end of the nineteenth century, French scientist Louis Pasteur had offered convincing demonstrations of the link between germs and diseases, and the exact conditions that allowed microbes to proliferate had become clear by the turn of the twentieth century. Scientifically-trained microbiologists brought laboratory methods out in the field and began to test systematically for the presence of bacteria. Across North America, public or medical health officers were emboldened to improve sanitation.

Nevertheless, health officers faced a lot of resistance. In 1911, Dr. William John McKay submitted to a meeting of the Board of Health of the city of Saskatoon, Saskatchewan, a shocking report on the city's butchers. He described a dire situation where hogs intended for slaughter would feed and wallow in the mix of blood and water seeping from the killing room while the overflow headed for the river nearby, polluting the intervening ground. It only got worse since the wagon piled up with offal was open to the air, leaking bloody slime and attracting flies. The slaughterhouse was a flimsy shack littered with all manner of animal refuse. The worker's overalls, carving knives, and knife sheaths were caked with blood and fat. Dogs had the run of the place, sniffing the carcasses which were also beset by flies.

However dreadful the conditions, butchers and meatpackers dragged their feet when it came to improving them. The very centralization of slaughter in places like the Chicago Union Stock Yards meant that fewer and fewer consumers were in touch with the former ritual slaughter every autumn of the animals they ate. What was out of sight easily stayed out of mind. In 1906, US author Upton Sinclair published a best-selling novel, *The Jungle,* that shocked North American readers with its portrayal of the crude conditions at a Chicago meat-packer. This finally led to the passing of new laws to better protect consumers.

CONCLUSION: ABOLISHING DISTANCE

Throughout the nineteenth century, railways transformed the landscape in an increasing number of ways. Beyond the obvious physical features of the railroad system (tracks, bridges, tunnels, and embankments), they also favoured the introduction of yet more new species in once remote corners of North America. While steam shipping in this period often brought only minor pests, other species such as the house sparrow and starling from Europe were introduced deliberately.

The common carp was brought over from Asia via Europe in the nineteenth century, perhaps as early as 1831, and it was disseminated for a time as a food-fish. Yet, it may be the most environmentally destructive invasive fish in the United States, as well as the costliest. When carp feed, they uproot native aquatic vegetation, which disturbs the sediment and muddies the surrounding water. This tends to ruin the habitat of native ducks and fish, including valuable commercial species.

Similarly, the water hyacinth was imported from Brazil because of its decorative lavender flowers, but this floating plant has gone native and invaded many freshwater lakes and rivers in the southern United States. As it proliferates, it prevents sunlight from reaching underwater habitats and it can also deplete the water's oxygen content. Both actions are detrimental to the survival of many native aquatic species. More recent invaders can be even more worrisome, from the snakehead fish to Asian carp introduced to aquaculture ponds in the southern United States in the 1970s.

On the grandest scale, the railways were a force for the European settlement of the temperate part of North America. The famous closing of the American frontier in 1890 was the result of an accelerating settlement process that swept over half the continent north of the boreal forest in half the time it had taken for European settlement to creep from the Atlantic to the Mississippi. The original grasslands were largely replaced by fields and pasturelands, just as the original inhabitants were pushed aside to let newcomers build cities and towns where the buffalo roamed.

The political import of railways was no less significant. Railway hubs were strategic targets during the US Civil War and the greater density of railways north of the Mason-Dixon Line helped the North overwhelm the South. In Canada, the transcontinental railway served as a bargaining piece to establish a new confederation in 1867 and the unfinished line still helped Canadian troops move quickly to subdue the Northwest Rebellion in 1885.

In the end, railways transformed North American lifestyles. They abolished distance by allowing people to visit more places in a lifetime than ever before, to extend the range of regular travel (for work or pleasure), and to be supplied with the products of locales far beyond the region from which they would have drawn their sustenance formerly. In doing so, it has been argued that they created a new distance between humans and their environment. Since people no longer depended as closely on the fruits of their immediate surroundings, their relationship with nature was weakened. In the abstract, railways were only one more technology mediating between humans and their environment, but they were certainly one of the most powerful ones of the nineteenth century.

BASIC DEFINITIONS OF RAILROAD TECHNOLOGY

Boiler: a device comprising two chambers, one inside the other; the fuel was burned in the inner chamber [the *firebox*] connecting through flues to the smoke box and then the smokestack; the outer chamber was filled with the water to be turned into steam by the heat of the burning fuel.

Cab: the small cabin at the back of the locomotive where all the controls are found; the locomotive engineer and the fireman shared the space inside the cab; the engineer was in charge of the engine's operation, while the fireman regulated the feeding of the boiler with fuel and water to produce the required *head* of steam. The first engines could be fuelled by hand, but once they became bigger, a mechanical stoker (such as a screw conveyor [Archimedean screw] or auger) was used to move the large quantities of coal needed.

Fuel: wood or coal used to fire the boiler of the locomotive engine.

Gauge: the distance between the rails of a given railway track.

Grade: the slope of the railway tracks.

Locomotive: the railway carriage powered by a steam engine and used to draw a train of cars along rails; high-pressure steam from the boiler entered cylinders on each side of typical locomotives; as the steam exerted force alternatively on both sides of the piston inside each cylinder, it moved the piston rods back and forth to create the rotary motion of the wheels.

Tender: the railway carriage attached to a locomotive and used to carry fuel, water, etc., in order to generate steam in the boiler.

Water: used by the boiler of the locomotive engine.

FURTHER READINGS

Dale F. Lott, *American Bison: A Natural History*, 2002.

CHAPTER 6

The Age of Systems

▶▶▶▶▶▶▶▶▶▶▶▶▶▶▶▶▶▶▶▶▶▶▶▶▶▶▶▶▶

MORE THAN THE SUM OF THEIR PARTS

The helter-skelter pace of innovation and technology transfer during the first decades of the nineteenth century made for an economic and social patchwork. In nooks and crannies, ranging from the Californian backcountry to the Arctic, North America hosted small aboriginal bands that still lived beyond the reach of European traders and retained a Stone Age culture. Others pursued a largely traditional lifestyle based on hunting and gathering though it increasingly incorporated industrially-produced trade goods such as guns, metal knives, and patterned cloth. During the first half of the century, nomads of the Plains forged a largely novel lifestyle using European guns and horses, while homesteaders gradually extended the farming model of the Eastern seaboard west of the Appalachians. Throughout the Northeast, competing canal, railway, and telegraph networks proliferated. In the hands of independent companies and owners, they were born of a building frenzy that created a technology-based economy as sophisticated as any in the world.

The next stage involved the standardization and unification of the many enterprises founded to take advantage of new technologies and resources. Yet, innovation hardly slowed down during the second half of the nineteenth century. Steam engines became more efficient and more powerful, allowing steam propulsion to displace almost every other means of navigation. By the end of the nineteenth century, steam liners and tramp steamers replaced most types of sailing ships at sea, even the speedy clippers used to haul tea from China. On lakes and rivers, steamboats took over from teamboats and many makes of keelboats or flatboats. Better steam engines also led to better locomotives while making it possible to apply steam power to agricultural machinery. By the end of the nineteenth century, the invention of the internal combustion engine presaged further advances in motorization, opening up new possibilities in personal transportation, on land or in the air. The invention of the telephone extended the capabilities of the telegraph, while chemistry helped guide the development of cheap steel, the creation of dynamite, and the synthesis of the first artificial dyes.

By then, though, the technologies of the early Industrial Revolution were no longer speculative ventures and financiers such as J. P. Morgan did not hesitate to backstop the rationalization of entire industries or networks. The transportation systems of the nineteenth century had wrought great changes, but improved integration of their operations achieved even more. Their manifold consequences did more than transform the workplace, leading to new ways of living. Less obvious or intrusive, new media and communication systems such as telegraphs, postal services, and cheap print publications evolved to cater to the needs of the new economy.

During the early years of the nineteenth century, electricity was still a laboratory phenomenon, an experimental plaything or a subject for classroom demonstrations. By the end of the century, it promised to become the basis for a momentous addition to the technologies already enlisted in the cause of humanity's comfort.

The first practical application of electrical science was probably the lightning rod in the eighteenth century, followed closely by attempts to use electricity for healing or the relief of chronic medical conditions. By the middle of the nineteenth century, electroplating became a lucrative niche used for the newly invented electrical battery, while arc-lighting found applications in theater, illuminated outdoor monuments or allowed night work on construction sites. However, electricity most concretely transformed communications by the end of the nineteenth century. Though it required relays and signal boosters, the electric telegraph outdid every previous communications technology. The signalling potential of electrical current led to other applications, including fire alarms and burglar alarms. As railway traffic soared, railroad timetables could best be coordinated by electricity's speed. Eventually, the telephone followed.

Early breakthroughs by researchers such as Hans Christian Ørsted, André-Marie Ampère, and Michael Faraday led to the parallel development of the electric generator and electrical motor by the second half of the nineteenth century. One consequence was to make waterpower essentially portable: electricity generated at one site could be transferred to drive an electrical motor at another. Previously, waterpower and steam power could only be transferred over short distances, basically within a single building. With electricity, motive power was delocalized. Above all, the inventions of the generator, the light bulb, and the electric streetcar allowed electricity to break through to wider markets. By the end of the nineteenth century, it became clear electricity would transform industrialized societies.

While railway engineer Sandford Fleming helped to turn railroad time into world time, another Scottish-Canadian, Alexander Graham Bell, was the first to patent a telephone. Yet, while telegraphs and telephones had down-to-earth applications, they also fed communicational utopias. In 1858, the first transatlantic telegraph cable was celebrated in Ottawa by speeches and the flight of a balloon a kilometer into the air. Though the celebrations were premature since a permanent telegraphic link between the Old and New Worlds would not be established until 1866, the telegraph already began to transform the nature of war during the 1846–1848 Mexican-American War. Not only were political leaders in Washington able to follow nearly in real time the actions of US troops, but journalists relayed war news to the newspapers at home, fostering among the general public a new sense of involvement in the military operations happening far from them.

The telegraph became the era's equivalent of the internet and it became a lynchpin of the large technological systems that were developed in North America in the course of the nineteenth century.

ABOLISHING TIME, WITH COMMUNICATION

If new means of transportation abolished distance, the new means of communication helped to abolish time, as did new technologies such as photography, sound recording, and moving pictures that could capture a moment and preserve it. The result was a new readiness to work with people in other locations, who might never actually meet in person but who were part of a coherent, coordinated structure.

Previous chapters considered the agrarian impact of European settlement—as settlers either brought new crops to the Americas (wheat, rice, and sugar cane among others) or discovered new crops there (maize, tobacco, and potatoes among others). While Europeans transformed the living landscape by felling trees, clearing fields and meadows, growing crops from abroad, and raising imported animals, they also introduced technologies that had less direct effects on the environment. Expanding settlement and transportation systems affected forest ecosystems, Prairie dwellers dependent on bison, and aquatic life.

Canals involved the manipulation of water flows, sometimes on a vast geographic scale. In North America, most of the early canals were small enough not to drain extensive quantities of water, and canalization work along the rivers to make navigation easier was less intrusive than flood control measures implemented in the late nineteenth and early twentieth century. Nevertheless, canals both affected existing riverine habitats and created new ones. They linked hydrographical basins and they helped some species to travel into new creeks, lakes, and rivers, whether the fish and mollusks came from the river one valley over or from the other side of the globe.

Railroads also transformed the landscape. They required cuttings and embankments that created new features of the land. However, it was harder for new species to hitch a ride on the trains travelling over the rails. To go from one locale to another, species needed help. There are few hideaways on trains! On the other hand, the speed of trains was such that one moment of inattention or one foolhardy decision could lead to a new species taking root hundreds or thousands of miles away from its place of origin.

While agricultural techniques were intended to yield food and necessities for the farmers, canals and railroads were built to carry goods for commerce. Since they improved on either the speed or the efficiency of previous methods, they proved able to convey far greater quantities of goods between increasingly arbitrary points on the world's surface. Still, while they facilitated the movement of bulk goods, higher-value products were still favoured, so that trade initially involved shipping whiskey, cured hog carcasses, livestock, or dressed meats rather than the corn used to produce all of these.

As roads, canals, and railroads formed an ever-growing network, they fostered the development of industry in North America.

FOSTERING INDUSTRIALIZATION

Indeed, they were not the only factor in the transformation of the context of everyday life. The distinguishing feature of the Industrial Revolution, the mechanizing of manufactures, changed profoundly the nature of work for thousands of men, women, and even children.

The economic importance of manufactures and industries grew slowly during the first half of the nineteenth century. At its outset, the most common manufactures in North America were still household ones, found inside farmhouses and other private dwellings. Even if not all households made everything, enough were set up to supply themselves and the surrounding community. Major manufactures were still those that transformed and processed farm products, turning linen into cloth, tobacco into snuff, wheat into flour, or grain into beer.

In the short term, the most direct impact of the rise of mechanized factories was felt not so much by consumers as by workers, especially by skilled ones. Before, artisans and craftsmen had worked at home, and mechanics had often owned their tools. As machines and machine-tools for factories became more expensive, mechanics could no longer afford them.

In the longer term, the Industrial Revolution had tremendous consequences for the standard of living of those it affected. While its fruits were not equally shared, for the first time it allowed a large population to outpace the rising demands resulting from population growth. In other words, industrial economies grew faster than the population, leading to genuine wealth creation. All that was needed was a sustained rate of annual growth of about 2% to 3%. In the nineteenth century, Great Britain achieved such sustained growth and its gross national product was multiplied by ten. Due to population growth, per capita income only increased by a factor of three or four, but this was enough to foster additional improvements in public health and education.

Industrialization is closely associated with mechanization. In England, the textile industry mechanized early. In the young United States, the flour milling industry was a pioneer of mechanization.

Another set of key developments happened in the United States arms industry. In 1798, the fear of war with France impelled the government to invest money in gun manufacture. One of its contractors was Eli Whitney, the inventor in 1793 of a *cotton gin* (a machine designed to separate the seeds from cotton fibres and reduce much of the human effort previously associated with this work). In 1799, Whitney promised to invent machines that would fashion the parts of the muskets he was committed to produce. These machines would "give expedition, uniformity, and exactness to the whole."

These characteristics would become the hallmarks of what was called the "American System of Manufacture." Expedition involved producing great quantities quickly. Uniformity involved producing muskets that would all be identical. Exactness implied something more—that the parts of the musket would be turned out to such exact specifications that they would require no adjusting or fitting. The last two characteristics essentially defined the ideal of interchangeability.

The ability to produce interchangeable parts multiplied the value of any production run. Previously, each production item had been an individual object with its own tolerances. Each part would have to be manually fitted to work with the rest, which was highly skilled work. If a part broke, a replacement part had to be adjusted anew. On a battlefield, a broken musket might have to be thrown away or sent to a distant workshop. With replaceable parts, repairs became possible on-site.

Eli Whitney himself never really developed the necessary machinery. A competitor called Simeon North (who got a contract for pistol manufacturing) developed a milling machine in 1816 to finish parts to exacting standards with a special, hardened steel cutter.

Two consecutive superintendents of the Springfield Armory, between 1802 and 1813, introduced the division of labour (so that various employees worked only on some parts of the finished product) and piece rates (which paid workers for the number of parts produced rather than for the time spent on the job). The next superintendent hired Thomas Blanchard in 1819 to create a special lathe able to cut irregular wooden shapes (gunstocks) by following the outline of a model placed in the machine. Finally, another subcontractor, John H. Hall, tackled the production of breech-loading rifles and designed additional special purpose machinery, including specialized fixtures (vises) and gauges to check for the uniformity of each part.

By 1822, "armory practice" had become a complete model that inspired other industries, such as clock making and the production of sewing machines. In the North American context where skilled workers were scarce and commanded high wages, anything that allowed owners to replace them with unskilled workers was favoured and so industrialization accelerated.

Insofar as the new milling machines and mechanized installations needed a source of power (whether it was steam or waterpower), they needed to be close to that source of power. Until then, much manufacturing had been done by hand (as the word implies) and often at home or in a home workshop. Spinning wheels or looms would be operated by one or two people, and the merchant made the rounds of his operators' homes to gather the finished product (cloth, for instance). This was called "putting out."

The new "factory system" involved gathering machines and their operators under one roof, close to the source of power needed to move the machines. The resulting manufacturing process cut down on the unnecessary transportation of supplies between individual homes and incidentally allowed the employer to keep a closer watch on the employees.

Around 1820, the earliest textile factories, or "mills," typically employed 30–80 people, most of whom were children between seven and fourteen. (Their fathers were often also employed by the mill owners, but outside the mills—working on farms, repairing machinery, weaving on handlooms or supervising other employees.) Later, in places like Lowell (near Boston), as the level of mechanization increased, the running of the mills was delegated to professional managers, and the workforce changed to include young unmarried women. The Lowell mills enjoyed great success for a few years, until patent protection lapsed and competition intensified. The US-born female workforce resisted attempts to make them work harder, and employers turned progressively to a new source of workers, immigration. In New England, after 1850, that meant hiring more pliable Irish and French-Canadian immigrants. In short, the scale of operations increased and also became much more impersonal.

The "factory system" spread to other industries: boot and shoe manufacturing, papermaking, even butter and cheese making, and meatpacking. Many of the mills and industrial sites were rural in the United States, whereas they had been urban in Great Britain. In Great Britain, cities were often the places best supplied with coal. The easy availability of waterpower and water transport along the eastern seaboard, in the shadow of the Appalachians, explains this as well as ideological choices. The greater availability of coal shipped by rail, as well as other factors, resulted in a later shift away from the initial countryside locations.

> **BOX 1 ▶ From Water Power to Steam Power (1856)**
>
> *"Most of our manufacturing towns and villages are indebted for their rise to water power. They are built on rivers and creeks where there are falls of water for driving machinery. It has now become a serious question with many manufacturers, using water power, that their supply of water is becoming more unstable every year, as the forests are cleared off. Many streams once flowing with power for the miller are now only water-worn channels. But manufacturers have not decreased in our country, thanks to the power of steam. With a plentiful supply of fuel (coal), steam forms a constant trusty power for driving machinery, and a steam factory can be erected independent of rare natural localities, like water-falls. Steam factories can be conducted in or near cities and commercial marts."*[1]
>
> (Founded in 1845, the *Scientific American* magazine was initially more concerned with industrial and technological progress than with science. In the October 1856 issue, it connected the clearing of forests with greater fluctuations in river flow and the shift to steam power provided by coal burning.)

As long as a destination was within easy distance of a canal or railway, great distances mattered less and less. As steam boats, steam ships, and locomotives took over, it became possible to travel throughout half of the continent in a few days, or to get either goods or news to a recipient in the same time, as long as the sender had the financial means. The (relative) reliability of the new transportation modes, when

---

[1] "Steam versus Water Power," *Scientific American*, volume 12, number 6 (18 October 1856), p. 45.

compared to the vagaries of sailing ships or boats propelled by muscle power alone, also brought into being a new concept: scheduling.

Once upon a time, leaving on a trip meant that you knew when you left but not when you arrived. Steamboats (and increasingly steamships) as well as trains were able to follow schedules. Indeed, for trains sharing tracks and arriving in the same train stations, schedules were crucial. For the users of steam boats or locomotives, such schedules meant that farmers and shippers worked to deadlines in a way that had been reserved until then to workers in the new factories of the Industrial Revolution.

As distance was made more and more manageable, time became the chief challenge of businessmen shipping their products over great distances.

LONG-DISTANCE RELATIONSHIPS

On the other hand, quicker transportation meant new relationships could be fostered between friends and partners residing in widely separated cities. Trains and steam ships made possible the democratisation of mail. The exchange of messages (letters) carried between distant places goes back to Antiquity, but only the Roman Empire's elite could afford to carry out an actual correspondence using a system meant to carry state messages. (Entrusting a letter to a friend travelling in the right direction was also possible, but it only made for one-way communication at best.) In later ages, various networks of messengers offered primitive postal services at high prices, so that only the very powerful and the very rich could afford to engage in correspondence. Steamships and trains revolutionised the economics of mail. By the middle of the nineteenth century, postage stamps were introduced and by the end of the century, an international postal union was set up to negotiate and oversee reciprocity accords between different countries.

With the development of modern communication systems, we move one level up in terms of intangibility. Information is all that will be carried, and yet that is enough to modify the experience of presence. In Canada, Prince Edward once ordered insubordinate soldiers flogged by telegraph. When the phone was invented, telepresence became an infinitely more powerful experience.

Moving information at the speed of light also abolishes distance, but it is something of a semblance. To speak by phone is either speaking with a ghost—someone who is not physically there—or it is a form of astral projection—sending your own consciousness to another place without going there physically. The asymmetry in these descriptions and the modern day's experience of the Internet lead us to think of the context for phone conversations or for Internet surfing as a virtual space. When speaking to someone on the phone, you are sharing an imagined state of proximity. When surfing, you are moving through an imagined landscape of websites connected in ways that can be almost grasped.

Distance is indeed abolished, but it is also replaced.

Telegraphs: From the Duke of York to the Duke of Kent

If railroads were highly complex and extensive *technological systems*, the development of telegraphy and telephony fostered networks similarly unprecedented in their intricacy. Less intrusive than the great transportation systems of the nineteenth century, they catered nonetheless to their needs. The telegraph especially was a godsend to railroads, which needed to coordinate the movements of fast-moving trains over great distances.

In fairness to its predecessors, the telegraph is properly called the *electric* telegraph. Various means of long-distance communication had long been known. The key was the relay principle. Sound was used in some cases: shouted calls relayed from one field to the next in densely settled areas, the whistling language of the natives of the Azores, drums in Africa, bells in Europe, gongs in Asia . . . Messages were also carried by human runners, by riders, or by birds such as doves and pigeons. Visual signals were also common, such as smoke signals and beacon fires. Flags had also been used for a long time to convey basic meanings with the help of colour, shape, and design. The potential usefulness of flags for conveying messages was boosted in the 17th century by the invention of the spyglass. The British Navy was among the first to take advantage and devise a detailed code using pennants flown from its ships, to be observed from neighbouring ships with the help of spyglasses.

The Duke of York (the future King James II of England) is credited with first establishing a signal code with a regular system during the Dutch War of 1665. The system is thought to have employed specific flags raised on various parts of the ship. The British Navy continued to use variations on this system until the 1780s, when a system using combinations of flags was developed and then codified by Lord Howe in 1782.

A few years later, the French engineer Claude Chappe conceived a land-based equivalent which became known as the semaphore, though it was also generally known as an (aerial) telegraph. A series of towers equipped with signal masts and staffed by dedicated men allowed messages and reports to be relayed with astonishing speed for the time. The first line started operating in 1794 and France's network lasted until the mid-nineteenth century; it was closed down only when the electric telegraph was shown to be a reliable (and much faster) alternative. In Great Britain, the government saw the advantages of having such a network and it set up in 1795 a line of telegraph towers to facilitate communication between London and the ports of the south coast during the war with France. The system was designed by a clergyman and amateur scientist, George Murray, who used six wooden shutters, to be either shut or open.

The new telegraphs inspired new hopes. An entry in the 1797 *Encyclopaedia Britannica* noted that, "The capitals of distant nations might be united by chains of posts, and the settling of those disputes which at present take up months or years might then be accomplished in as many hours."

In Canada, the first major (aerial or optical) telegraph line dates back to 1798. During the war with Revolutionary France, the British forces based in the Maritimes and commanded by prince Edward, the Duke of Kent, linked Halifax by telegraph to the crucial lighthouse on Sambro Island in the Atlantic, and also to Fredericton. (A dedicated shuttle carried messages across the Bay of Fundy, between Annapolis and St. John.) The system was openly based on the flag system of the Navy, though the use of wickerwork balls made for a more complex code. Spyglasses were employed to decipher the messages over intervals of 10 to 25 km. (At night, lanterns were used.) Prince Edward thought of extending the system to Quebec City, in order to link together the principal colonies of British North America, but it would have required too much manpower. The Peace of Amiens in 1802 ended the scheme.

In the United States, a similar line-of-sight telegraph system was tested between Boston and Martha's Vineyard in 1800. While there were plans to extend optical telegraph lines from Maine to the Gulf of Mexico, their cost was prohibitive and little was done.

By 1809, the British garrison in Quebec City operated a system built along the lines of the Halifax network, running upstream and downstream from the Citadel. When the wars were over, part of that network was maintained with the help of the city's merchants who wanted to know ship arrivals ahead of time. In 1837, a bilingual newspaper naturally called *Le Télégraphe* took advantage of the small network to keep track of ship movements on the St. Lawrence as they approached Quebec City.

Prince Edward, the Duke of Kent and Commander-in-Chief of British North America, was an early believer in working at home (from his personal lodgings some distance up the sound from Halifax) and on the road with the help of the visual telegraph network he'd established around Halifax. We have a letter by one of his staff officers, Captain Lyman, writing in February 1800 from Halifax to Edward Winslow in Fredericton:

> *"The Duke returned on Saturday, what he has been about so much longer than he had proposed I have not heard, but I am told they have established telegraphs all the way to Annapolis, so that there was a continual communication kept up of ordering and counter orders while he was away even to the approval of courts martial and ordering the men to be flogged. I was at Barracks on Saturday to pay a visit to Col. Burrows when on looking out the window I saw preparations making that I did not understand, on asking what it meant the Col. told me it was a punishment going on. Expressing my surprize [sic] at it during the Duke's absence, I was told the men were to be flogged by Telegraph. So though an hundred miles off, the Duke was acquainted with what was going on, and giving orders the same as usual."*

The instructions given out for making signals in Halifax in 1799 read as follows:

> *"The following signals are made in the Citadel when vessels are coming into Halifax Harbour:*
>
> One Ball—For one square rigged vessel.
> One Ball half hoisted—For two square rigged vessel.
> Two Balls close—For three square rigged vessel.
> Two Balls separated—For four square rigged vessel.
> A Pendant of any colour—For five square rigged vessel.
> A Pendant under one Ball—For six square rigged vessel.
> A Pendant over a Ball half hoisted—For seven square rigged vessel.
> A Pendant under two Balls close—For eight square rigged vessel.
> A Pendant between two Balls separated—For nine square rigged vessel.
> A Flag of any colour—For ten or more.
>
> *The above are hoisted at the East or West Yard Arm, according to the Quarter the Vessel first appears in, and as soon as the Vessel can be described one or more of the following Colours are hoisted at the Mast head.*
>
> A Union—For a Flag Ship with or without a Squadron.
> A Union with a Red Pendant over it—For a two decker.
> A Union with a Blue Pendant over it—For a frigate.
> A Union with a White Pendant over it—For a small armed vessel.

A Red Flag pierced White—For a Packet.
A Blue Pendant—For a merchant ship.
A Red Pendant—For a merchant brig.
A White Pendant—For a Topsail Sloop or Schooner.
A Red Flag—For a Neutral Man of War.
A Red Flag with a Blue Pendant under it—For a Neutral Merchant Ship.
A Red Flag with a Red Pendant under it—For Neutral Sloop or Schooner.

Enemy's Signals

A French Jack—For an Enemy's Fleet
A Blue Pendant under a French Pendant—For an Enemy's Ship.
A Red Pendant under a French Pendant—For an Enemy's Brig.
A White Pendant under a French Pendant—For an Enemy's sloop or Schooner.

N.B. No Signals can be made with those for describing Enemy's Vessels except when they are in our possession, in which case, a Union Jack will be hoisted over the Signal."[2]

THE COMPLICATED DEVELOPMENT OF THE ELECTRIC TELEGRAPH

Earlier chapters rarely dealt with individual inventors. Canals evolved incrementally. Railroads were technological systems of even greater complexity, so that different people in different countries often had a valid claim on this or that improvement to a given component of the system. The electric telegraph might seem like a different matter, but it was a sufficiently complicated invention to have required several inventors.

Electricity was studied intensively during the 18th century. It was noted by April 1746 that a line-up nearly a mile long of monks linked by iron rods seemed to be traversed instantly by an electric shock produced by an accumulator. By 1753, a Scotsman suggested that electricity be used to transmit signals by making each wire or other electrical effect correspond to a letter. In Spain, Francisco Salva is thought to have set up an experimental line with multiple wires between Madrid and the spring residence of the royal family as early as 1795. In England, twenty-eight-year-old

---

[2]Cited by James H. Morrison, "The Duke of Kent's Astonishing Telegraph", *The Beaver* (December 1991-January 1992), p. 32.

Francis Ronalds built experimental lines using up to 15 kilometres of iron wire in order to connect dials and transmit signals. In July 1816, he wrote to the British Admiralty offering to demonstrate it. The Secretary of the Admiralty replied, "Telegraphs of any kind are wholly unnecessary, no other than the one in use will be adopted."

By the 1830s, two types of electromagnetic telegraphs had been developed: the needle system and the armature system. The first employed the deflections of small magnetic needles placed at the receiving ends of the wires through which a current was sent. The second placed an electromagnet at the end of the wire, so that the current put through the electromagnet might produce a mechanical effect.

Russian diplomat Pavel Schilling drew on the work of an early experimenter in Munich, Soemmering (around 1810), to design a single needle telegraph that became known to scientists throughout Europe and became part of lectures on electricity in various locations. The son of a British doctor who had known Ronalds, William Cooke attended such a lecture in Munich and came back to England determined to build a practical electric telegraph. With the help of a university scientist, Charles Wheatstone, he succeeded by June 1837, patenting an invention that needed only to be marketed.

By then, the competition was fierce. Electric telegraphs were being thought up by numerous inventors in Europe and North America. In 1832, during a six-week trip across the Atlantic, Samuel Morse (1791–1872) conceived a particularly efficient code using only dots and dashes produced by depressing a single key (no need for magnetic needles or cumbersome dials) suitable for an electric telegraph; however, it would take him until 1837 to find the right partners (a university chemist by the name of Leonard Gale and the son of an industrialist, Alfred Vail) in order to perfect the corresponding apparatus and start marketing it in 1838–1839.

The code designed by Morse and Vail assigned the fewest numbers of dots and dashes to the most common letters in English (*e* was a single dot and *t* a single dash, and so on). When the code was adopted by railway companies in continental Europe, German telegraphers modified eleven codings to match the most common letters in German. This modified code was adopted by the Austro-Germanic Telegraph Union in 1851, and it was later the version of the Morse code that was adopted for international use in the age of radio.

However, the original Morse code continued to be used by railways in the United States and Canada, where it naturally became known as "railway Morse." It was used for many decades, enduring in Canadian National Railway offices until 1972 as a potential backup to the phone system.

However, early electric telegraph inventions were often unable to transmit a signal very far and remained impractical prototypes, but the development of railways created a need for quicker means of communication over long distances. There were many ways of avoiding train collisions—an obvious one was to build double sets of tracks, each reserved to trains going one way. The expense, however, was such that single tracks were preferred if they could be made safe.

Some telegraph promoters duly noted that railway tracks, occupying continuous parcels of land between major cities, offered the perfect location for laying telegraph lines. Initially, the electric telegraph was mainly used to synchronize clocks in all the train stations of a given railway company. The messaging capability of telegraphs was also used to allow neighbouring train stations to communicate and transmit timely warnings. The use of the electric telegraph to provide stationmasters, human signallers, train operators, and mechanical signalling devices with information as to the location of trains on a length of track was not fully adopted until the second half of the nineteenth century. Many railroad companies were skeptical and resisted the adoption of such telegraphs to directly manage train traffic until the rising toll of accidents compelled them to rely on yet another telegraphic application.

However, once train stations started to use telegraphs to exchange information, the small differences in local times became significant. Some train mishaps of the nineteenth century were caused by misunderstandings and discrepant times. This would motivate railway managers and engineers such as Canadian Sandford Fleming to turn railroad time into world time.

Originally, the electric telegraph swept into Canada on the heels of its growing success in the United States. After years of effort, Morse had been able to send messages between Baltimore and Washington in 1844. The race was on to establish lines wherever they could be financed. A demonstration in Toronto on June 24, 1846, led local businessmen to invest in the construction of a line between Toronto and Buffalo, which was already connected to New York. The line between Toronto and Hamilton was opened on December 19, 1846; by mid-January, Toronto was communicating directly with New York.

In Montreal, the chamber of commerce first examined four competing projects offering lines to Halifax, Portland, Saratoga, and Toronto. The Toronto line was started in February 1847 and opened in August of the same year. Another company incorporated to build the line to Halifax, fulfilling Prince Edward's old dream. And a line to Quebec City was completed by December 1847. During the first full year of operation, 33,000 messages were exchanged between Toronto and Quebec City.

By 1851, one could send a ten-word telegraph message from Montreal to Trois-Rivières for one shilling and sixpence or all the way to Quebec City for one shilling and sixteen pence. A few years later, the first experiments in laying telegraph cables underwater led to a grander scheme—laying a cable under the Atlantic all the way from Europe to North America. When the first transatlantic cable was completed, President James Buchanan of the United States and Queen Victoria exchanged greetings (transmission taking ten to twelve hours from end to end). Celebrations from New York to Quebec City to Ottawa marked the momentous event on September 1st, 1858. Speeches proclaimed the hope that such a cable would help the world's peoples become brothers and result in such amity and harmony that it would help civilization advance and improve the material welfare of Christian countries. (The cable broke down after a month; a new one was only set in place in 1866, after the US Civil War delayed the undertaking.)

In 1871, Montreal entrepreneur and inventor George-Édouard Desbarats followed the example set elsewhere and invited young women to take telegraphy courses at his new school in Old Montreal. Desbarats even had a private line connecting his office on Place d'Armes and his workshop on Saint-Antoine Street.

While telegraphs fed communicational utopias, they also had down-to-earth applications. The electric telegraph was being applied by then to a fire alarm network, connecting alarm boxes to fire halls. US inventor Elisha Gray made significant money selling such fire alarms in Chicago after the great fire that almost destroyed the city in 1871. In 1892, there were 137 signal boxes spread throughout Quebec City, most of them on street corners.

THE TELEPHONE

The invention of the telephone was slightly less complex, but only slightly less. A Scottish-Canadian, Alexander Graham Bell (1847–1922), was the first to patent a telephone. He was nearly beaten by a rival, Elisha Gray (1835–1901), a professional inventor associated with the telegraph industry, but he benefited from the fact that Gray's bread and butter were telegraphic inventions. His real interest was in the field of "harmonic telegraphs," which Bell had also worked on, but the telephone patent was secondary for him. The telegraph industry dominated by Western Union was huge and it had already rewarded him handsomely for earlier inventions. Western Union wanted a device capable of sending several messages over the same line at the same time. It did not want another way of sending a single message over a single line, even if it could transmit the human voice!

As a matter of fact, the telephone was one of several devices—the others being the multiple telegraph and the musical telegraph—that could be based on the same physical phenomenon known to a number of contemporaries. In France, Charles Bourseul is said to have described the principle of the telephone in a periodical, *L'Illustration*, in 1854; however, Bourseul was an employee of a telegraph company and he was told by his bosses, in no uncertain terms, that he should stick to his work. In Germany, a professor of physics and music, Johann Philip Reis, actually built a device around 1861 he called a "telephone" though it was essentially a musical telegraph, able to transmit musical notes which were received as a melody. However, it could not transmit recognizable words.

The technical challenge associated with the telephone was the building of a transmitter able to convert the human voice into an electrical signal. A different challenge was associated with the "harmonic telegraph," which seemed to be the key to a multiple telegraph able to combine on the same line several signals transmitted at different pitches. Sending was not a problem, but decoding the signal at the other end, by disentangling the different frequencies, was the main hurdle faced by several inventors, and chiefly Elisha Gray.

Bell himself had been encouraged by his backers, including his future father-in-law, to invent such a harmonic telegraph. But the appeal of the "telephone" sidetracked him. Gray had thought of the telephone, but he concentrated on the harmonic telegraph and seems to have filed a "caveat," an intent to patent, just in case. However, Bell had filed an actual patent application three hours earlier and proceeded to market his invention.

Gray did not pursue the telephone until very late in the game, even though it was a logical extension of his work on the multiple telegraph. Until the tele-

FIGURE 1 ▶ An early three-box telephone, with the electric circuitry in the top compartment, the batteries in the bottom, and the transmitter in the middle. *(Picture by author in Brantford, Ontario, 2007.)*

phone started showing its potential, the multiple telegraph seemed to be the key to riches because the telegraph companies already covered the entire country. It was an existing market, and a lucrative one.

Alexander Graham Bell, born in Scotland, had moved to Canada in 1870 before finding a job in Boston.

He would do part of his work in Canada, and later buy himself a summer residence in Nova Scotia. He is acknowledged today as the inventor of the telephone. It has been suggested that Bell stole a look at Gray's patent application and corrected after the fact a small but crucial detail in his telephone patent. Initially, Gray had yielded the priority to Bell without complaint, after his case was voided by the courts, but when this allegation aired years later, Gray became quite embittered and renewed the controversy in his old age.

FIGURE 2 ▶ The family home of Alexander Graham Bell in Brantford, Ontario. *(Picture by author in 2007.)*

While Bell's work was crucial, he depended on the technical expertise of his assistant, Thomas Watson, and on the financial backing of such as Gardiner Hubbard, the father of Bell's wife.

Later, telephone lines were improved with the amplifiers of Michael Pupin in 1900, and then with the triode and repeater designed by Arnold in 1906. These improvements allowed the telephone system to span the continent.

THE WIRED CENTURY

By the time electrical lighting was developed by Edison, the nineteenth century was already the century of wiring. Telegraph wires had come first, strung from post to post across the land. They connected train stations, a few businesses, and many telegraph offices. Secondary systems (such as fire alarm networks) made use of them, but, for the most part, telegraph wires multiplied because each wire could only carry one message at a time.

The telephone soon added its own set of wires to the landscape. During the Bell monopoly era, between 1877 and 1893, businesses owned two thirds of the phones, but limitations similar to those of the telegraph also meant that cities needed to be criss-crossed by even more wires.

When Edison opened his first electrical lighting network in downtown Manhattan in 1882, he tried to keep the power lines underground, but they soon appeared overhead.

The development of electric streetcars or trolley-buses, pioneered by Frank Sprague in 1888, demanded the stringing of live wires overhead, so that major cities in North America became thoroughly and intrusively *wired*.

THE AGE OF SYSTEMS: INVENTING SYSTEMS

Technological systems are often created by entrepreneurs who play a crucial role by linking the efforts of inventors and engineers by taking an overall view of the distinct contributions of each. If the nineteenth century was the heyday of the independent inventor, it was also an era defined by the contributions of engineers who increasingly enjoyed the benefits of a specialized education. However, the contributions of both would have been less productive without the entrepreneurs who lined up funds, organized systems, and made sure the whole enterprise was profitable. All or some of these roles could merge in a single, talented person, such as Edison, but they are sufficiently distinct to often absorb all of an individual's creative energies.

Inventors conceive and design the physical components of systems. Their inventions are concrete, may be patented, and may or may not be intended to fit into a given system. The archetypal inventor was a free-lancer who came up with inventions that he or she would then try to turn into money-makers—or sell off. By the end of the nineteenth century, inventors were being made a part of companies (such as Bell) that were pioneering the modern research and development (R&D) department.

Entrepreneurs innovate. Economists and historians of technology distinguish innovation from invention. To innovate is to turn the prototype of an invention into a workaday product for the marketplace. Entrepreneurs innovate while developing and managing the business structure that will make this a paying proposition. They attempt to make money with inventions, providing the funds or the hard work or the managerial skills (or all three) needed to turn the technical idea of the inventor into something that will be adopted by society at large. Often, this may mean that the invention will be fitted within a larger technological system.

Sometimes, the inventor may also be an entrepreneur, as in the case of Thomas Alva Edison (1847–1931). He led the effort that invented an effective electric light, then designed a system that would deliver high-voltage current to lighting customers, then founded companies to manufacture the parts of the system and to supply them (at a profit), and then set up companies to provide the electric service. And he also raised the needed capital from various investors.

Sometimes, the entrepreneur is no inventor; he or she just spots the potential of somebody else's inventions and works hard to turn it into a product, bring it to market, and find a way to make it commercially profitable. Among many other things, Edison invented an improved phonograph, but he thought its principal use would be as a dictation machine for businessmen; it was somebody else who recognized the potential of the phonograph to play music.

Engineers build or design what is to be built as part of a technological system. They may be part of the initial inventive efforts or of the innovation process. They provide the technical know-how to turn the ideas of inventors and entrepreneurs into practical designs that are simultaneously safe, effective, and efficient—and commercially viable. Some engineers build bridges and dams, and others improve or oversee the production of manufactured objects (light bulbs, locomotives, chemical products, etc.). Some engineers make things work, tending to steam engines, power plants, assembly lines, and other machinery. Some engineers make discoveries in the name of utility, though this category may include specialists nominally from other fields, such as the chemists who develop tests to determine whether drinking water is safe or the geologists who map iron ore or oil fields.

Like inventors and entrepreneurs, some engineers wear more than one hat. Engineers may patent new processes and products, thus becoming inventors. They may also found consulting firms or manufacturing companies, thus becoming entrepreneurs.

Ruth Schwartz Cowan defines engineers as people who do for the sake of production what scientists do for the sake of knowledge. "Put a slightly different way, this means that engineers are people who have systematically acquired knowledge about the natural world and who put that knowledge to use in achieving some practical goal."[3]

However, inventors, entrepreneurs, and engineers were all needed to create technological systems during the nineteenth century. In fact, the creation of such systems did much to define the distinct roles of each.

Yet, in the end, the success of the system-builders doomed the independent inventor, sharply circumscribed the possibilities open to entrepreneurs by creating

---

[3]Ruth Schwartz Cowan, *A Social History of American Technology* (Oxford University Press, 1997), p. 120.

monopolistic companies, and turned the engineer into an employee. Large technological systems could only be run and managed by equally large corporations.

Inventors were hired to head research laboratories or sold their inventions outright to the companies. Entrepreneurs were left with fewer opportunities when corporations controlled most of the market and strove for monopolistic control.

As for engineers, they became professionals. For much of the early nineteenth century, North American engineers outside the US Army Corps had been free agents. They were a rare commodity, and their skills commanded respect. Whether they ran large construction projects (bridges, canals, railroads, aqueducts, sewers) or designed the most powerful machinery of the day (locomotives, stationary steam engines, steamers), they could pick and choose their jobs. Many headed their own shops, took on contracts of their own choosing, and were effectively their own bosses.

Passed in 1862, the US Morrill Act donated large tracts of federal land (in proportion to the population) to states that would establish colleges "for the Benefit of Agriculture and the Mechanic Arts." Naturally, these "land grant colleges" developed courses not only for young farmers and would-be mechanics, but also for engineers to be. By 1872, there were 70 academic engineering colleges in the United States. By 1880, the number had risen to eighty-five. By 1900, about 10,000 young men (and a few young women) were being admitted to the freshman classes of such colleges.

The US decennial census recorded 7,000 engineers in 1880. Forty years later, it found 136,000 engineers. Many were school-educated. Fewer and fewer engineers had trained directly in the shops of the old engineering elite. By the late 1920s, it was estimated that only a quarter of all engineers who had graduated before 1909 were consultants or proprietors of their own business, the implication being that the younger engineers were even less likely to be independent.

By then, professional societies had been formed to define the standards expected from engineers. The American Society of Civil Engineers (1852, relaunched in 1867), the American Institute of Mining Engineers (1871), the American Society of Mechanical Engineers (1880), the American Institute of Electrical Engineers (1884), and other associations all wished to certify professional status, to define educational standards, and to recommend countrywide industrial norms in their respective fields. In practice, however, engineers had largely become part of the systems they had contributed to create originally.

The Telegraph System

The first extensive technological system to enter North American lives tied together train stations, businesses, and cities both metaphorically and literally since the telegraph required wires to carry messages from one place to another. The speed with which messages could be exchanged introduced a growing divergence between transportation and communication. Previously, communication had remained beholden to the fastest available means of transportation. Now, transportation would grow to depend on the fastest available means of communication for its coordination. The telegraph created a new technological arena with additional consequences for politics, culture, and markets. Information ceased to be local.

After the first demonstrations of the new technology, a number of different companies bought licenses from Morse and entered the field to push lines between cities. Alternative technologies, such as the printing telegraph, were also promoted, but in all cases, both governments and major investors declined to back the electric telegraph in a serious way, forcing rival inventors to sell as many licenses as possible. By 1849, almost every state of the Union east of the Mississippi had telegraph service, though in an often fragmented form. While other innovative technological networks were initially controlled by the originating entrepreneur, who could rely on their patent rights to discourage encroachment, the telegraph system was quickly rationalized so as to epitomize the 19th-century industrial empire.

Around 1850, one of these competing companies, the New York and Mississippi Valley Printing Telegraph Company, launched a series of mergers or takeovers of its competitors. In 1866, it changed its name to that of the Western Union Telegraph Company. During the decade after the Civil War, Western Union acquired an almost complete monopoly on telegraph service in the United States. It was able to send messages to an office almost anywhere in the United States. In essence, Western Union benefited from the snowball effect that is more properly described as the accrual of increasing returns to adoption. As a true network, a telegraph network provided more value to its users the more extensive it was, by allowing to reach more people at lesser expense (due to economies of scale, in part).

During the second half of the nineteenth century, only one company challenged Western Union's monopoly. The Postal Telegraph Company specialized in providing pick-up and delivery services for telegrams, though it never managed to corner more than 25 percent of the telegraph business in the United States. In 1866, when Western Union was incorporated, it controlled almost 22,000 telegraph offices, depended on

1.3 million kilometres of wire strung from telegraph poles, often along railroad rights of way, and handled about 58 million messages annually. Internationally, by the first decade of the twentieth century, the United States ranked slightly ahead of European countries such as France and Germany for the total volume of the telegraphic messages, and just slightly behind Great Britain.

By 1920, the Western and Postal duopoly managed more than 1.6 million kilometres of wire and 155 million messages. Other companies used those lines on a contractual basis to deliver distinct services: railroads coordinating train movements, investment banking houses, wire news services (which included the original Wall Street stock ticker). Between 1860 and 1880, the telegraph became crucial to political and economic life in North America. The war between the United States and Mexico in 1847 was the first war to have rapid news coverage, and the Civil War generals increasingly depended on the quick flow of strategic information over telegraph lines. After the completion of an effective Atlantic cable in 1866, the speed and frequency of communication between nations accelerated, changing forever the character of diplomatic negotiations. The role of ambassador lost much of its original importance, when statesmen thousands of miles away became able to follow a situation in real time and intervene themselves.

Within North America, communication itself changed as organizations grew to depend on a technology that placed a premium on brevity. While it allowed for the creation of commercial enterprises with agents and dealings throughout the continent, the telegraph also fostered more impersonal relations between people who were likely strangers to each other. Thus, while patent and corporate law had to evolve in response to the new situations created by the telegraph system, people too were required to accept a less collegial management style and the reference to an authority (as in the case of the Duke of Kent in Halifax) that was physically remote.

Markets themselves were affected. While new transportation technologies meant that costs plummeted, the telegraph could provide nearly instantaneous intelligence on commodity prices across North America by the middle of the 19th century. As a result of both developments, prices were no longer mainly determined by the local conditions, but by national or even international ones. Supply and demand in Pittsburgh or Montreal no longer primarily drove the price of products. Markets increasingly shifted from trading goods between places with different prices to considering the uncertain future of prices.

Ruth Schwartz Cowan concludes: "In short, by 1880, if by some weird accident all the batteries that generated electricity for telegraph lines had suddenly run out, the economic and social life of the nation would have faltered. Trains would have stopped running; businesses with branch offices would have stopped functioning; newspapers could not have covered distant events; the president could not have communicated with his European ambassadors; the stock market would have had to close; family members separated by long distances could not have relayed important news—births, deaths, illnesses—to each other."[4]

The Railroad System

The railroad network got its start at a slightly earlier date than the telegraph system, but it did not extend its reach as fast. The capital cost of laying tracks was much higher. On the other hand, the advantages of railways over canals were obvious—they were fast, they did not depend on proximity to waterways, and they did not stop operating when rivers flooded or canals froze in winter.

The first railway boom exploded during the 1840s. Railroad-building schemes were being concocted and discussed in parlors and banks, state houses, and farm houses all over North America. By 1860, the United States had almost 50,000 kilometres of track.

However, though railway lines were numerous, they were often poorly integrated, especially before the Civil War. Many lines were designed for short-haul cartage, connecting major cities with their agricultural hinterland. Each route was owned by a different company, each company had its own rolling stock, and each used a track gauge (width) that seemed best for its locomotives and cars. So, in 1849, it took nine transshipments between nine unconnected railroads (and nine weeks of travel) to get freight from Philadelphia to Chicago. In 1861, the trip between Charleston and Philadelphia required eight car changes because of different gauges.

This was great for local teamsters, porters, and innkeepers, but less than convenient for travellers and those in the freight business. Integration got underway after the Civil War. The railway system continued to expand and the United States completed a transcontinental connection (with the Union Pacific Railroad in 1869). By 1880, there were 150,000 kilometres of track in the United States.

By 1920, when the US railroad system peaked with just over 400,000 kilometres of track, a true network had come into being, based on a hub-and-spoke system combining the longer trunk lines (running from coast to coast, east-west) with the shorter feeder lines (limbs) that connected localities with the trunks.

---

[4]Ruth Schwartz Cowan, *A Social History of American Technology* (Oxford University Press, 1997), p. 153.

Integration was the result of consolidation. In 1870, there had been several hundred railroads, many of which were in direct competition. By 1900, virtually all of the trackage in the United States was either owned, controlled, or managed by just seven (often mutually cooperative) railway consortiums. These grand alliances had been constructed by businessmen such as J. P. Morgan and Cornelius Vanderbilt, who were not builders but investors.

As ownership became concentrated, ground-breaking decisions became easier. By 1890, a standard gauge had been adopted and almost all railroads had converted to a width of 4 feet, 8 1/2 inches. Along with the creation of central stations, this eliminated the need for passengers and freight to make repeated transfers, thus increasing the effective speed of travel, even without technical improvements in the performance of locomotives. So, while population tripled in the United States, freight tonnage on the railroads went up eleven fold.

The Petroleum System

Though petroleum had been known for thousands of years, the petroleum age started around 1859 in North America. Ten years earlier, Canadian inventor Abraham Gesner (1797–1864) had distilled kerosene from oil as an *illuminant* capable of replacing whale oil lamps and candles. In 1854, having moved to the United States, he was awarded three patents by the United States Patent Office for three different kerosene mixes, each being "a new manufacture or composition of matter for illuminating and other purposes." He specifically noted that he obtained each from "petroleum, maltha, or soft mineral pitch, asphaltum, or bitumen." (Four years earlier, British inventor James Young had obtained a patent for a similar process.) And in 1857, New York businessman Michael Alexander Dietz (1830–1883) perfected a kerosene lamp with a flat wick superior to other lamps using whale oil—such as the ones the Dietz company run by his brothers were making at the time!

The oil obtained as a by-product from brine wells and tar pits suddenly acquired much greater value.

In Enniskillen Township, Ontario, the brothers Charles and Henry Tripp had learned of tar-like gum deposits from the Geological Survey of Canada. They acquired the rights and were distilling the gums and resins by 1853. By 1854, they had formed a company, the International Mining and Manufacturing Company. Though their products were innovative and rewarded at the Paris World Fair in 1855, the Tripp brothers did not make money. There were no railways or even decent roads out of the Enniskillen swamp, so that cartage was inordinately expensive.

The Tripps sold out to James Miller Williams, a coachmaker from Hamilton. In 1858, Williams dug into the gum beds to find their source. At a depth of 4 metres, he struck oil. This was the first oil well in North America. (The drilling of oil wells goes back centuries in China and Iran.)

The timing was perfect for Williams. The Great Western Railway had just completed a line from London to Sarnia, passing through the village of Wyoming nearby. The oil could now get to market and a boom town called Oil Springs quickly grew up around the site. By 1861, 400 wells were producing anywhere between 50 and 800 barrels a day, at a time when barrels were selling for $10 apiece, a sum that amounted approximately to a week's wages at the time. After 1867, though, the Ontario oil industry moved a few kilometres north to Petrolia as the wells near Oil Springs began to dry up.

In 1859, however, Titus Drake struck oil in Pennsylvania and started an even larger oil rush in the United States. Oil was sold to machine shops and factories as a lubricant, and to households and businesses as a source of lighting fuel. The Civil War accelerated the pace of drilling (the whaling industry was hampered by naval operations). By 1862, some three million barrels of crude oil were being processed.

Growth persisted after the war. In 1872, the number of processed barrels had trebled.

Transportation initially depended on the moving of barrels by horse cart or river barges to the nearest railroad-loading points. The barrels were then loaded into freight cars for the trip to cities where the crude was being refined and sold. It was a cumbersome process—the barrels might leak, the barges capsize, and the wagons sink into the mud.

Pipelines were quickly tested as a solution and the first one to operate was built in 1865 over a ten kilometre span. Pipelines were extended throughout the 1870s and 1880s, but they remained mostly short-haul lines, connecting oil fields to the railroads. Tanker cars were developed after 1870.

Thus, the pipeline network was integrated with the railway network, and also with the telegraph network. Oil companies used the telegraph system to monitor the price for oil in various markets and also to keep track of the flow through their pipelines.

The logic of networks also led to a quasi-monopoly situation in the petroleum system. John D. Rockefeller realized that the petroleum industry depended on the petroleum transportation system. Starting with part-ownership of an oil refinery in Cleveland, he negotiated a rebate with one of the two railroads then serving Cleveland. Using the rebate, he was able to coerce other Cleveland refiners into selling out and soon controlled the city's oil refining capacity. As he acquired oil refineries in other cities, he became able to negotiate exclusive deals with the railroads that barred them from carrying oil to refineries he did not control.

When drilling companies tried to build pipelines to railways Rockefeller did not control, he responded by gaining a monopoly on the indispensable tank cars. By 1879, he had been so successful that the stockholders of pipeline companies were forced to sell out to him. In that year, Rockefeller and his associates controlled 90 percent of the refined oil in the United States. By 1900, the Standard Oil Company he owned was building long-distance pipelines for the transportation of crude oil and only relied on railways for the transportation of refined oil.

Nevertheless, the petroleum system expanded beyond Rockefeller's control with new discoveries in Texas, Oklahoma, Louisiana, and California, while the development of the internal combustion engine created a new and growing market.

By the end of the nineteenth century, the petroleum system was pervasive. A large number of North Americans, especially those living outside cities, used one of its products, kerosene, for heating, lighting, and cooking. And industry became dependent on other petroleum products to lubricate machinery.

ELECTRICITY UNBOUND

Whereas other technologies had been bound and contained within fairly coherent systems, electricity proved to be different. Until Edison tackled the problem of electrical lighting, the demands of technologies such as those of the telegraph or the telephone required comparatively little electrical power. In many cases, batteries could provide the power required.

Lighting was a different matter. Generators were needed, of a size that placed major demands on the ultimate motive force (steam engines, waterpower). However, once such generators were built and shown to be effective, the floodgates were opened to a surge of new uses for electricity.

Electricity made transporting power easy. Previously, power derived from water (via wheels or turbines) and steam could only be transferred over short distances. Mills and factories were sited near sources of waterpower (hence the importance of Ottawa's Chaudière falls, which originally powered a grist mill, a sawmill, and a hemp mill). Even steam engines needed a regular supply of water to replenish their boilers. Furthermore, steam engines or waterwheels were connected to belts, shafts, and pulleys crisscrossing factories, making for a crowded and noisy work environment. With electricity, motive power was delocalized. It was no longer necessary to cluster a factory's machine around the power source (water turbine, steam engine) or even to build a factory in the vicinity of a water source.

However, electricity's first major role in everyday life was to produce light. Edison fought an epic battle to turn this into a profitable proposition. His first plants lost money, but the returns on later plants made the effort a money-maker and repaid the sums spent to acquire rights to key patents (including those of Canadian inventors Henry Woodward and Matthew Evans). Returns increased with adoption as more people bought in, as the initial research costs were amortized, and as Edison's engineers grew more proficient at building plants and generating electricity efficiently.

Though the direct current (DC) generators developed by Edison had a short range, the alternating current (AC) generators adopted by rail magnate George Westinghouse were able to produce power that could be transported over dozens, even hundreds of miles. The AC motor designed by Nikola Tesla (1856–1943) and the multiphase AC system originating in ideas also patented by Tesla would eventually form the basis for today's North American power distribution system.

Edison fought hard to convince the public AC was unsafe. In 1888, he was offering 25 cents to local children in New Jersey to bring in dogs. The dogs were then wired and zapped, first with DC, and then with AC. Since it took 1000 volts of DC to electrocute the typical mutt, but only 300 volts of AC, Edison argued vigorously that AC was dangerous. Edison's passion for demonstrating the dangers of AC led him to electrocute larger animals, which led to the invention by others of the electric chair for human executions, even though Edison was not in favour of capital punishment.

However, the Westinghouse designs prevailed. They could serve towns and villages and isolated houses that could not benefit from the short-range Edison power plants. And since one Westinghouse plant could do the job of a dozen Edison plants, they were far more economical, using less copper and other materials. Among the first long-distance lines were those built in California and those linking the Niagara Falls power plants to the Hydro Ontario network.

It was the age of wires—telegraph and telephone lines hung between poles and buildings, filling the sky over city streets. Edison decided to bury his power lines, but other utilities soon added power lines to the maze of wires running above the streets.

Electric light, just like electricity in general, was enormously popular. In France, people struck by the wonders of electricity spoke of it in magical terms (it was the "Fée Electricité"). Later, Edison's electric light turned into an entry point for other household instruments powered by electricity. Bulb sockets were used at first to power other early electrical devices: fans, teakettles, sewing machines, toasters, irons, and vacuum cleaners. By the turn of the century, the electrical vibrator for women (originally invented by Joseph Mortimer Granville before 1883 as a general purpose medical massage device but turned into an aid for the medical relief of female "hysteria") was another common device sold to home users through advertisements in such publications as needlework catalogues. The modern plugs and wall outlets evolved around the turn of the century before becoming fixtures in every modern home.

FURTHER READINGS

Thomas P. Hughes, *Networks of Power: Electrification in Western Society, 1880–1930* Baltimore: Johns Hopkins Press, 1993.

CHAPTER 7

The One Best Way to Mass Production

▶▶▶▶▶▶▶▶▶▶▶▶▶▶▶▶▶▶▶▶▶▶▶▶▶▶▶▶

NEW MARKETS

In the second half of the nineteenth century, new technologies led to a delocalization of consumption. Improved food preservation methods and the mastery of the cold chain allowed for the export of beef and cereals from North and South America. With the help of new machines, farming was mechanized, increasing surpluses for export. In some cases, especially that of wheat, every step (plowing, planting, cultivating, harvesting, threshing, winnowing, and hauling) had been mechanized to some degree by 1880.

By then, the application of horse power (either pulling machines such as reapers or working on treadmills to operate them) was already giving way to the application of steam though steam engines tended to be too heavy and unwieldy for many uses. In an age of dirt roads and wooden bridges, their usefulness was limited in many locales. Within half a century, tractors powered by internal combustion engines would take over in turn. In some cases, manufacturers jumped straight from the horse era to the gasoline era. In 1891, two Canadian farm equipment companies founded respectively by Daniel Massey in 1847 and by Alanson Harris in 1857, merged to create the Massey-Harris company. Until the First World War, the new firm mainly marketed horse-drawn reapers and mowers, but in 1910 it acquired the

Devo-Macey company and added gasoline engines to its range of products. These engines were sold as stationary sources of power to be hooked up to various items of farm machinery such as threshing machines. It was only after the start of the war, as the demand for wheat escalated, that the company began selling tractors powered by an internal combustion engine though it faced a serious competitor in the mass-produced Fordson models of the Ford Company.

In the United States as well, the total number of trucks and tractors on farms only began to surge towards the end of the First World War. In fact, the number of horses on US farms peaked during the First World War. Indeed, it wasn't until the early 1950s that trucks and tractors became more numerous than horses. The rise in the number of tractors continued unabated into the 1970s, after which it fell back as family farms lost ground and higher oil prices discouraged the accumulation of unnecessary units. Between 1980 and 2001, the total remained below 50 million, significantly less than the peak of about 55 million of the late 1960s. In Canada, between 1961 and 2001, the number of tractors remained between five and ten million, significantly more than might be expected based on a comparison of each country's population.

Not all agricultural activities were successfully mechanized, though. As late as the 1960s, some crops—such as cotton and tobacco—continued to require essentially manual labour. And tobacco was an extremely labour-intensive crop, requiring about 370 hours of labour per acre in the nineteenth century. Even there, though, tobacco products like cigarettes benefited from mechanized production methods and their sales price came down somewhat.

Nevertheless, the overall reduction of human labour was significant. In the case of wheat, the reduction may have been as high as from 61 to 3 hours per bushel. As agricultural yields came close to doubling on US farms in the last third of the nineteenth century, production rose and this rise was made only greater by the opening of the frontier's last available lands. Between 1866 and 1898, wheat acreage approximately trebled and yields nearly doubled, making for a production of 675 million bushels compared to 152 million bushels earlier. Yet, the relative value of agricultural products did not grow at all, because the value of industrial products climbed even faster. In fact, relative agricultural output regressed. In 1869, 53% of US production was agricultural and 33% industrial. In 1899, half of the United States output came from manufacturing and only a third came from farming.

This double increase in total acreage and yields per acre multiplied the harvests many times, which had some important consequences.

First, the increased production allowed a smaller number of farmers than ever before to support an ever expanding city population. The change to a predominantly urban country happened within 50 years in the United States. In 1870, 54 percent of

US inhabitants were farmers or farms labourers. By 1910, it was down to one in three. In 1870, only a quarter of the US population lived in cities, but that proportion reached 46 percent by 1910. Urbanization passed the 50 percent level between 1910 and 1920.

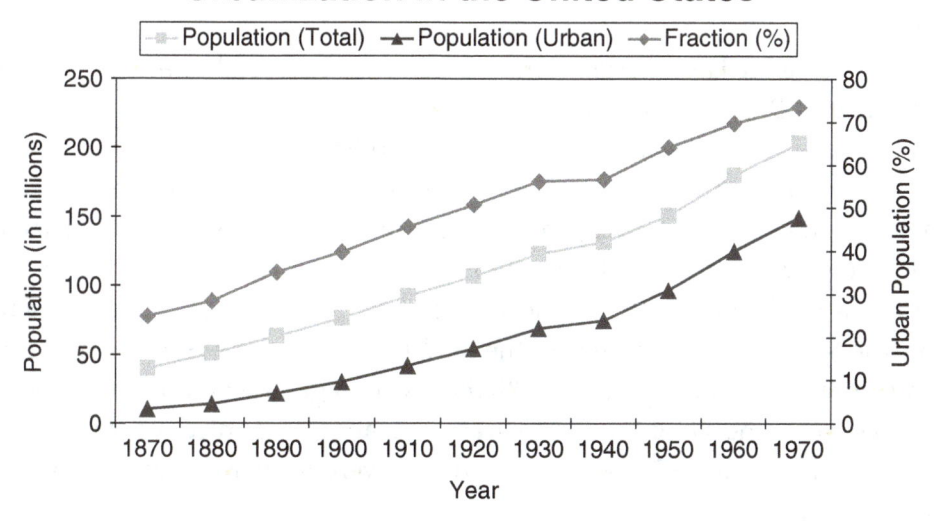

FIGURE 1 ▶ Between 1870 and 1970, most of the growth of the US population happened in cities, leading to an increasingly urban country.

In Canada, the same threshold was reached slightly later.

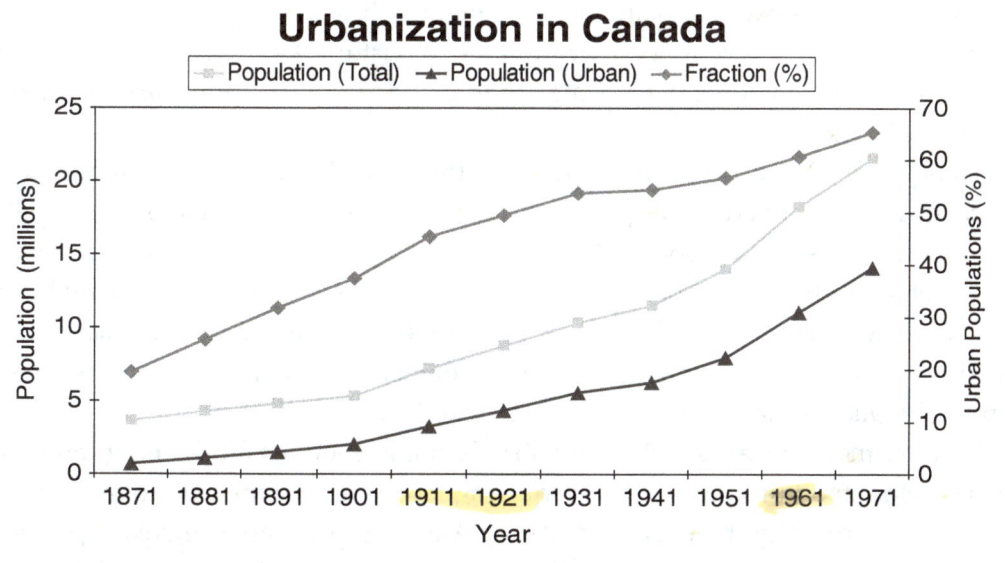

FIGURE 2 ▶ Between 1871 and 1971, much of the growth in the Canadian population happened in towns and cities, leading to a largely urban country.

In 1871, only 20 percent of the Canadian population was urban, but that proportion reached 45 percent by 1911. However, it should be noted that the definition of an urban area differed in each country. In the United States, a settled area had to number more than 2,500 people to be considered urban by the census authorities. In Canada, an urban area was defined as a settled area with more than 1,000 people.

Indeed, while the US frontier is considered to have closed by 1890, the settlement of the Canadian Prairies was still at full flood by the turn of the twentieth century, though this did not impede the growth of cities in Eastern Canada.

The expanding number of people living off the farm both increased the number of consumers for manufactured products and the available workforce for factories. Second, farms grew larger—a farmer working by hand could harvest 7.5 acres per worker in the field, but 135 acres if the same farmer relied on machinery. As a result, some farmers were either pushed off the land (leaving for the cities) or became tenants. In Kansas, between 1880 and 1900, the percentage of tenant farmers rose from 16.3% to 35.2%. At the same time, the rural population accounted for less and less of the total population. In 1870, 54% of US citizens were farmers or farm labourers. By 1910, it was only one in three.

Furthermore, increased production also led, necessarily, to lower prices. All other things being equal, lower prices make for a better standard of living. As city-dwelling consumers profited the most from cheaper produce, dressed meats, and factory-made goods, they found life in the cities pleasant enough and their children—healthier and living longer—swelled the urban population. These lower prices were also part of the equation that made it necessary to seek export markets. At the same time, by becoming dependent on international markets, farmers became part of an ever broader network.

Thus, by 1880, the urban population in the United States was growing accustomed to eating canned meat, peas, and corn, and to using condensed milk. The Heinz Company supplied bottled ketchup and pickles. Campbell's would soon start to market soup. Beer had once been made at home, especially on the farm; but by 1873, there were some 4,000 industrial breweries. Even factory-made crackers and cookies were becoming familiar. In Canada, one early patent for Viau cookies, still popular in Quebec, dates from the late nineteenth century.

In short, mechanization using industrially-made goods made farming more productive. More food production (and requiring fewer people) made it possible for the population, especially in cities, to increase. And this population increase provided manufacturers with a larger market, thus encouraging manufacturing activity.

The growth of cities required new infrastructure as the habits inherited from the small towns of the colonial era proved inadequate as populations exploded. During the second half of the nineteenth century, many large North American cities banned their citizens from keeping or raising animals (hens, rabbits, pigs, and cows) for food. This was one less presence in the streets and one less source of animal droppings in the streets, lanes, and yards of cities. Public lighting—first gas, then electric—became common. Sewers were built to keep cities clean and reduce the spread of disease. Before the germ theory of disease, it was thought that the bad smells emanating from privies and cesspools might actually spread sickness. Aqueducts were built to provide clean drinking water, but also a supply of water with which to fight fires. Finally, the expansion of public transit provided by streetcars, originally horse-drawn, later electric, made it possible for the mobility of city residents to keep pace with the growing size of cities.

As modern cities became dependent on technological systems to provide their citizens with transit, water, electricity, and gas, the figure of the city engineer appeared, working either for city hall or a company dealing with the city government.

MASS CONSUMPTION AND ENMESHMENT

By the end of the nineteenth century, as a result of the increase in consumer numbers and farming for export, consumers a continent away increasingly dictated the choices of farmers and workers. Indeed, the twentieth century was to be distinguished by this *enmeshment*.

Remember that the pre-modern situation was one where survival was local. A village, a farm, or a homestead had to be, in the short term, almost completely self-sufficient. In the 17th and 18th centuries, most day-to-day needs were met with local products. Settlers might depend on outside sources for some of their technology (especially metal implements), but transportation and communications were too difficult and unreliable to be counted on to provide a daily supply of material objects, let alone food and drink. Therefore, the early settlers had to be able to get most of what they needed from their gardens, fields, and domesticated animals; from their immediate relatives, friends, and neighbours; and from the surrounding woods and wetlands within a two- or three-hour walk. They depended on themselves first, and then on a limited number of people.

The modern situation is increasingly different. Turning on the lights, turning the tap, driving a car, taking the bus, buying food at the supermarket—at each step along the way, we depend on the work of others. Our confidence in them is key and it is the hallmark of the rich, democratic countries. After all, the crucial feature of democracy is a willingness to trust others, even if their views are different, to the point of entrusting them with power and the rule of the country. The French Republic's motto was *"Liberté, Égalité, Fraternité,"* which translates as "Liberty, Equality, Fraternity (or Brotherhood)." Usually, democracy emphasizes the first two. But the third term is arguably the one most closely linked to the working of modern technological systems.

The call to brotherhood calls us to trust each other like brothers and sisters. Back in the 18th century, Adam Smith argued that everybody's self-interest combines to yield a harmonious society, as if guided by an "invisible hand." But we still need to trust that others understand what is in their own self-interest.

Technological systems require a similar sort of trust, implicit and mutual, especially since they extend the need for trust far beyond the people we meet every day. An advanced technological society is a society where, at one level, many will have to consider their fellow citizens like family in order to have confidence that water will run in the aqueducts and be drinkable when it comes out the tap, electricity will be carried by power wires without undue interruptions (or illegal tapping), and roads will not be cut by potholes or fallen trees. Trust can be abused of course. Systems cannot work without trust, but single actors or agents within the system may take advantage of that automatic, default trust. Sophisticated systems develop safeguards to strike a compromise between absolute trust and complete distrust.

If modern-day citizens find themselves enmeshed in these networks of interdependency and far-reaching trust mitigated by assorted precautions, it is the result of decades of work that went into building the necessary technological systems.

A world characterized by this form of enmeshment, where each and everyone depends on many people near and far for their goods and services, might appear to be more fragile. At first glance, it seems that being cut off from crucial supplies would be easier and more serious. The consequences of a failure on the other side of the world would be dramatic. But interdependency in a fully enmeshed world also means that help or replacement goods can come from many other places which have a vested interest in everyone's survival. The logical consequence is that a globally enmeshed world civilization, if it is truly more resilient, can only be threatened by a global problem or collapse.

The early technical systems of the nineteenth century affected many lives, but only transformed a few. Canals were few and far between, only requiring a small workforce. The telegraph only operated out of offices at prices that made communication by telegraph a luxury only used by the poor in cases of dire necessity (announcements of births, deaths, marriages, accidents, etc.). On the other hand, the telegraph made it possible for everybody to read about news of events in distant cities and other countries. The telephone was both rarer and more public. By 1893, there was one telephone for every 250 citizens of the United States, but aside from the telephones owned by the rich, they were often found in pharmacies, liquor stores, and stables that catered to all walks of life. The railroads probably played a greater part in people's lives, though a train ride was still a once in a lifetime occasion for many people at the end of the nineteenth century.

Nevertheless, daily life was being transformed at the turn of the nineteenth century. Petroleum products (and hydrocarbons of various other origins) were being consumed in many homes, especially as kerosene for lighting, heating, and cooking. Though electricity was gaining a foothold, gas ranges and gas lighting were still popular. Though Edison's phonograph had been tagged, like the early telephone, as an invention for businessmen, sound recordings of music provided increasing competition for the dictation machines sold to the high end of the market. Bicycles appeared in the streets, forcing fashions to change and helping cities breathe a bit. The development of photography, especially by Eastman (Kodak) in the United States, turned the picture camera into an increasingly available gadget. In short, the potential for mass consumption was becoming clearer.

Whereas urban clerks of 1820 walked to the office of a family business lit after dark by candles or oil lamps, adding figures in a ledger by hand or writing letters with a quill pen, employees of 1900 took a streetcar to work, might use an elevator to get to a gas lit office (some might even enjoy electrical lighting) belonging to a large industrial concern or railroad company, with men working side by side with women, using fountain pens and typewriters, telephoning customers, dealing with telegrams, and adding figures with a hand-cranked calculating machine.

MASS PRODUCTION: FROM PROTESTANT THRIFT TO FIGHTING WASTE

And yet the methods of production were found to lag. They were, to use the terminology of Thomas P. Hughes, a *reverse salient* (a problem to be solved for progress to continue to advance on a broad front; note that a bottleneck can be a reverse salient, but that a reverse salient is not always a bottleneck). Invention was not the problem—it had become more and more systematic, from Edison's Menlo Park to the permanent research labs set up by Eastman and professional inventor Elmer Sperry. The patent offices published gazettes and new intermediaries known as patent attorneys or lawyers had sprung up to take care of the paperwork. Consumption was not a problem either. That left production.

In the age of electricity, industrial plants could be laid out without having to depend on belts, shafts, and pulleys to transfer motion from turbines or steam engines. Electrical motors could be positioned where they would do the most good. Mills and factories had originally been found near sources of waterpower (hence the importance of Ottawa's Chaudière falls), but the new sprawling factories demanded increased attention in order to become efficient. A generation of experts took on the job of improving the performance not only of manufacturing machinery but of the workers themselves.

And the solution found to production's inefficiencies led to an ever greater enmeshment of technological systems and of the people within technological systems. The Protestant ethic, which was starting to be noticed by sociologists like Weber in Germany, had always emphasized the virtues of thrift. So, it is not surprising that an enemy of waste such as Frederick Winslow Taylor (1856–1915) found an enormous audience for his message that anything less than the fullest possible output was injurious to employers and workers alike. Waste meant that products were scarcer and more expensive than strictly necessary; it also meant that workers did not earn as much as they could.

However, it was his claim to be scientific both in his approach and in his methods that helped him to sell his philosophy abroad. Protestant thrift was just penny-pinching. Efficiency was something greater that reduced effort and useless fatigue while increasing production. It was not necessarily miserly—while some workers might be laid off, the remaining workers would be paid more. Who could say no to better pay and more production, achieved not by "slave-driving" but by strictly objective methods?

BEFORE SCIENTIFIC MANAGEMENT

The attention to detail brought to inventing and organizing networks such as those of the railroads, the telegraph, the telephone, or electric lighting was brought to bear on manufacturing by the believers in scientific management, including Taylor and the Gilbreths.

The results were not an unmixed blessing. Workers had long been used to enjoying some control over the pace of their work. Whether as farmers or independent artisans, they had been the ones deciding how hard they worked and how long they worked within the constraints of the weather and of orders to be filled.

When they started finding work in factories during the Industrial Revolution, before and after 1800, workers first needed to learn punctuality. Clocks were still relatively uncommon and watches wholly unknown outside the wealthy elite. People working in the fields had no clocks, and craftsmen worked to deadline. Getting workers to show up every day, by a particular time, was the first challenge.

The second challenge was determining who controlled the actual work—the employer or the worker? The struggle over control took the form of arguments over what was "pacing," or "soldiering." (It was called "soldiering" because peacetime soldiers whose everyday lives centered on the barracks or the garrison were thought to produce relatively little of any value. A veteran soldier volunteers for nothing.)

Let us take the example of industrial workers in the iron, machine, shoe, and textile trades. Around 1830, they were paid piece-rates rather than day wages. (They were paid by the number of units—metal implements, ingots, machines, shoes, articles of clothing—they produced, and not by the hour.) Now, when the employer introduced new technology or production techniques, he was soon inclined to reduce piece-rates since the worker was supposed to be producing more with the same investment of time and effort. Even if all the workers were pushed to work faster, the evidence was clear that the new standard, the "new normal," would soon be taken for granted and the rates reduced. Naturally, workers were disinclined to produce at anything like their maximum rate of work or speed, fearing in essence, that they would never enjoy very long the fruits of efficiency increases.

Merritt Roe Smith describes several forms of pacing: "Working to collectively defined 'stints,' taking unauthorized breaks to have a smoke, go to the john, share a cup of whiskey, or purchase cakes being hawked outside the mill gate by a local baker, looking for missing tools, sharpening and repairing other tools, and reading newspapers while at work are common examples of pacing."

WAS SCIENTIFIC MANAGEMENT "SCIENTIFIC"?

The joke goes that any field or discipline that has *science* or *scientific* in its name is probably not a science (political science, for instance). Yet, it should be understood that *scientific* did not quite have the same meaning in the United States of that era as it does today.

Looking back, when Rufus Porter created the magazine he called *Scientific American* in 1845, he presented it as "The Advocate of Industry and Enterprise, and Journal of Mechanical and Other Inputs," and his sales pitch specified that:

> *"Each number will be furnished with from two to five original Engravings, many of them elegant, and illustrative of* New Inventions, Scientific Principles, *and* Curious Works; *and will contain, in addition to the most interesting news of passing events, general notices of the progress of Mechanical and other Scientific Improvements; American and Foreign Improvements and Inventions; Catalogues of American Patents; Scientific Essays, illustrative of the principles of the sciences of Mechanics, Chemistry and Architecture; useful information and instruction in various Arts and Trades; Curious Philosophical Experiments; Miscellaneous Intelligence, Music and Poetry."*

Thus, *scientific management* only claimed at first to be objective and systematic, relying on the spirit of scientific inquiry rather than on specific laws of nature. Taylor articulated the analogy by asserting that his system rested upon clearly defined laws, applied universally (to all forms of work), and produced inescapable results.

FREDERICK WINSLOW TAYLOR

Frederick Taylor was the central figure in making efficiency, waste, and scientific management part of public debate. After working as a machinist and a foreman, Taylor had developed a career as an efficiency expert. He realized that a few seconds or minutes gained here and there, when it came to operations repeated thousands of times, could transform into major savings. To eliminate wasted time, Taylor proposed rearranging the equipment a worker needed and setting piece rate wages based on optimum production to give the worker a fair rate of pay as well as an incentive not to "soldier." (The faster workers received a better piece-rate than the slower ones.) Taylorism was soon associated with the idea of the "one best way" to do a job, which involved eliminating waste motions while keeping only the most efficient of the existing motions used by actual workers.

However, his use of the stopwatch and insistence on surveillance (by specialized bosses who replaced general foremen), his preference for breaking down skilled trades into smaller and easier jobs, and his small number of more concrete measures (to reduce unnecessary walking, bending over, etc.) had a limited appeal. Part of the gains in productivity came from merely driving the workers to maintain their highest possible output, by taking time management out of their hands. If some of these gains were not sufficiently returned to the workers, there were definite limits to the improvements that could be achieved, due to the resistance of the workers (and their unions) and to the intrinsic limitations of the production methods, which were not being changed.

Taylorism could be extraordinarily intrusive. Taylor called for a study of the character, the nature, and the performance of every workman. Workers who had once enjoyed a great deal of independence within factories, especially the skilled tradesmen who brought in their own tools, felt clearly threatened. And though Taylor underlined that he didn't want to imperil the health of workers, he obviously had an ideal worker in mind, an "ox" who would be able to put in large amounts of physical work while leaving the planning to the managers. While Taylor was aware of job injuries, he seemed to take little account of the effects of fatigue, repetitive strain injuries, and workplace conditions. He was asking workers to give up the certainties of a job they knew they could do at a reasonable pace for uncertain returns, since there was no guarantee their exhaustion would be compensated by a fair share of the profits. By creating modular jobs, that left little room for the worker's initiative, he was also depriving them of control over their own working conditions.

Frank Gilbreth (1868–1924) and Lillian Gilbreth (1878–1972) are remembered today for being the famous husband-and-wife team that pioneered motion study as an alternative to the time study advocated by Frederick Taylor. Though Frank Gilbreth also used a stopwatch and was part of the early development of scientific management, he was later disowned as a disciple by the heirs of Taylor because of his reliance on cinematographic motion study techniques.

The Gilbreths were known for their use of micro-motion study analyzing the minutest gestures and breaking down a process into therbligs before moving on to any sort of method study. When it came to improving efficiency, they did not hesitate to change the way a job was done to whatever would be fastest and most efficient.

Just like Taylor had worked as a machinist, Frank Gilbreth had worked as a bricklayer and later as a construction entrepreneur, while Lillian Gilbreth was an industrial psychologist by training. Together, they were the champions of job simplification through the economizing of effort and the minimizing of stress, the setting of meaningful work standards and the creation of incentive wage plans.

The result was to be greater output for the employers, but not at the expense of the satisfaction of the employees, since fatigue was to be reduced and earnings increased. Their use of motion pictures to turn ordinary workers into stars of the workplace appears to have made for better relations with the workers whose jobs they were analyzing. They also advocated measures such as lecture series and suggestion boxes to improve the workplace atmosphere.

By 1912, the Gilbreths were pioneering micromotion study by filming a worker's operations against a cross-sectioned background while a chronometer recorded the time. By examining the film through a magnifying glass, frame by frame, Gilbreth could time each of the worker's motions to a few milliseconds. As a side benefit, the grid pattern on a white background created the semblance of a laboratory in which the work was to be studied "scientifically:" without saying a word, this bolstered the argument that such work was truly "scientific."

In 1913–1914, Frank Gilbreth perfected the cyclegraph: a miniature electric light mounted on a ring could be attached to the fingers of a worker so that the worker's motions showed as bright lines on a single time-exposed photograph. The Gilbreths went on to develop the chronocyclegraph, which interrupted the flow of current to the light in order to obtain, in the resulting sequence of flashes, a record of the time and direction of the motions. A stereochronocyclegraph created a three-dimensional image of motion by using two slightly offset cameras.

By 1915, Frank Gilbreth had formulated a basic alphabet of work motions (*therbligs*) reducible to sixteen categories: search, find, select, grasp, position, transport load, assemble, use, disassemble, inspect, preposition (for next operation), release load, transport empty, wait (unavoidable delay), wait (avoidable delay), and rest (for overcoming fatigue).

Their idea of the better way to do a job, by reducing strain and stress, even attracted attention in the Soviet Union after the communist takeover. Yet, the increases in efficiency produced in this way were not costless—they required new spending on a new profession, that of the efficiency expert. Though the efficiency improvements paid for increased spending on capital equipment, new supervisors, and new management methods, they obviously added a new layer in technological arrangements.

And the resulting productivity increases drove up economic output without increasing overall employment. As this coincided with a lull in the sort of new product development that might spawn new industries and with an unequal sharing of profits to the detriment of most workers, this was a factor in the major economic downturn known as the Great Depression.

After Frank Gilbreth's early death, Lillian kept working in the same field until the 1950s and was the first woman elected to the US National Academy of Engineering. Two of their children authored books, including *Cheaper by the Dozen* (Thomas Y. Crowell, 1948), about their childhood under the watchful eye of Frank Gilbreth, who was known to film his children as they did the dishes in order to find ways for them to do their chores more quickly.

It should be noted that Lillian Gilbreth's professional career was not that singular. Many women went to university in that era and earned degrees. In fact, in fields such as the pure sciences, the proportion of women graduates reached impressive levels by the time of the Depression, levels that were not seen again for 50 years.

Anti-nepotism laws of the time played a role in the eclipse of women at the professorial level in universities. Out of a fear that relatives (including spouses) of professors might enjoy an undue advantage when it came to hiring, many colleges and universities put in place rules and guidelines to forbid such relatives from applying. Female university graduates who had married other graduates found themselves barred from university positions unless their husbands found a position elsewhere or accepted life at home and a career unfulfilled.

If Taylor had his heyday at the time of the great railway debates around 1911, he was soon to be displaced by a new industrial hero: Ford.

CHAPTER 8

In the Year of Our Ford: The Automobile Era

▶▶▶▶▶▶▶▶▶▶▶▶▶▶▶▶▶▶▶▶▶▶▶▶▶▶▶▶▶▶

THE AUTOMOBILE BEFORE THE AUTOMOBILE

Inventing the automobile was comparatively easy. More than one solution was found in the course of the nineteenth century to the problem of powering a vehicle over roads. As was mentioned, the first steam vehicle was built by Cugnot in France in the 18th century. Many more steam-powered coaches, trucks, and carriages were built during the nineteenth century. Electric cars were also developed by the end of the century, as well as cars driven by internal combustion motors. For a time, all of them competed for dominance.

In the United States, Oliver Evans designed and built an amphibious steam-driven vehicle as early as 1805. In Canada, the first known automobile was built by Henry Seth Taylor, from Stanstead, Quebec, in 1867. A steam-powered carriage, it was shown off in country fairs, more as a curiosity than an actual prototype. As steam engines became smaller and more efficient, they were increasingly used to drive road vehicles. Many isolated attempts are known. In 1899, for instance, Vancouver mechanics converted a horse-drawn carriage into a vehicle propelled by a steam engine burning gasoline.

Before World War I, the Stanley Steamer produced in Massachusetts was a steam car still competitive with cars powered by internal combustion engines or electric batteries. According to one argument, its fate illustrates the role of contingency in the evolution of technology. Its steam engine's need for water meant it had to use the horse and cattle troughs found along streets and roads. When a hoof and mouth disease outbreak led to the banning of such troughs (thought to spread the disease), the Stanley Steamer company was forced to redesign its engine so as to recycle the initial water supply.

By the time a closed cycle had been designed, gas-powered cars had taken an unreachable lead and many of the steam car manufacturers remained small concerns that were crushed by the methods of mass production. The typical steam car was more complicated to get started though easier to operate once in motion (no transmission shifts). After World War I, conventional gas-powered cars in the same price range were not only easier to start, but routinely achieved higher speeds (80 km/h versus 60 km/h) as well.

During the 1920s, the last companies making steam cars either converted to internal combustion (White) or went under (Doble, Stanley). Some late entrants (such as Brooks Steam Motors Ltd, established in Stratford, Ontario, 1924–1929) appear to have been highly speculative ventures, if not outright frauds.

Electric cars were never really in the running, in spite of the best efforts of the Edison companies which pushed electric vehicles for many years, showcasing a fleet of electric trucks for urban deliveries. Belief in the potential of electricity propelled more than one early inventor. In Canada, electrician William Still built the first known electric car in 1893 in Toronto, in part to demonstrate the capacity of the new type of battery he had invented. His car ran well enough to encourage investors in Canada and the United Kingdom to back a small manufacturing firm that ended up closing in 1902. Even though the performance standards expected of cars were still low, electric batteries of the time could move a car, but not any significant payload or over a long distance before exhausting their charge. As long as electric cars were compared to horse-drawn vehicles, they remained competitive, but other motor vehicles increasingly outclassed them.

By the end of the nineteenth century, internal combustion engines had gone through nearly 40 years of development since the first gas-burning prototype built by Belgian Étienne Lenoir and the theory of the four-stroke engine outlined by French inventor Beau de Rochas in 1862. Engines using the explosions of a gaseous mixture to actuate a piston, obviously inspired by 17th-century experiments, were built even earlier by such inventors as the Niepce brothers in France around 1806 and Alfred Drake in the United States around 1855. The first workable internal combustion engine was put together by German engineer Nicholas Otto in 1876; its power and light weight made it ideal for vehicles. Less than ten years later, it was propelling cars. The Diesel engine was invented a few years later, achieving high thermodynamic efficiency.

Within ten years, European companies were producing cars on a commercial basis and several countries such as France developed the beginnings of small automaking industries. Whereas North America had pioneered the use of the steamboat and steamship, it was clearly a follower in the case of cars, as it had been with steam trains.

In the United States, the first horseless carriage is usually attributed to the brothers Charles E. and J. Frank Duryea, bicycle mechanics who in 1893 copied a design by German car builder Karl Benz. Their background highlights the importance of the bicycle industry at the time. Another pair of brothers involved with bicycles was the Wrights, who built the first real airplane by combining glider technology with the internal combustion engine in 1903. And bicycle manufacturing led to the installation of the interchangeable parts system in many shops, supplied the machine tool industry with a crucial outlet in the 1890s, and experimented with new techniques such as sheet metal stamping and electric resistance welding.

In fact, adapting an internal combustion engine to vehicle propulsion was sufficiently simple that a growing number of North American tinkerers were tackling the job on their own by the turn of the twentieth century. In Canada, bicycle mechanic George Foss constructed a gasoline car in 1901 in Sherbrooke, Quebec, while stove manufacturer Tom Doherty did likewise around the same time in Sarnia, Ontario. In 1899, the Canada Cycle and Motor Company (CCM) was created by a merger of the bicycle division of Massey-Harris with the Canadian branches of four US bicycle makers, which allowed it to gain the rights to the successful De Dion gasoline engine through one of the US parent companies. It manufactured three- and four-wheeled vehicles driven by a De Dion motor as well as a steam-powered vehicle made in Hamilton using a US design. In 1902, it took over the Toronto company making Still's electric car so that it was briefly in a position to market cars reliant on steam engines, electric motors, and internal combustion engines. While it became a Toronto sales agent for Henry Ford after 1903, CCM launched a true gasoline-powered car originally called the Russell in 1905. Using a high-end British motor, the later Russell-Knight flourished briefly as a Canadian-made luxury model until it was hit by a recession in 1913. The Russell Motor Car Company spun off from CCM in 1911 sold a few cars to the Canadian army during the First World War and obtained a contract for experimental armoured vehicles, but poor sales forced it to merge with the US Willys-Overland Company in 1916.

Other commercial attempts are known in Canada, but the United States was already moving ahead. The Pope Manufacturing Company in Hartford, Connecticut is usually acknowledged to have been the first to make automobiles for sale in 1897. Within two years, Albert Pope, a prosperous bicycle manufacturer, had produced five hundred electric cars. By 1899, about thirty US firms were also engaged in manufacturing a variety of electric cars, "steamers," and "benzine buggies." They benefited from the country's staggering diversity of machine shops with experience in turning out everything from farm implements to electric apparatus. Canada's smaller economy, still dominated by farming and natural resource extraction, did not enjoy the same array of skilled technicians, which is why Canadian entrepreneurs so often needed to import outside expertise.

Even when the internal combustion engine prevailed over the alternatives (steam, electric), the choice of fuel was still somewhat open. Besides gasoline, ethanol was considered to be a viable possibility by people like Henry Ford. Chemists also investigated the conversion of waste straw and other vegetable matter into biogas down to the interwar years. While the technical feasibility of the process was demonstrated, it could not compete with the increasing availability of gasoline. In Canada, some companies are still striving today to perfect the conversion of cellulose (from straw) into ethanol using enzymes at a competitive price. Other companies are resorting to other technologies and feedstocks in the hope of having renewable fuels supply 27 percent of the world's transportation needs by 2050, instead of the current two percent.

MASS PRODUCTION

Like many others, Henry Ford yielded to the attraction of automobiles in the 1890s, both as a technical challenge and a new source of thrills. He first made his reputation as a builder and driver of fast cars. He formed the Ford Motor Company in 1903 at a time when automaking was undergoing an astounding expansion in the United States. Between 1900 and 1908, about 485 car manufacturers went into business and half of them were still around in 1908 when Ford launched the Model T. It cost less than comparable cars ($825–$850), but it could generate twenty horsepower, which was exceptional for cars in that category, and it featured a number of amenities for the everyday driver. Ford advertisements did not lie when they claimed, "No car under $2000 offers more, and no car over $2000 offers more except the trimmings."[1]

---

[1] Ruth Schwartz Cowan, *A Social History of American Technology* (Oxford University Press, 1997), p. 228.

While there was still room for improvement, the main challenge for automakers at the outset of the twentieth century was no longer mainly technological. The issue was cost. An automobile was a complex piece of machinery that could only be built by skilled labour. In 1901, a single Mercedes car required the full-time work of two well-paid craftsmen in Germany. Ford's initial offering, the 1903 Model A, was simple enough that a worker could complete twelve of them within a given year. This involved sacrificing quality to an extent that European manufacturers refused to countenance, sticking for another generation with their more artisanal production methods. Led by Ford, US companies eventually opted to offer the best possible car at the lowest possible price, which opened a new, mass market for their wares.

Building automobiles for the masses was a harder problem than merely designing or inventing them and it stimulated the development of the modern assembly line. Some of the principles of mass production were already known in the 18th century when Adam Smith described how a pin factory, by breaking down the job of making pins into several specialized tasks, was able to turn out many more pins than an equivalent number of workers could have done if each had been charged with making pins from start to finish. The Cincinnati and Chicago meatpacking plants evolved "disassembly" lines to process animal carcasses. Late in the nineteenth century, Taylor introduced the stopwatch in factories to determine the optimal pace at which a given job should be done.

Taylor himself was mostly concerned with efficiency, which entailed reducing costs and resulted in better profits. Ford placed more emphasis on production. Both courses of action improved productivity. Productivity is usually defined as the ratio of total production to total costs, however defined. (The classic economic definition restricts it to the value generated by an hour of work, but there are other definitions.) This means it can be increased by increasing production or reducing costs or both.

Taylor's drive for efficiency increased productivity, but not necessarily production (doing the same with less, one could say). Ford, on the other hand, focused on efficiency as a way to increase production (doing more with less or with the same). Instead of improving efficiency as a way to cut costs and increase profits, he improved efficiency as a way to increase production and cut prices so as to dominate the market. This was not a decision that could be made by Taylor and his colleagues; as efficiency experts, they were essentially hired as consultants, not to make strategic choices.

But Ford was an entrepreneur with a vision. The United States enjoyed a larger internal market than almost any other developed country by the first decade of the twentieth century. On average, per capita incomes were also higher than elsewhere, meaning that even more Americans should be able to afford an automobile. As a result, mass production was particularly well-suited to the North American context. Ford realized this. His workers were more efficient than other workers in the fledgling automobile industry, but he was also ready to hire enough of them to boost production and achieve volumes that would let him lower prices. And Ford didn't stop with just making each individual job more efficient; he oversaw a wholesale rethinking of car production.

Ford and his engineers added little that was new to mass production, but they pulled together every strategy known to industrial managers and efficiency experts. The subdivision of tasks was carried very far and each job was timed carefully. Parts were interchangeable and manufactured precisely to fit the first time. Parts were always within reaching distance or nearly so. Machines were developed to replace actions formerly performed by humans. Travel was minimized—the moving assembly line brought the work to the worker instead of it being the other way around. This was the distinctly American contribution to the development of the automobile—not the manufacture of a truly innovative vehicle, but the mass production of utilitarian models made with interchangeable parts, and so cheaply that they could be targeted at the mass market. The end result was a product that was designed to vary as little as possible.

Ford established Fordism at the new manufacturing plant built in Highland Park near Detroit, Michigan. By mid-1913, flywheel magnetos, transmissions, and motors were being constructed on assembly lines initially devised on a trial basis. The time needed to assemble a magneto was dramatically reduced from twenty to five minutes. Within a few months, assembly-line production of parts was outrunning the final assembly of the chassis, and so the chassis too was turned over to assembly line production. From October to December 1913, the time required to complete the chassis fell as a result from 12 hours and 30 minutes to 2 hours and 40 minutes. Part of the impressive cost savings financed Ford's celebrated pay rates, but another part was passed on to customers in the form of lower prices. Even during a period of inflation, the price of the Model T dropped from about $850 in 1908 to $360 by 1916. (It dropped down to $290 by 1927, in spite of renewed inflationary pressures.)

The eight-hour shift defined by Ford as a work day became the new standard. Long sought by the labour movement, the eight-hour day was now shown to be perfectly compatible with profitability. On February 20, 1930, this was confirmed in Canada by the passage of the *Fair Wages and Eight-Hour Day Act* after nearly 20 years of debate, giving workers under federal jurisdiction the eight-hour workday.

Though Ford wanted to bring automobiles to the masses, workers did not always like his new model for industrial work. Ford thought and stated that some men and women were willing, or even loved, the repetitive, mind-numbing labour of assembly line production. Was that because there really were different types of people or was it because there were different types of desperation? Ford's workforce included many black Americans, in part because they could rarely find equivalent work elsewhere. It might well be argued that ultimately, Taylor's and Ford's job simplification prepared industry for the use of robots.

In any event, Fordism ended up losing by winning. Ford captured such a huge share of the market that most of his competitors (outside of luxury car builders and special-purpose constructors) were forced to move over to some version of his system. However, Ford had created such a rigid system in the name of production cost-cutting ("Any customer can have a car painted any colour that he wants so long as it is black."[2]) that he opened avenues for his competitors to exploit. Chief among them was Alfred P. Sloan of General Motors, who was sufficiently attuned to consumer sensibilities to realize the importance of offering a way for buyers to feel different—product choice being indispensable to self-definition. General Motors therefore produced different yearly models (a "car for every purse and purpose") in a variety of colours for different markets. In 1923, Sloan became the leader of the combination of companies assembled under the aegis of General Motors (Cadillac, Buick, Chevrolet, Delco, Frigidaire, and several more) and he reorganized the whole company by splitting the production divisions for parts and finished automobiles, and by creating separate agencies for research, advertising, and product planning. By 1927, GM outsold Ford. In fact, a single division of General Motors—Chevrolet—sold more cars that year than the whole of Ford.

MASS PRODUCTION IN CANADA

While automobile manufacturing in Canada is dwarfed by the scale of the US industry, Canada has held its own with other car-producing countries. Between 1905 and 2005, Canadian car assembly plants turned out 88 million vehicles. During the same period, the Italian car industry accounted for 75 million vehicles. Yet, while Italian brand names such as Fiat, Ferrari, and Lamborghini are known worldwide, there are no real Canadian equivalents as a result of the structure of its automobile

---

[2]Henry Ford and Samuel Crowther, *My Life and Work* (Doubleday, Page, 1922), p. 72.

industry, dominated by branch plants of foreign companies (U.S., Swedish, Japanese, Korean), by joint ventures between local investors and foreign manufacturers, and by licensing agreements allowing Canadian manufacturers to benefit from outside expertise.

Various federal and provincial governments have shaped the evolution of Canadian automobile manufacturing, allowing it to grow in spite of the small domestic market. During the first third of the twentieth century, a 35 percent import duty on finished vehicles along with lower duties on parts provided key support for Canada-based manufacturers. A flood of small European cars in the 1950s forced the federal government to revisit this policy and the 1961 report of the Bladen Royal Commission led to the Canada-US Auto Pact, in force from 1965 to 2001. The agreement traded regulated access to the Canadian market by the Big Three automakers (Ford, GM, Chrysler) for unlimited access to the US market while requiring the Big Three to maintain their Canada-based production of cars at 1964 levels. While it appeared to be a good deal for Canada on the face of it and proved over time to be quite beneficial, the Big Three agreed to it in order to reduce future trade disputes.

As a result, the Canadian automobile industry tended to be limited to assembly and parts manufacturing. Very little development or design work actually happened in Canada. The US car manufacturing boom of the first decade of the twentieth century discouraged local entrepreneurs such as CCM and inspired instead the first joint ventures between Canadian businessmen and US companies. The difference between the import duty on car parts and the one on the finished car meant that, if assembly could be done cheaply enough, a car made with US parts and assembled in Canada would sell for less in Canada than the same car assembled in the United States. Furthermore, British policies adopted in 1897 mandated the almost entirely free trade of goods between all parts of the British Empire. As a result, a car made in Canada could be exported free of any duties to other parts of the Empire while a similar car made in the United States would face tariffs.

In 1904, a young Canadian entrepreneur from Windsor, Ontario, approached Henry Ford with a proposition. Gordon McGregor would build Ford-designed cars in Walkerville, just west of Windsor. Some parts were sourced in Canada to lower costs further. This was the beginnings of the company that became known as Ford of Canada. By the outbreak of the First World War, it was producing more than half of all the cars made in Canada and, with the aid of US sales personnel, was exporting almost half of its production, either to other parts of the British Empire or to countries in the southern hemisphere, since Ford of Canada had more cars available in winter, when Canadian sales slowed to a near standstill, than its US counterpart. By then, the Canadian company was sharing in the success of the Ford Model T.

From the start, the tariff on US parts pushed Canadian car manufacturers to buy as many Canadian parts as possible. This allowed Canadian businesses to become part of the supply chain of automakers in Canada from the first. Car manufacturing was still a small business. In 1914, vehicle registrations in Canada totalled only 89,944 in a country with a population of almost eight million. Registrations tripled during the First World War, with Alberta and Saskatchewan ranking just behind as high wheat prices allowed western farmers to buy new cars. Car ownership in the Prairies rose so fast that Ford of Canada built an assembly plant in Winnipeg in 1916. Ford of Canada profited greatly from the war. While the Canadian army disdained using it opting instead for Cadillac models, other Allied militaries obtained nearly 125,000 Ford Model Ts and Ford of Canada accounted for almost a third of the total.

FIGURE 1 ▶ The Canadian Ford Model T testified to the attraction of the star product of mass production. *(Picture by author at the Canadian Museum of Science and Technology in Ottawa, Ontario, 2010.)*

By 1922, when its founder Gordon McGregor died, Ford of Canada was facing its first real competitor in the mass market niche. Samuel McLaughlin, the heir to a family of carriage-makers in Oshawa, Ontario, first struck a deal in 1907 with US businessman William Durant to produce Canadian versions of Durant's Buick line of cars. The Buick was more expensive than a Ford and fewer were sold, but the business prospered. However, the Chevrolet Motor Company founded in 1911 by Durant began manufacturing the low-cost Chevrolet 490 in 1915, selling it for ten dollars less than the basic Model T. McLaughlin and Durant agreed to a new partnership. By 1916, the Oshawa plant was making three times as many Chevrolets as Buicks, using assembly line technology. In 1918, Durant bought out the McLaughlins in order to make the Oshawa installations part of General Motors of Canada. GM of Canada shared in the prosperity of the 1920s as Canadian car ownership rates rose steadily.

Registered Motor Vehicles in Canada
(In Thousands)

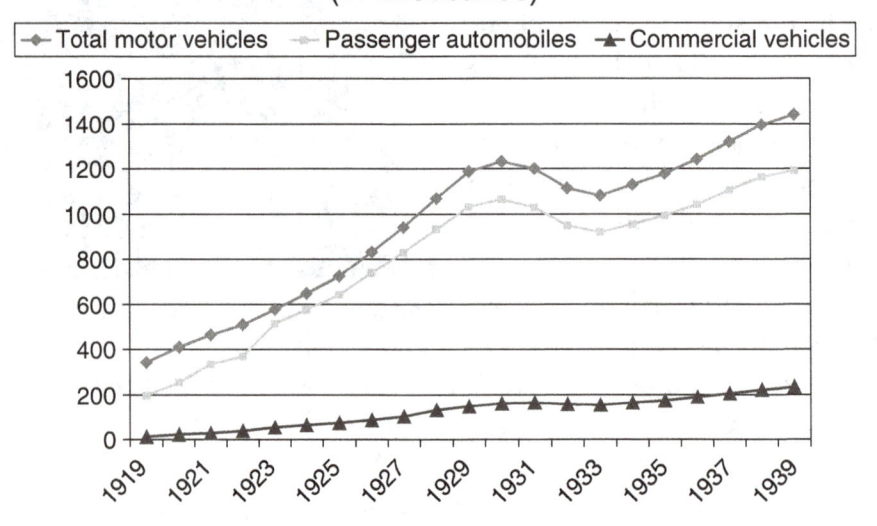

FIGURE 2 ▶ During the interwar period between 1919 and 1939, the number (in thousands) of registered motor vehicles in Canada increased almost four-fold, which was largely due to the rise in passenger automobiles. *(Data source:* Historical Statistics of Canada, *1983.)*

Chevrolets alone outsold all Canadian Ford cars in 1927 when Ford of Canada shut down its plants for half a year to launch the replacement of the Model T. By 1929, the Ford family acquired a majority of the stock in Ford of Canada and Canada's two largest automakers were then firmly controlled by US corporate interests.

THE TECHNOLOGICAL EVOLUTION OF THE CAR

As an artifact, the American automobile evolved rapidly after World War I as GM accustomed consumers to yearly changes, at times technically substantial and at times purely cosmetic. As a result, automakers raced to introduce new features. The Depression only increased the benefits of moving ahead of the crowd since car makers were competing for a scarcer buyer. Yet, due to the expense of retooling an assembly line and rethinking fully integrated plant operations, changes had to be evolutionary rather than revolutionary.

The Model T was still something of a horseless carriage beholden to its design at a time when there were more bicycles and horse-drawn carriages than motor cars on the road. By the time the United States entered World War II, the cars found on American roads had been shaped by a new concern for comfort and streamlining.

Their engines were larger than those of contemporary European cars, which were often constrained by taxes based on horsepower. As roads improved, speeds could increase and required more power. By the 1920s, motors grew from four to six cylinders. In spite of the Depression, models from the 1930s began to offer eight cylinders. The bodies of American cars were also more likely to be all-steel, and to be roomier, since the price of steel was lower than elsewhere. The introduction of continuous hot-strip rolling in 1924 in steel mills superseded the older method of producing steel sheets by having experienced hands pass the steel back and forth through sets of adjustable rollers. The new process made for a more uniform product available in greater quantities. Thanks to new, durable paints, new colours besides black became available.

As paved roads multiplied, new car models no longer needed to be designed for the deep ruts of dirt tracks. The Packard Motor Company introduced hypoid gearing in the late 1920s, making it possible to build low-slung cars. The automatic transmission launched by GM in 1939 and subsequently sold to other car manufacturers capped more than 30 years of gradual improvements and over a decade of sustained work based on patents for the epicyclic gearbox, the torque converter, and hydraulic coupling.

THE SOCIAL AND ECOLOGICAL IMPACT OF PAVED ROADS

On a larger scale, providing cars and trucks with fuel (which demanded the creation of a network of gas stations), and then with roads (eventually snow-free in Canada), and then with highways modified the North American landscape.

It was in Paris, in 1838, that asphalt was originally used to pave streets (on a concrete foundation) as an alternative to medieval cobblestones, granite blocks, hard bricks, or macadam. This asphalt was a naturally occurring material (rock asphalt) found *in situ* at Val de Travers, in Switzerland. Over the next thirty years, major cities in the United Kingdom, France, and Belgium adopted or experimented with asphalt paving, and they imported increasing quantities of mined asphalt from Trinidad, in the Caribbean. New York experimented with asphalt paving in 1869 and other North American cities followed suit progressively.

By 1880, the invention of the bicycle created a new class of road users who began to agitate for better roads between cities. While the lobbying efforts of cyclists and their associations did not result in significant road improvements, they did lead to the creation of university courses on road construction for engineers and to the launch of the federal Office of Road Inquiry (ORI) in the United States in 1893. Within a few years, car owners added their voices to the cyclists and farmers who were calling for better roads. The ORI became the Office of Public Roads in 1905 and it played a greater role in advising local authorities as to the best road design and construction practices. By 1910, most of the asphalt used for paving in the United States was not imported from natural sources, but was a mix including petroleum fractions from refineries producing gasoline for cars.

At the turn of the century, the United States had something like 3,000,000 km of rural roads, but only 220 km were paved. Even in 1915, the new transcontinental Lincoln Highway was mostly a gravel road, with a few miles of concrete and macadam (even brick). Planning to cross the country, fourteen travellers left in cars from New York on May 15, 1915, and arrived in San Francisco 104 days later. In 1919, Thomas Harris MacDonald became the head of the United States Bureau of Public Roads and he would oversee decades of effort to remedy the poor state of US roads until his firing in 1953. In 1921, the Federal Highway Act allowed the US government to finance one half of road improvement costs while state governments financed the rest. Gasoline taxes funded work both on roads and on streets in cities.

MacDonald was able to take full advantage of advances in the mechanization in road construction. Before the First World War, much of the work was still done by men wielding hand tools, with the help of horse-drawn vehicles. By 1925, motor trucks, power shovels, concrete mixers, and finishing machines for shaping concrete significantly reduced the labour needed to complete a length of paved road.

MacDonald could also rely on the vocal support of the Auto Club, ceaselessly clamouring for more paved routes. During the Depression years, public investment in infrastructure (especially roads and streets) increased markedly. Between 1928 and 1950, the stock of public streets and roads in the United States almost doubled. Most of the growth (over four percent annually on average) happened before the United States entered the war in 1941. Before the Second World War, however, few of these roads were true divided highways. Nevertheless, by then, a newly mobile society had come into being. There were enough cars on the roads to carry the entire population of the country. Yearly gasoline consumption per car rose from 1790 litres in 1925 to 2267 in 1930, and then to 2775 in 1940. This was mainly due to the increased size of engines, but the increased availability of good roads also made for more driving. While this resulted in more air pollution, it did reduce the number of horses on farms and in cities. Cleaning city streets became easier as each fewer horse also meant five to ten kilos of manure no longer soiled the pavements.

As roads became more common and automobile travel as well, new facilities were devised to cater to drivers and their passengers. Gasoline stations multiplied in cities and then the countryside. Trips to national parks rose fourfold during the 1920s. Travelers camped out of their cars, extending tents or awnings to increase living space, or they rented space to pitch a tent on a campground.

One of the first motels in the United States opened in 1925 in San Luis Obispo, California, roughly halfway between Los Angeles and San Francisco. Originally known as the Milestone Mo-Tel, it was designed as a cross between a campground and a true hotel. Travellers would spend the night in separate cabins or a small apartment, each unit being provided with indoor plumbing. Within a few years, many other roadside inns offered similar amenities and the establishment's name became a generic noun. After the Second World War, many withered and closed as the expansion of the interstate highways changed traffic patterns. New accommodation standards and increasing volume led to the creation of national chains of motor lodges such as Holiday Inn (1952) and Howard Johnson's (1954). The Howard Johnson's brand had previously been associated with restaurants often set up by the turn-offs of the first divided highways such as the Pennsylvania Turnpike in 1939. The postwar interstate highways favoured the rise of fast food restaurants such as McDonald's.

North Americans wanted to drive everywhere as they discovered the wonders of individual, high-speed mobility. The drive-in restaurant, where food was brought to the car so that people could eat without leaving their vehicle, first appeared in Dallas in 1921. Chains of drive-in restaurants flourished down to the 1970s. The first drive-in cinema, where people watched a movie without leaving their car, opened in Camden, New Jersey, in 1933. In the United States, drive-in cinemas multiplied after the Second World War, their popularity peaking around 1958. They lost ground as the suburbs grew and increased the price of the land they sat on. By the 1970s, the switch to daylight savings time pushed back the start of showings, limiting their audience since features started too late for families with young children.

Drive-in restaurants and cinemas were part of a new culture that North American youth embraced eagerly. Able to drive at sixteen, young men and women could pile into a car and vanish into the distance, far from the watchful gaze of adults. A car was the means to a new sort of independence, allowing adolescents a greater scope for job-searching, geographical exploration, and sexual experimentation. By the last half of the twentieth century, the most common destination for young drivers was equally likely to be a fast food restaurant or a shopping mall.

The first shopping center intended to serve drivers may have been the Country Club Plaza, built in Kansas City in 1923. Subsequently, many downtown stores opened suburban branches where parking was less expensive and land was cheaper.

Shopping malls grew in size. In northern climes, enclosed malls became popular until the sheer number of ever larger stores burst the confines of single buildings. Sprawling power centres recreated the downtown shopping district of old by doing away with almost everything that wasn't either parking or square footage for stores.

By the time of the Second World War, divided highways were celebrated in the United States as vital to the economy and to defence. The country's inhabitants drove an increasing number of motor vehicles (97 million in 1967) and covered an increasing number of miles (960 billion in 1967). Carefully laid-out highways would reduce the mileage between major cities (by up to 25 percent in some cases) and would reduce the driving time even more (thanks to the absence of all traffic flow interruptions). They would also be safer than the old primary roads (the median strips made head-on collisions least likely) and they were also easier on the cars (reducing fuel and maintenance costs). Indeed, by 1967, studies suggested that the accident fatality rate on the completed portions of the interstate highways was 2.8 deaths per 100 million vehicle-miles as opposed to 6.9 for the older roads.

Originally, the US interstate highway system alone was planned to span 65,000 km when it was to be completed in 1975. It is no coincidence that President Dwight Eisenhower's chief transportation adviser was Lucius D. Clay, chairman of General Motors. The rise in the number of cars as the system was being built was probably the mere extension of a long-established trend, but it is highly likely that the availability of new divided highways made cars more useful and promised to make driving simpler.

Officially known as the "National System of Interstate and Defense Highways," it required at least 6,500 square kilometres of land for right of way, an area larger than the state of Delaware. The law passed in 1956 under President Eisenhower mandated a partnership between the federal and state governments. Through the Bureau of Public Roads, the federal government paid 90 percent of the costs and retained a right of approval and oversight. The individual states determined the routes and designed the highways. The original target date for completion was 1972, though it was later pushed back to 1975 as costs rose, new standards (for safety, especially) were implemented, and urban opposition organized. In Boston, for instance, the Inner Belt (which would have become Interstate 695) was cancelled in 1971 by Massachusetts governor Francis W. Sargent due to strong opposition by community activists as this eight-lane highway would have run through thirteen neighbourhoods. Under pressure, the US Congress passed laws that allowed public transit projects to be financed in part out of funds allotted for interstate highway construction.

Other countries have made choices between faster commutes and the existing urban environment. For instance, in 1993, an East London neighbourhood faced demolition when the M11 highway was planned, extending from Wanstead to Hackney, in order to connect existing highways. Ancient woods were to be razed, up to 350 homes torn down, and thousands of people moved in order to accommodate a six-lane highway designed to shave six minutes off previous travel times. In spite of spirited opposition, the project went ahead in 1994.

Though Canada did not develop long-distance divided highways to the same extent (the 1948 federal law mandating a Trans-Canada Highway catered to the lowest common denominator by supporting nothing more than a two-lane, paved road), various provinces did invest in the construction of highways, both for travel between cities and within cities. As in the United States, this led to the razing of some neighbourhoods. For instance, in Quebec City, the local Chinatown was almost entirely displaced by the construction of the Dufferin-Montmorency Highway in the early 1970s.

It is estimated the entire United States now has over 6 million kilometres of public roads (and counting). Their combined surface is about one percent of that country's land area, the equivalent of a state like South Carolina. As a consequence, these roads—in addition to the dividing strips, shoulders and ditches often found alongside them—have become a major ecological force.

Roads divert streams and drainage, changing water tables. They are conduits for the emission of carbon dioxide, ozone, and smog, as well as smaller quantities of heavy metals and toxic dusts. The heavy elements can grow to surprising concentrations in the higher plants, while the dust is enough to kill lichens and mosses. The roadside, even when it is not dosed with herbicides or kept cropped mechanically, is an environment all its own, often harsh and open to plants quite different from the dominant species of the neighbouring area (if only because the seeds of common weeds are spread by cars and trucks).

In the US Northeast, where salt is abundantly used on driveways, parkings, and roads, chloride concentrations (salinity) in streams rise during the winter, up to a quarter of typical values for seawater.

In wooded areas or when a road cuts through a wilderness, the habits of wild animals are disrupted. Roads divide up habitats into smaller, more isolated parts, and the vehicles using them produce enough noise to drown out the more subtle cues used by wildlife. In Alaska, caribou will sometimes migrate along cleared roads, exposing themselves to trucks and predators. In North Carolina, black bears move away from busy roads, just like grizzlies in the Rockies. Most dramatically, roads kill the unwary animal trying to cross them. As early as the 1960s, it was estimated that a million animals a day were dying on the pavement of North American roads, including amphibians, birds, and mammals—but excluding insects. Unsurprisingly, vultures flock to roadsides to take advantage of the abundance of carrion.

On the whole, landscape ecologist Richard Forman from Harvard University estimates that the ecology of 20 percent of the United States is directly affected by the presence of roads. Most obviously, while roads as artifacts have an impact, they also provide access. When they reach into wilderness areas, they may allow for tourism and resource exploitation (logging, mining) to affect previously untouched areas.

Still, the human environment has been most obviously affected by automobiles. Outside the old cities and their downtowns once designed for pedestrians and horse-drawn carriages, a new landscape has been developed to host aliens—four-wheeled vehicles massing hundreds of kilograms that go everywhere from the home to the workplace or the shop. Asphalt or concrete roads have been laid down, shopping centres have replaced main street shops, parkings have multiplied, and gas stations or garages have popped up everywhere. Increasingly, people live and work without entering the downtown cores, sometimes commuting from one far-flung suburb to another.

The fuel demand of cars translates into the need for a world-spanning infrastructure, leading from oil wells to local gas stations. It is estimated that only 13 percent of the average modern car's fuel energy actually turns the wheels, the rest being lost as waste heat, friction, and noise, or being used to power accessories or idling.

As a result, modern cities sprawl, strip malls (and car dealerships) colonize freeway exits and suburban boulevards, and the air grows hazy with a new kind of smog. While the massive resources (glass, steel, rubber, and electronics) invested in each automobile end up in dumps or need to be recycled.

The modern suburb, served by automobiles and not by streetcars or railway like some suburbs in the early twentieth century, is a creation of the car. There is some debate as to the role played by car and tire manufacturers in buying up streetcar companies and offering instead bus service, a switch that led to the disappearance of streetcar tracks in cities and the opening of city streets to . . . car traffic. What is not arguable is the expense, both in primary resources (metal, plastics, oil, wood, and concrete) and in secondary resources (land and diverse ecosystems), that is consumed by suburbs requiring large infrastructure improvements (paved streets, sewers, streetlights, and sidewalks eventually) serving a relatively low number of people per square kilometre.

THE HUMAN USE OF HUMAN BEINGS

Part of the mass production system was the classification of human beings. Taylor had already advocated studying "the character, the nature, and the performance" of every worker. The Ford system went further. Employees were given the jobs they seemed best fitted for. In this respect, Ford was at the forefront of his era's belief in human classification.

This belief drew on developments on several fronts.

Oldest of all was the rise of scientific racism, dating back to the 18th century. European scientists had encountered people who were unlike them. In the spirit of the Scientific Revolution, some applied to the science of humans the same methods used by the biologists who classified plants, insects, or animals. They identified salient traits, measured them or counted them, correlated them with other traits, noticed which ones went together most often, and then inferred that one trait followed from the other. And so they felt able to draw general conclusions from the observations of a single thing. Such classifications yielded reasonably trustworthy results in chemistry or botany, but they sometimes generated basic confusions. However, making mistakes with the proper classification of chemical compounds or ferns was far less serious than when it involved human beings.

Nevertheless, Western anthropologists and psychologists at the turn of the twentieth century still felt confident they knew how to classify people. Their assertions fed the contemporary passion for intelligence measurements, symbolized by the vogue of the IQ (Intelligence Quotient) test. By then, the IQ test proper had outgrown its origins in psychiatry and child pedagogy to be applied to immigrants to America and to soldiers during World War I.

Originally, French psychologist Alfred Binet (1857–1911) had designed a test intended to identify children whose lack of success in normal classrooms suggested the need for remedial measures or special education. A first version of the test was published in 1905, but it was the 1908 version that assigned an age level to each task. (In 1912, German psychologist W. Stern argued that mental age should be divided by chronological age, thus yielding an *intelligence quotient*.) Importantly, since Binet believed that special education could improve a child's performance, the Binet test did *not* measure some fixed, innate mental ability. The test was concerned with identifying children who needed help, not ranking normal children—or adults.

In the United States, H. H. Goddard extended the Binet test to adults and to immigrants. By 1913, physicians working at the Ellis Island immigration centre in New

York were using his version of the intelligence test to reject "feeble-minded" immigrants.

This was the era of eugenics and New York was also the home of the Cold Spring Harbor Laboratory from 1904 to 1939, the base of the Eugenics Record Office and the headquarters of a national movement to improve the human race through selective breeding. *Eugenicists* at Cold Spring and elsewhere believed that the unfit had to be prevented from passing on their defective genes for blindness, criminality, insanity, and stupidity. They often expressed the wish that they could sterilize the "submerged tenth," the most unfit 10 percent of the population, but first it was necessary to identify them. The extended intelligence tests could be applied to the identification of stupidity. Keeping out undesirable immigrants was also part of the eugenic agenda.

Eugenics was considered to be progressive. It was based on the newly emerging science of genetics and on the work of Francis Galton, a cousin of Charles Darwin. Eugenics was embraced by universities, funded by major endowments, and endorsed by the US Supreme Court. In some US states and Canadian provinces, doctors and mental institutions were authorized by law to sterilize people they judged to be unfit to pass on their genes (in some cases, their patients were mostly guilty of being poor and ignorant, or of being the wrong race). In other cases, doctors overseeing patients interned in asylums and prisons are suspected of having conducted experiments on behalf of eugenicists.

In 1916, Lewis M. Terman carried out his own revision of the Binet test, by increasing the number of tasks and by extending the scale from mid-teenage years to "superior adults." He also advocated generalized testing and believed in matching jobs to the abilities of test subjects, even when the latter were of inferior intelligence:

> "The evolution of modern industrial organization together with the mechanization of processes by machinery is making possible the larger and larger utilization of inferior mentality. One man with ability to think and plan guides the labor of ten or twenty laborers, who do what they are told to do and have little need for resourcefulness or initiative."[3]

This statement by Terman in 1919 came after the systematic testing of almost two million adult men by Robert M. Yerkes in the army camps set up by the United States during its participation in World War I. The goal had been to build up a copious, useful, and uniform body of data that would set the art of intelligence measurement on

---

[3] Paul Michael Privateer, *Inventing Intelligence* (John Wiley & Sons, 2008), p. 12.

a firmer footing. The tests used by Yerkes and his psychologists were the first mass-produced written tests of intelligence. The default written text was known as the Alpha test, while a more pictorial version for illiterates was known as the Beta test. According to the results of these tests, the psychologists graded each man from A to E, with plusses and minuses.

The first wave of US psychologists testing for intelligence tended to believe that intelligence was both strongly congenital and an innate quantity fixed for life. Ford's system was not so rigid, but it still tended to slot people into ready-made places just like car parts were to be fitted into their assigned places. Even though Ford did not use the IQ test, he obviously believed that there were distinct types of people.

CHAPTER 9

Mass Consumption and Technology in Daily Life

▶▶▶▶▶▶▶▶▶▶▶▶▶▶▶▶▶▶▶▶▶▶▶▶▶▶▶▶▶

DOMESTIC TECHNOLOGIES

By 1900, new technologies had brought about a delocalization of consumption. Clipper ships, more powerful steamships, express trains, and the first motor trucks added one more increment of speed to the effectiveness of the existing canal, railway, and road networks. Their added speed underpinned the effectiveness of the postal service, brought fresh fruits and vegetables from the farm to the city table in a matter of hours and days, and allowed tea from China to reach North America or England before the leaves could lose any flavour. Improved food preservation methods and the mastery of the cold chain allowed for the export of beef and cereals from North and South America to Europe and beyond. Consumers a continent away increasingly dictated the behaviour of farmers and workers.

It is easy enough to recognize the large-scale effects of technology when species go extinct and landscapes are transformed wholesale. However, technology also enters our daily lives in subtler fashions. Sometimes overlooked, domestic technologies constrain our behaviour from the time we wake up. By the early twentieth century they raised people's expectations (running water and refrigeration at home), changed their daily habits (electric lighting and washing machines), and fed our pastimes (photography, phonograph, cinema, and radio).

161

The debate over technological determinism is most acute in this private sphere as it clashes with our belief in personal autonomy. While we cannot bend a technology to our every whim, a sufficiently complex technology rarely determines how it will be used. Edison spent time and effort on recording devices because he expected to make money selling them as dictating machines for businessmen. However, the first prototypes drew fairground crowds entranced by the sight of a machine reproducing the sound of the human voice. Thereafter, Edison followed the lead of competing inventors such as German-born Emil Berliner and concentrated instead on sound production for entertainment rather than pure utility. By 1900, it was possible to produce faithful copies of the original recording. Sales boomed and the first recording stars were born, such as Italian tenor Enrico Caruso whose voice and operatic hits suited the limitations of the medium. The horn used to channel the sound to the diaphragm whose vibrations drove the recording stylus could only capture relatively loud sounds, excluding bass frequencies and the full complexity of orchestral music. Duration was also limited. The flat disc perfected by Berliner in 1887 outlasted the cylinder marketed by Edison, which still registered no more than four minutes in its improved 1909 version. Longer pieces, such as symphonies, would remain the preserve of the concert hall until the development of the long-playing record after World War II proved to be the last triumph of the analog technology pioneered by Edison in 1877.

While the phonograph eventually enjoyed its greatest popularity as a source of music in the home, movie technology moved the other way. At one point, Edison envisioned the rich using movie cameras to make home movies. Once again, though, the public flocked to watch movies as soon as they were available in 1893, even when Edison's primitive Kinetoscope could only be used one person at a time and forced the viewer to bend over a peephole to discover the relatively tiny moving images. Since Edison had failed to seek international patents on his device, perhaps because he had fused a number of European innovations, inventors outside the United States took full advantage and the brothers Lumière in Lyons, France, came up with a simple and effective projector in 1895. Even though it was scorned by Edison who feared it would saturate the potential customer base, the projector crowded out the original Kinetoscope within a year of its arrival on the market and cinema catered thereafter to mass audiences.

While the phonograph entered the home, the movies drew people out of home. The first very short movies, sometimes no more than a minute long, were included as short features of vaudeville houses. Around 1905, the nickelodeons became the first specialized movie theatres, though many were small enough to fit in the back of a cigar store. For the price of a single vaudeville ticket, a workingman hoping for action or slapstick comedy could catch four or five twenty-minute long film showings.

It wasn't until the second decade of the twentieth century that entrepreneurs targeted a broader audience by creating upscale movie palaces, gaudily decorated to seduce a richer class of customers. The massive US market became the springboard for movie companies that still exist today such as Fox and Paramount to produce silent movies that offered heavily promoted movie stars and complete stories. When the First World War savaged the movie industries of many formerly dominant European countries, the United States rose to global prominence as the purveyor of films with mass appeal. In 1918, US companies supplied 85 percent of the worldwide film market.

Other technologies entered the home without ceasing to be present in the work world. Radio was an information and entertainment technology that proved to be equally important as a means of communication and an entertainment medium. As its use spread, it created a public space that was immediately available to listeners. The telegraph had reduced the time required for point-to-point communication, but telegraph operators were the only ones to really experience the sense of virtual presence associated with nearly instantaneous communication. Once the telephone was no longer marketed exclusively to professionals and upper-class families, it allowed a growing number of people to experience an auditory form of telepresence. However constrained, the feeling of *being* with somebody who was not in the same physical location became familiar. Still, telephone users were tied to their machines and to the wires that connected phones. They could not choose the location they reached. Even with the public payphone introduced in 1889, the choice of locations remained limited.

Radio was inherently more flexible. It was not tied to wires, not even for power if batteries were used. Furthermore, once radio broadcasting took off, on-the-scene reporting could transport the listener to any location where a radio-journalist chose to set up. The sense of immediacy this fostered arguably shaped politics as Franklin Delano Roosevelt spoke to US audiences by radio, offering fireside chats at the same time as the speeches of Adolf Hitler in Germany were heard on radio sets in that country. The radio also brought music, radio plays, and soap operas inside homes equipped with radio receivers. No longer was it necessary to leave home to hear orchestral music, see a play, or laugh at vaudeville comedy. The old-fashioned storyteller or neighbourhood fiddler was no longer needed to enliven weekend gatherings. The piano survived as a source of musical accompaniment or training, but it was less and less often the centerpiece of an evening of song and music.

Like radio, a number of sometimes purely domestic technologies shaped daily life in ways that were guided in part by industrial designers and in part by the users themselves.

RADIO AS TECHNOSCIENCE

In 1913, *Scientific American* magazine ran a contest asking essayists to choose the ten greatest inventions of the last 25 years.[1] The invention that garnered the greatest support was wireless telegraphy, beating out airplanes, X-rays, automobiles, movies, phonographs, and the incandescent light. What radio had in common with inventions such as X-rays or the incandescent light was a close, causal relationship with the science of the day. Scientific laws and formal expertise played a supporting role in Edison's perfecting of the light bulb. X-rays were discovered fortuitously by several scientists investigating electrical discharges in Crookes tubes and they were described by German physicist Wilhelm Röntgen in 1895. The Crookes tube was a gas-filled tube provided with electrodes inside the insulating envelope and the study of such tubes led to the invention of fluorescent lights.

However, the existence of radio waves was predicted by Maxwell's equations for electromagnetism and German physicist Heinrich Hertz showed they could be detected. While radio waves are only a small part of the electromagnetic spectrum, ranging from the low frequency bound of three kilohertz to the high-frequency bound of 300 gigahertz, they were a wholly new class of phenomena in the eyes of nineteenth-century investigators, who were already familiar with the visible light spectrum and knew of its infrared and ultraviolet extensions. While their existence might eventually have been deduced from other observations, Maxwell's theory and Hertz's work supplied later workers with an initial understanding of radio that was far ahead of what the first steam engine builders had available to them when they sought to improve the steam machinery of their day. Indeed, for a good decade afterwards, the development of radio remained in the hands of scientists.

Research into radio was an international effort. British physicist Oliver Lodge used the coherer designed by French physicist Édouard Branly as a more sensitive detector of radio waves than the simple wire loop used by Hertz. The coherer was a glass tube which contained small metallic filings. If exposed to a radio wave, they *cohered*, forming a compact mass that allowed current to flow. Russian professor A. S.

---

[1] Wyman, William A., "What Are the Ten Greatest Inventions of Our Time," *Scientific American*, 1 November 1913, pp. 337-340.

Popov improved the coherer by reducing the potential for interference from sparks in the circuit and by connecting it to a large antenna. While North Americans did not contribute significantly to this work, it did not go unnoticed. In Toronto, Canadian astrophysicist Clarence A. Chant lectured about these developments in 1895, demonstrating a spark gap transmitter and a coherer connected to a galvanometer as a receiver in order to show that radio waves did behave like light waves. Less than ten years after the pioneering experiments of Hertz, this part of Maxwell's theory was now fully assimilated by the international scientific community.

While Hertz had been skeptical of his experiment's practical applications, other scientists did foresee its potential for wireless communication. However, the prevailing ethos of scientific research at the time encouraged them to freely disseminate their discoveries. In England, Lodge had to be convinced by others to patent some of his basic inventions. By the turn of the twentieth century, however, further progress in developing radio as a means of communication fell into the hands of practical men such as Guglielmo Marconi, Reginald Fessenden, Lee de Forest, and Valdemar Poulsen.

Though he lacked formal training, Marconi was mentored by Italian scientist Augusto Righi, who might be compared to Chant in his role as teacher and populariser. Fessenden likewise lacked scientific credentials, but he had been chair of electrical engineering at Purdue University and had worked for Edison. On the other hand, Lee de Forest was a graduate of Yale whose PhD dissertation in 1899 addressed the action of electric waves in antennae. What linked them was a common determination to turn a scientific phenomenon into a useful technology. What distinguished Marconi was entrepreneurial spirit. Within a year of his arrival in Great Britain in 1896, he argued with unshakable confidence, in front of gathered government officials from the Navy, the Army, and the Post Office, that his system could be used for communication. In the age of the telegraph and the telephone, he targeted the one area where signalling over a distance was still unimproved. Marine communication outside of visual range, whether from ship to ship, ship to shore, or shore to ship, was both vitally important in a world reliant on sea-borne trade and naval supremacy, and completely lacking.

Marconi justified his claims by achieving clearer transmissions and greater ranges than ever before by grounding his antenna and patenting new tuning methods based on work done by Lodge. His transmitter produced a signal by generating a spark across a gap between two conductors. Each spark released a burst of radio waves across a broad span of the electromagnetic spectrum, making it easy to detect but prone to interfere with the reception of other signals.

When Marconi managed to send a message across the Atlantic between Poldhu, in the United Kingdom, and St. John's, Newfoundland, in 1900, he demonstrated the empirical success of his apparatus, though scientists understood neither how his design modifications could improve its performance nor how he could have detected transatlantic radio waves that should have been hidden from view by the curvature of the Earth. Thus, Marconi's inventive efforts had outrun the scientific knowledge of the day and provided scientists with new facts to interpret.

This mingling of scientific and technological advances, each feeding off the other, is typical of what has been termed *technoscience*. The international dimension of both the scientific and the technological evolution of radio is also deemed to be characteristic of innovation in the twentieth century. They relate the technological cutting edge to the increasing complexity of science in the late nineteenth century. As science progressed, fewer scientists were in a position to master more than their own field of specialization, to the point where an advanced country might only have a handful of researchers working seriously on a topic like radio. While each of them might be pursuing a useful insight, only the combination of their ideas could result in true improvement. Similarly, on the practical side of things, only a few innovators in each country might be sufficiently attuned to ongoing research and have the necessary expertise to explore its practical applications. As the mingling of science and technology strengthens, the line between each may blur and scientific research may be undertaken with a view to solving a technical problem hindering the development of a technological application.

This is more likely to happen if scientific research is organized from above to assign a purpose to research and development efforts. Indeed, technoscience may be defined as goal-oriented as opposed to basic research into pure or fundamental science.

The organisation of research and development arose in facilities such as Edison's Menlo Park with teams of technicians and scientists collaborating on projects determined by their employer. Such a research laboratory usually focused on producing patentable inventions that could be commercialized.

By the early twentieth century, as the complexity of new products such as synthetic chemicals, electrical machinery, pharmaceuticals, and automobiles grew, US corporations created in-house research laboratories with multiple roles. For one, managers needed to have an immediately available source of expertise if they ran into a technical problem. Only if their own experts failed them would they turn to outside help, often by calling on university professors.

General Electric (GE) opened the first corporate research laboratory in 1901 and companies including Du Pont, Bell, and Eastman-Kodak followed suit. Industrial research laboratories aimed to produce patentable improvements to a company's most profitable products. Concrete improvements would allow them to stay ahead of the competition, either winning or preserving market share. However, as long as a potential improvement was patented, a company could also keep it out of the hands of the competition even if it did not use it. The largest corporations also allowed their research staff to pursue difficult projects with an uncertain pay-off. Such breakthrough inventions, if they occurred, could create new industries or save a company from obsolescence. By the time of the Second World War, ongoing research at the Radio Corporation of America (RCA) would lead to the invention of the electronic television.

Technological innovation may also be organized by government. As technoscience becomes costlier and more complex, only governments may be willing to underwrite the risks of research that may never lead anywhere.

In the case of radio, governments most often played a more traditional role—that of customer. In Canada, the federal government erected two Marconi radio stations on either side of the Strait of the Belle Isle separating Newfoundland from Labrador as early as 1901. They were intended to supplement the submarine telegraph cable connecting the Newfoundland network to the Canadian network as winter ice often damaged the cable. By then, Marconi had also signed two contracts with the British government, the first with the War Office to provide it with radio equipment for the Boer War and the other with the Admiralty. He had also come to a groundbreaking agreement in September 1901 with the marine insurance firm Lloyd's of London—the Marconi Company would supply it with radio equipment and operators while Lloyd's committed to use only Marconi equipment and to communicate only with Marconi-equipped radio stations.

In Germany however, the Kaiser intervened in 1903 to bring about the merger of two companies pursuing commercial radio. Thanks to continued government support, the resulting Telefunken system became a major competitor for Marconi and other foreign radio companies.

In the United States, Marconi's earliest competitor was a company founded in 1897 by Canadian entrepreneur William Joseph Clarke. By 1898, the United States Electrical Supply Company (USESCO) was selling spark transmitters and receivers. Clarke was an active promoter, using radio to report on the America's Cup yacht race in 1899 and demonstrating his radio equipment at trade shows, scientific meetings, and other venues, including the 1899 Canadian National Exhibition in Toronto. The US Army Signal Corps was one early customer.

FROM TELEGRAPHY TO TELEPHONY

By the end of the nineteenth century, wireless telegraphy was a reality. Inventors and entrepreneurs like Marconi steadily improved the technology to make transmission possible over long distances. In 1902, the Canadian government subsidized the construction of a Marconi radio station in Glace Bay, Nova Scotia, that would become a vital link for transatlantic messaging. In exchange, it obtained word rates that were about 60 percent lower than cable rates at the time. However, it was still necessary to send and receive only the dots and dashes of the Morse code, or a version thereof. The work of Reginald Aubrey Fessenden (1866–1932) made it possible to send and receive voice.

By the turn of the twentieth century, Canadian-born Fessenden worked for the US Weather Bureau which wanted a network of wireless stations along the eastern seaboard that would collect and disseminate meteorological data. As early as 1897, Fessenden had sought to improve the Branly-Lodge coherer and he went on to reconsider the wholesale reliance of Marconi and others on spark gap transmitters. After leaving the US Weather Bureau in 1902, he formed the National Electric Signalling Company with two Pittsburgh businessmen.

In December 1900, he achieved speech transmission by radio over a distance of one mile. He did so by enormously increasing the spark frequency, from eight per second in Marconi's apparatus to about ten thousand per second, thus approximating continuous wave generation. The next step was to build a high-current, very high frequency alternator that could generate a continuous radio wave. While Fessenden involved General Electric as early as 1900 and patented an early design in 1901, the first machine delivered in 1903 to the new company's Brant Rock, Massachusetts research station was not satisfactory. An improved version finally allowed successful tests of a radiotelephone. By 1904, the National Electric Signalling Company advertised radio telephone sets relying on the combination of a high speed alternator and quenched spark gap with a guaranteed range of 40 kilometres.

In 1907, a sufficient number of radio experimenters and hobbyists had acquired the necessary equipment to receive voice messages. New York experimenter Lee De Forest started broadcasts from the top of a hotel, and they were detected up to at least 100 km from their point of origin. Later that year, Fessenden tried broadcasting from his location on the Massachusetts coast, and his transmissions were received up to at least 350 km from their point of origin. A successful inventor, Fessenden was not enough of an entrepreneur to crack the head start of the Marconi system. His alternator-based system did not begin to make headway in the radio market until the early years of the First World War.

Instead, spark-based radios were first outclassed by a different device using an electric arc to convert direct into alternating current and produce oscillations of constant amplitude. Perfected by Danish engineer Valdemar Poulsen in 1903, the new invention quickly achieved greater broadcast power and impressive ranges, successfully transmitting speech and music in 1908 between Berlin and Denmark. In 1912, the Poulsen Wireless Corporation demonstrated the potential of the new technology by establishing a direct link between California and Hawaii. The next year, it contracted with Canada's Postmaster General to build stations in Ireland and New Brunswick and create a transatlantic radio link that would compete with the Marconi radio link between Ireland and Glace Bay, Nova Scotia.

During the First World War, radios using continuous waves dislodged the spark-based radios because they could achieve greater range with less power. Batteries were correspondingly smaller and aerials shorter which made the sets more portable and reduced the vulnerability of the antennae to enemy action. The far superior tuning capability of continuous wave transmission also reduced interference and allowed a greater concentration of radio stations. Official skepticism dissipated as radio signalling was tested against the traditional carrier pigeon and testers concluded that it required "less time than it took to get the bird in the air." After the war, the vacuum tube took over as the means to produce continuous wave transmissions. While the continuous wave emission won out as the superior choice, the inventions of Fessenden and Poulsen were eventually abandoned.

During the war, radio was mainly used at sea, but it also was used to connect with planes in the air once the bulky radio sets of the early years (the largest weighed up to two tonnes and the smallest might still weigh as much as an adult male) were replaced by sturdier and more compact devices. By 1916, radio began to be used in conjunction with telephone land lines to direct artillery fire either from the ground or the air. The Canadian Corps created a Wireless Section late in the year after earlier experiments. In 1918, the Canadian Corps used truck-borne radios to coordinate the army's advance into enemy territory during the war's final offensive. Whereas the British used radio only when telephone lines were unavailable, the Canadians used it at all times either as the principal or an auxiliary means of coordinating their military units.[2]

---

[2]Sharon A. Babaian, *Radio Communication in Canada: A Historical and Technological Survey*, Ottawa: National Museum of Science and Technology, 1992, pp. 9–13, 28–33, 76–77, 82–98.

After the war, the US government encouraged companies already involved in radio research to join in creating the Radio Corporation of America (RCA) in 1919. The immediate impetus was the frustration faced by the US Navy in dealing with the near-monopoly of the Marconi company over communications in and across the Atlantic, backed by the patents it held and the support of the British and Canadian governments. National security was invoked to push Bell, GE, and Westinghouse to pool their patents. The first two had already done much to improve the triode (a vacuum tube equipped with three electrodes) as a means of both radio reception and transmission, building on the breakthrough of Lee De Forest who had later joined Bell. While the US government mainly hoped to gain control of transoceanic wireless transmission, it created a juggernaut that would dominate the domestic radio market.

FROM FANS TO FARMERS

Radio created an early community of *fans*, as the amateur operators and early adopters were called. It flourished in the United States after crystal radios were shown to be a cheap and effective alternative to existing receivers. Patented as early as 1901, they were increasingly used by amateurs after 1906. They relied on a galena, silicon, or pyrite crystal to convert the oscillating radio signal into a direct current, along with a "cat's whisker detector" that involved the operator placing the tip of a conducting wire on the right spot of the crystal to maximise reception. Due to their low cost, they remained popular after the First World War.

In Canada, all radio operators, whether amateur, commercial, or governmental, required a license from the federal government. Licenses were often extremely specific as to power levels, frequencies, location, and type of use. Marine communication was the federal government's priority and radio was overseen by the Department of the Naval Service. In April 1912, the sinking of the *Titanic* demonstrated the importance of radio and an international conference held in London in June adopted a set of regulations that required even more stringent government oversight. Canada's Parliament passed a Radiotelegraph Act that was enacted in 1913, at a time when only 123 radio stations were licensed throughout Canada, of which 37 were coast stations responsible for shore-to-ship communication, 52 were ship stations, six were commercial or private stations, and 28 were amateur or experimental stations.

After the sinking of the *Titanic* and increasing complaints about radio interference, amateurs had been restricted to wavelengths shorter than 200 metres, a section of the radio spectrum considered to be of little use by the government and commercial operators. During World War I, North American amateurs were entirely barred from using their radios. After the war though, radio fans tackled a series of challenges and pushed their underpowered equipment past its expected limits by relaying messages from one station to the next or by making connections over vast distances by working at night. In one 1921 demonstration, thirty or more North American stations punched through a signal all the way to Great Britain. Other operators managed to connect with Africa, Asia, and even Australia. Within four years of the war's end, a convention of amateur radio operators attracted several hundred attendees from the United States and Canada.

The expertise required to use the early radios lent an added prestige to the messages some exchanged and to the broadcasts others succeeded in listening to. Many of these technically knowledgeable *fans* were part of the early audience for science fiction stories, especially since the founder of the first science fiction magazine had previously published a magazine for radio amateurs. Later, the nuclear bomb legitimized science fiction, whose authors could claim they had seen it coming. The American enthusiasm for nuclear bombs also echoed a long tradition of belief in superweapons going back to the nineteenth century and the transformation of inventors into heroes.

Radio sets boasted unprecedented advantages. Compared to the existing telephones (with their switchboards operated by humans) and telegraph offices, both reliant on a network of wires, the new wireless might require a greater capital cost (and time investment), but operating expenses were lower. Privacy was also greater, or perceived as greater while the number of hobbyists remained low. Radio operators could also communicate directly, point to point, without needing to go through offices or switchboard operators. It was even thought at first that there could be an unlimited number of senders and receivers.

In the United States, amateurs were numerous. During the 1910s, they began to improvise broadcasts for the benefit of anyone listening. Music, news, and monologues were transmitted from primitive stations set up in bedrooms or chicken coops. After the war, this was recognized by Westinghouse as a better business model. While a radio allowed two individuals to communicate like the telephone or telegraph, it could not guarantee privacy. The key was to turn this drawback into a selling point. In 1920, Westinghouse built a pioneering commercial broadcaster, KDKA, in Pittsburgh. A rooftop shack housed a hundred-watt transmitter. Other radio stations turned to commercial broadcasting, offering a medley of news, sports, religious, and musical programming. By 1923, such broadcasts from nearly 600 stations were heard by a million radio owners throughout the United States.[3]

In Canada, radio was progressively adopted by the same constituencies that had made for its success in the United States. As radio broadcasts offered more and more items of interest, either cultural or informative, radio was also adopted by farmers in the countryside, even though farms were often cut off from the electrical networks. However, the batteries used by the first radios could be recharged at the local service station or by farmers who owned a car or truck. It was only in the hillier or northernmost areas that radios proved less attractive. Hills blocked the signals broadcast from the city. Farther north, solar interference disrupted reception. After 1925, the availability of short-wave radio receivers, less affected by these specific problems, encouraged new users to try radio.

On the broadcasting side, Montreal was a radio pioneer in Canada. As early as 1919, an English-language station (XWA Montreal) was on the air. Renamed CFCF in 1920, it started regular broadcasts in 1922. In French, the Montreal daily *La Presse* launched CKAC in 1922; by 1929, the station's spread outside Montreal was confirmed by the establishment of a transmitting station in St. Hyacinthe, thought to have the most modern equipment in Canada.

In France, the first regular radio broadcasts from the Eiffel Tower in Paris started in December 1921. The first private radio broadcaster was created in August 1922.

In Ontario and in the West, Canadian households with the necessary means bought radios for home entertainment. Quebec families did not do so with the same enthusiasm. In 1930, Ontario farmers owned 3.75 times more radios than their Quebec counterparts. This may be due to some of the other uses of radio. In the Eastern Townships of Quebec, dairy farmers did not need to follow grain or cattle prices as closely as the wheat farmers and cattle ranchers of the West. Also, the early radio stations only broadcast in English. Even though classical music made up part of the programming, the language factor made them less interesting for francophones.

Radio was most strikingly a *wireless* technology. It became possible to communicate without any visible intermediary. It was the start of a dematerialization of the technological world, as the basis of new technologies (such as chemicals) was less and less visible or were "black-boxed," pushed under wraps so that only technicians were allowed to lift the lid off the inner workings of new machines.

---

[3] Susan J. Douglas, "Amateur Operators and American Broadcasting: Shaping the Future of Radio," in *Imagining Tomorrow: History, Technology, and the American Future.* Cambridge: MIT Press, 1986, pp. 35–57.

Other domestic entertainment technologies have often followed the same course as radio. Phonographs, television, stereo systems, videocassette players, and downloadable movies or television serials have made home life easier, eliminating the need for trips outside the home for purposes of entertainment, culture, or social mixing. They also grant individual users greater control over their entertainment, freeing them to listen to a favourite piece of music or watch a beloved old film without being bound by the scheduling of a concert hall, movie theatre, or television broadcast. As a result, individuals may determine the soundtrack of their own lives and this ability to choose artistic experiences at will no doubt favours greater identification with the works chosen.

At the same time, communication technologies also connect their audiences to a larger culture, so that consumption imperatives filter more rapidly to a greater number of people. What is more, the operation of these new technologies often demands a reliable supply of power, leading to an increased load on the power grid.

CONCLUSIONS

Mixed use technologies, such as the personal computer, have complex effects. As for useful domestic technologies (the washing machine, the dishwasher, the dryer, the vacuum cleaner, the iron and ironing board, etc.), they have often been sold on the grounds they would make life easier "for mother," but the actual effect has often been to allow mothers and wives to get more work done in the same amount of time, with no gain in leisure.

Pure entertainment and information technologies have changed the household from a place for sleeping, eating, getting dressed, and sometimes working into one that allows for cultural consumption and new forms of socializing. By the 1930s, families gathered around the radio to listen to cherished serials in the same way they might watch the Walt Disney movie of the week on a television in the 1970s or a downloaded episode of *Doctor Who* on a plasma screen in the 2010s. Phonographs, pick-up record players, transistor radios, high-fidelity stereo systems, and modern sound systems with ports for digital music have similarly allowed generations of youth to share music at home instead of going out.

Radio and television also extended the reach of politics, religion, and sports. Instead of needing to leave home to hear political speeches, attend mass, or take in a game, people could simply tune in to the news, a broadcast sermon, or on-the-air play-by-play. Intermittent involvement could turn into a full-time interest, to the possible exclusion of all others.

Did the small number of available radio stations and television channels foster the creation of a North American mass culture in the course of the twentieth century? There is no doubt that radio and television had become omnipresent by 1960. Television gained a solid foothold in the United States as early as 1949 when two percent of households already owned a set, but this grew to 64 percent within six years. In Canada, about 66 percent of Canadians were able to watch Canadian Broadcasting Corporation (CBC) television in 1955. By then, the Canadian television ownership rate (0.074 per capita) was just behind the British rate (0.082 per capita). By 1959, 90 percent of US homes owned a television set, a level matched by Canadian homes by 1967. Canadian television ownership continued to lag somewhat the pace set by the United States down to the end of the twentieth century (**Figure 1**).

International Television Statistics
(TV Receivers per Thousand in North America)

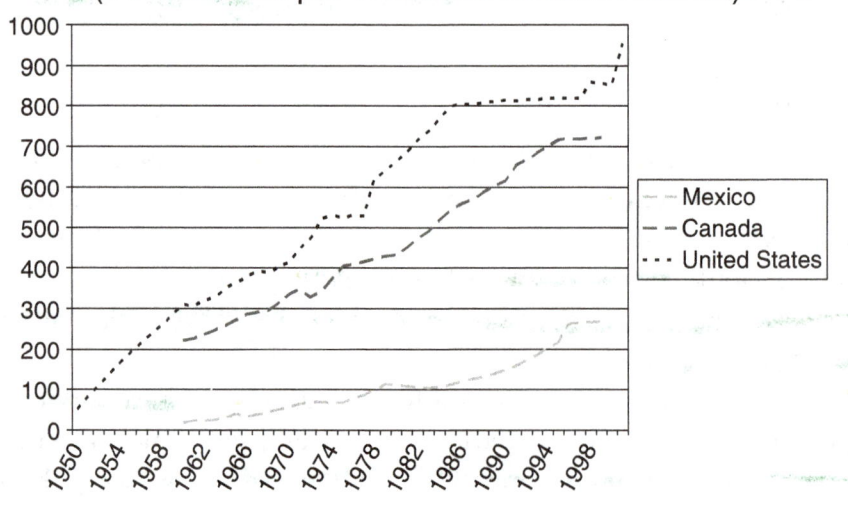

FIGURE 1 ▶ Television receivers (per thousand inhabitants) in North America between 1950 and 2001. *(Data source: CHAT database.)*

Broadcasters did want to appeal to the largest possible market and most offered family-oriented fare that could be enjoyed by people of various ages and backgrounds. Nevertheless, regional, linguistic, and cultural diversity was present. Both popular and classical ("serious") music was aired. Westerns, soap operas, science fiction serials, educational programming, and plays drawing on classic authors from Shakespeare onwards all won a share of air time down to the 1980s. While some have described the resulting culture as middlebrow, the range was vast and only excluded extreme intellectualism or violence and vulgarity. There was room for Elvis Presley as much as for Vladimir Nabokov. Artistic movements later considered to be too challenging to be appreciated properly were still part of the general conversation, as well as public intellectuals ranging from Lewis Mumford to Marshall McLuhan.

As the number of television channels multiplied afterwards, specialization increased and the mass audience of earlier times fragmented. Radio listeners opted for certain formats (news and talk, country music, soft rock, religion, jazz) just as the television audience divided according to network, political preference, and specialty channel.

The price to be paid for the expanding diversity of programming was the rise of commercials, sponsorships, and pledge campaigns. Outside of relatively rare government-funded cultural and educational programming, advertising, corporate branding, and appeals for public donations necessarily interrupt radio and television offerings. The influence of advertisers and sponsors has often been criticized, but it remains perhaps the last standard-setter outside of the courts.

CHAPTER 10

The Atomic Age

▶▶▶▶▶▶▶▶▶▶▶▶▶▶▶▶▶▶▶▶▶▶▶▶▶▶▶▶▶

PLANNING AND PREPARING THE FUTURE

The mass mechanization ushered in by the First World War quickly extended beyond transportation. Technologies that became widely available for the first time (private cars, aircraft, mechanical refrigerators for the home) combined with new media (newspaper supplements, "slick" and "pulp" magazines, radio, movies that were no longer silent, and even television by 1939) to foster a new sense of the possible. The ground was also laid for the acceptance of change and novelty through other means. In mid-century North America, both advertising, popular fiction, and forward-thinking visionaries proposed captivating conceptions of the future, many of them embodied in the showpieces of the 1939–1940 New York World's Fair. They appealed to a society increasingly enjoying the fruits of technology in daily life, from personal amenities and comforts (running water, electric lighting, phonographs) to collective infrastructure (paved roads and highways, hydroelectric dams, airports) at a time when technological progress was the only source of optimism in a world wracked by economic crisis and global war.

In North American society, the technological imagination of the early twentieth century was the product of a culture rooted in the 18th-century Enlightenment that began by celebrating the inventor as a benefactor of all humanity. Throughout the nineteenth century, the inventor in the United States took on a distinctive cast. Presented as self-taught, the heroic male inventor was celebrated as the ideal of the self-reliant, democratic US citizen, succeeding through hard work and native genius, without the assistance of government or the advantages of higher education. As successive inventions broke down old limits and turned fairytale wonders into realities, technological progress came to stand for all progress. Popular culture increasingly equated the inventor with a transcendent figure—Edison was the "Wizard of Menlo Park."

As it became clear that the present no longer resembled the past, the logical conclusion was that the future would not resemble the present, and that it would be arguably as much of an improvement over present-day reality as the present was an improvement over the bad old days. Even though the future lacks by definition any precise, objective reality, it turned into a setting for the hopes and dreams of the late nineteenth century. The twentieth century was talked of, by authors ranging from Victor Hugo to H. G. Wells, as an era of stupendous achievements. The year 2000 was imagined as a time of omnipresent aerial transportation, of learning by direct electrical stimulation of the brain, and of many other futuristic marvels.

While written works of science fiction go back to the 17th century, the future only appears sparingly in pre-1800 stories. The very appearance of fictional time machines in the nineteenth century seems to reveal a profound conviction that time could be mastered by mechanism. The future is still a timid presence in the imaginative works of Jules Verne, which were read avidly in North America by young readers. Like contemporary authors of US dime novels, Verne has inventors who are present-day characters. At most, their fantastic devices are displaced in time by a few years. Often, they are to be found in remote parts of the world. This echoed the practice of many popular science and technology magazines of presenting various speculative schemes and projects that might be undertaken within a few years, funds permitting. More than a few were turned into reality during the ensuing decades by entrepreneurs and inventors.

By the end of the nineteenth century, grander leaps into the future are found in literature and journalism alike: public screens used for advertisements or political propaganda, multilevel cities, bucolic suburbs linked by train to busy downtowns, skyscrapers filled not with offices but with housing, aircraft commutes, and even floating cities. Even these turned out to inspire real-life efforts as planners and organization men gained increasing sway.

The previous decades going back to the days of Fitch and Watt were taken as proof that an inventor's airy conceptions could be turned into tangible reality. While early builders and inventors might have proceeded with a minimum of planning and a maximum of onsite improvisation, engineering was taught in colleges and universities as the art of designing, calculating, and planning. Bridge collapses and train accidents reinforced the emphasis on preparing for the worst-case scenarios. Expected bridge, tunnel, and dam lifetimes extended into ever more remote futures. The city engineers in charge of aqueduct, sewer, and electrical systems were tasked not only with maintenance but also with allowing for future urban growth. By the early twentieth century, city planners were not only designing housing tracts or whole neighbourhoods, they wished to guide the evolution of entire towns and cities.

By the Second World War, a number of examples of large, planned communities were under construction or already existed in locations ranging from Vienna, Austria, and Lyons, France, to the suburbs of Montreal, Canada, and Washington, DC. In North America, many consumer items as well as larger artifacts reflected a new concern for not merely the appearance of objects but also the message their styling might convey as well as the way they might be used. The new look of technological objects by the mid-twentieth century heralded the success of a new breed of innovator—the industrial designer.

Design is often thought to influence only the appearance of objects, but for many everyday objects, form cannot be separated from function. A standalone bungalow, a townhouse, and an apartment in a high-rise building are all places to live in, but they offer different experiences and affect their surroundings in different ways. A highrise development can be served by public transit, but suburban split-levels are usually associated with personal cars, garages, and freeways. There are so many possible ways to build even the simplest of objects that designers are free to place more weight on some factors than others, and select some outcomes at the expense of others. In particular, industrial designers juggle with trade-offs directly affecting the performance of their creations.

The discipline of design started with nothing more than a preoccupation for esthetics. In England, Christopher Dresser (1834–1904) was a designer influenced by the reform of the British decorative arts, but his work grew to include work on the shape and appearance of manufactured objects. By 1889, his studio functioned in essence as an industrial design firm. The British example inspired German designers through Hermann Muthesius, who had been to England. Along with Peter Behrens, the first industrial designer employed by a large corporation (AEG), in 1907 Muthesius created the *Deutscher Werkbund*, an association dedicated to combining art, craft, and industry in order to create "artistic" industrial products that could be exported abroad. In Great Britain, the 1915 Design and Industries Association gathered all those involved with industrial design: designers, manufacturers, architects, advertisers, and merchants. By 1937, the United Kingdom had a national register of industrial designers.

A past member of the *Werkbund*, Walter Gropius launched the enormously influential Bauhaus movement in Germany after World War I, with the idea of applying design to everything: architecture, posters, furniture, paintings, sculpture, household implements, among others. If British design was all about lending practical devices a suitable and functional form, the Bauhaus tended to impose a general look on all objects.

DESIGN AND DEPRESSION

In the United States, industrial design emerged as a full-fledged profession after World War I, but it took over centre stage during the Depression when increased competition made it imperative for companies to differentiate the looks of their products.

The shock of the Depression in North America cannot be understated. In 1929 prices, real output fell from $103.1 billion in 1929 to $73.7 billion in 1933. Private construction (residential housing and business) did not recover until the 1950s. Over four million passenger cars had been produced in 1929, a level that was not equalled again until 1950. (Chaplin's 1936 movie *Modern Times* illustrates the effect of this crash on former assembly line workers.) Unemployment shot up from 3.2 percent in 1929, peaking at 25 percent in 1933, and it remained as high as 19 percent in 1938. In such a context where the market had effectively shrunk, any edge counted.

The investment in design was part of other investments by the largest corporations of the day (RCA, AT&T, IBM, Dupont, Alcoa, Ford, GM, Kodak, and General Electric). Relying on their own privately funded research and development, they turned out new or improved consumer products (the television, nationwide long-distance calling, nylon, Plexiglas, Lucite, cars with power steering and automatic transmissions) and in some cases returned to profitability before the beginning of World War II.

By 1944, sixteen professional designers, including Raymond Loewy and Henry Dreyfuss, were able to form a Society of Industrial Designers. Unlike many of their European colleagues employed by large companies, US designers were consultants for the most part. This may explain the cross-fertilization that is so evident in the work of designers such as Buckminster Fuller and Norman Bel Geddes. Indeed, Bel Geddes was a dominant figure of the interwar period. In 1932, he penned an important book, *Horizons* (Little, Brown, and Company), on the streamlining used for the era's new locomotives and thus encouraged the streamlining craze of the time—in ways that made a modicum of sense for cars, trains, and planes, but really did not for more mundane consumer products. Bel Geddes came up with a series of grandiose schemes (such as huge hydroplanes) that culminated in his model city for 1960, "Futurama," created for the World's Fair of 1939–1940. Other dreams for the future were embodied in the World's Fair "Democracity," a combination of metropolis and garden cities linked by highways.

The designers working on the largest scales, imagining cities, residential suburbs, urban lay-outs, and modern high-rises drew on the ideas put forward by visionary architects, artists, and assorted thinkers—such as the Italian Futurists—who had been reflecting on the possible uses of new materials and building techniques since the turn of the twentieth century.

European and North American cities seemed to be growing unstoppably, and the dreary tenements of New York were not an inspiring vision of what the future could hold. They were crowded (when they weren't overcrowded), noisy, often dirty, and lacked any kind of greenery.

The ideal of the "garden city," mixing houses, tree-lined streets, and gardens, had been presented at the end of the nineteenth century by Ebenezer Howard and a first attempt to turn the ideal into a reality was begun at Letchworth, in Great Britain. Both in Britain and in the United States, those who could afford it had long built their homes outside cities, on the model of the aristocracy's country estates. In the nineteenth century, trains and streetcars had allowed a first wave of homeowners to live in outlying villages and the countryside, while commuting to work downtown. They took advantage of cheaper land to build comfortable homes surrounded with sizable yards and gardens. Developers might invest in the creation of a whole neighbourhood for the well-heeled, but little thought was given to creating suburbs for the masses, built wholesale to reduce costs, until after the Second World War. The "garden city" advocated by the heirs of Howard was something new because it would offer the advantage of greener surroundings to more people than ever before.

The "garden city" was an attractive ideal, but it was far from perfectly realized by the new suburbs. As motor cars and buses made it possible for more employees to commute, many found housing in the subdivisions being developed by the 1920s. Suburban bungalows were a far cry from the genteel homes of nineteenth-century commuters, but neither were they tenements or flats in a treeless city block.

By the 1930s, the "garden city" was linked by planners (such as French architect Jacques Gréber) with the ideal of the "greenbelt," a ring of greenery (woods, fields) to be maintained around downtown cores in order to restrict development. Suburbs built within the greenbelt or beyond it would respect the environment and serve strictly residential purposes. One such suburb was built in Maryland on the outskirts of Washington, DC, and actually called Greenbelt, as part of research by the US Federal Housing Authority in the best way of building subdivisions designed for the automobile while providing low-income families with economical housing. The actual building of these model suburbs was also intended to provide much-needed work during the Great Depression, but it turned out to be undertaken first to provide housing for war-time employees in Washington.

The "garden city" model aimed to improve living conditions, but it failed to convince many people that it could accommodate the large numbers of people flocking to cities, pushed off the land by the rising efficiencies of industrial farming, and attracted by the jobs offered by new industries.

The solution put forward by some at the outset of the twentieth century was the "vertical city:" immense high-rises set in the middle of parks and gardens, thus combining green space and accommodation for large numbers of residents. At the time, high rises were still exceptional, a few reaching ten, twenty, or thirty floors in North American cities. Most were designed for banks, offices, and hotels. While French architects like Swiss-born Le Corbusier, Auguste Perret, and Tony Garnier envisioned such vertical cities as a practical solution, others liked them for their modern, aesthetic qualities. In Italy, Antonio Sant'Elia drew tall buildings whose strong, simple, and geometrical shapes echoed the abstract artworks of later artists such as Mondrian and Vasarely.

Industrial designers do not introduce new technological devices. They rarely offer new motors, new tools, new machines, or new sciences. However, they may be said to work entirely at the systems level. By determining what function a technology must serve, they make choices and either include or exclude

FIGURE 1 ▶ The Sterling Building (*c.* 1910) and the Kensington Building (1975) stand side by side, underlining the differences between old and modern schools of architecture. *(Picture by author in Winnipeg, Manitoba, 2008.)*

both specific devices and specific materials in and from a given product. In 1939 at the World Fair, they got the chance to imagine how the world of 1960 would look. In so doing, they actually influenced how it ended up looking and the post-war architectural style reliant on metal and glass was often startlingly different from early twentieth-century still beholden to Beaux-Arts ideals.

Many of their dreams were realized during the ensuing decades. The hopes for better living through technology even survived the shock of Hiroshima and atomic power was incorporated in North American dreams of a clean and shining Jetsons future. After World War II, the future visions of science fiction took on a darker cast. Once the Soviet Union detonated an atomic bomb of its own in 1949, the spectre of a war fought with nuclear weapons gave rise to stories set in a post-apocalyptic world often featuring societies which had reverted to an agrarian lifestyle. Indeed, even nuclear tests proved to be deadly. In 1953, fallout from nuclear tests in Nevada was detected as radioactive rain in Troy, New York. In 1954, a thermonuclear bomb test at Bikini Atoll in the Pacific scattered fallout that contaminated a Japanese fishing vessel downwind from the site, killing one crewman within days.

To mollify incipient public opposition throughout North America, extraordinary efforts to find a silver lining to the creation of the fission and fusion bombs received unprecedented support. Nuclear technology was developed to yield power plants using fission reactors, cancer-curing isotopes bred in nuclear facilities, and radioactive farms. Nuclear engineers promised to come through with atomic cars, planes, and rockets as well as fusion reactors producing energy that might one day be "too cheap to meter." Some influential scientists pushed the idea of using nuclear bombs as dynamite on steroids to dig tunnels or canals, to melt the Albertan tar sands or even to dissipate the Los Angeles smog.

In 1953, faced with a developing nuclear arms race and signs of concern at home, the United States attempted to put more weight on the peaceful possibilities of atomic power. They proposed a new deal which would (a) restrict the proliferation of nuclear bombs by cutting off nuclear weapon know-how to countries that did not yet possess the Bomb; (b) offer in exchange access to nuclear technology for peaceful purposes under the supervision of a UN agency that would verify that it wouldn't be used for military purposes; and (c) commit all countries, including those with nuclear arsenals, to working towards nuclear disarmament.

In a speech at the United Nations on December 8, 1953, President Dwight Eisenhower called for the creation of what became the IAEA (International Atomic Energy Agency) in 1957 and proclaimed that, "The more important responsibility of this atomic energy agency would be to devise methods whereby this fissionable material would be allocated to serve the peaceful pursuits of mankind. Experts would be mobilized to apply atomic energy to the needs of agriculture, medicine, and other peaceful activities. A special purpose would be to provide abundant electrical energy in the power-starved areas of the world."[1]

The Atoms for Peace program comprised a series of different governmental initiatives to pursue nuclear power. Atoms for Peace also inspired an outpouring of ideas for applications that would counterbalance the threatening image of nuclear weapons. Nuclear energy was to be applied to food irradiation, curing cancer, plant breeding, blight and pest control, among other initiatives; the more forbidding the menace of nuclear weapons, the more extraordinary the proposals to turn them into an asset. The ideas put forward ranked from the grandiose (using nuclear-powered desalting plants to irrigate the arid coastal lands of the world) to the unlikely (digging a sea-level Panama Canal with bombs).

Food irradiation to destroy pathogens and prolong shelf-life should not be confused with the use of radioactivity to induce useful mutations. The latter idea was not new at the time of Atoms for Peace. By 1925, Lewis J. Stadler (1896–1954) of the University of Missouri was subjecting corn tassels to X-rays and observing genetic effects. Later work with ultraviolet exposures led to the experimental use of radioactive isotopes producing gamma rays and benefited from US government funding as part of Atoms for Peace, with the IAEA then starting in 1964 to promote radiation breeding worldwide. The resulting mutant varieties include up to 75 percent of the red grapefruit grown in Texas, disease-resistant cocoa, premium barley used in Europe for beer and fine whiskeys, wheat used for bread and pasta, and the semi-dwarf Calrose 76 rice variety grown in California. Over the years, useful varieties of beans, oats, pears, peas, cotton, peppermint, sunflowers, peanuts, sesame, bananas, cassava, and sorghum have also been created by radiation breeding. They were characterized by better yields, taste, appearance, size, resistance to disease or pests, or adaptations to different climates or soils.

Along with nuclear reactors, radiation breeding may be one of the most durable legacies of the adaptation of nuclear technology to peaceful use. Other ideas (nuclear-powered planes or cars, earth-moving with nuclear bombs) have fallen by the wayside. Even today, though, arguments are still made for peaceful or world-saving uses of nuclear bombs, as NASA did in a March 2007 report, "Near-Earth Object Survey and Deflection Analysis of Alternatives," proposing to use them to deflect asteroids threatening to hit the Earth.

---

[1]Eisenhower, Dwight D., "Atoms for Peace Speech." IAEA.org http://www.iaea.org/About/atoms forpeace_speech.html (accessed January 10, 2014).

Yet, it became increasingly clear by the 1960s that radioactivity was dangerous. Before World War II, a short-lived fad for watches with luminescent dials led to the use of radium in some cases and the workers painting the dials, often cleaning the delicate brushes with their fingers or lips, later came down with various cancers. And the sale of radioactive water as a health drink lead to widely publicized premature deaths. The deaths from irradiation at Hiroshima and Nagasaki, as well as the deaths caused by nuclear fall-out from bomb tests, fixed those dangers in the public mind to the lasting detriment of nuclear technology.

ORGANIZING RESEARCH

The grand hopes raised in connection with nuclear power were grounded in the obvious accomplishments that resulted from the growing exploitation of scientific results by inventors, engineers, and technicians. The great inventors of the nineteenth century had often struck partnerships with scientists, such as that of Morse with Vail. Thomas Alva Edison had employed scientists like Upton as part of a formal research establishment.

However, many other nineteenth-century inventors, from Stephenson down to the Wright brothers, had little or no formal education. They were often experienced tinkerers who drew on new technological resources to come up with novel designs. Books were published in the nineteenth-century which included long lists of simple machines and "mechanical movements." These were the building blocks of many humbler improvements and mechanical designs.

The new faculties of science and engineering in US universities began to respond to the needs of industry around the twentieth century. At first, they had responded to labour needs by turning out trained engineers and graduates with a basic grounding in science, mathematics, and practical skills who might find work of a technical nature. The professors within those universities also came to the help of local industry facing practical problems by undertaking focused research projects. In return, businesses would provide financial support. In effect, universities substituted for commercial research when companies could not afford to have their own research laboratories, or needed something more. Before World War II, however, this type of research was still conducted on a case-by-case basis and many professors pursued their own problems.

However, it was not so easy to keep track of the new discoveries made by scientists and to think of their potential applications. Many of these had been quietly accumulating obscure papers for scientific journals, and dusty notebooks in laboratories. The Second World War was pivotal—it spurred both new research (jet propulsion, rocket propulsion, the nuclear bomb) and systematic efforts to collect, examine, and apply older work (radar, antibiotics, new chemical insecticides, analog and electronic digital computers). Completely new research establishments were built up. Teams of scientists and engineers collaborated in coordinated fashion. More than ever before, university professors were called upon to share their time between teaching tasks and useful research. All of them were directed to work closely with industry to ensure that what was found could be produced and manufactured in large quantities.

In 1940, even before the United States entered World War II, Vannevar Bush convinced President Franklin Roosevelt to create the National Defense Research Committee (NDRC), chaired by Bush, to conduct research but not development work on weapons systems. When this proved insufficient, Bush created and headed an even larger organization, the Office of Scientific Research and Development (OSRD), which subsumed the NDRC. Originally, Bush had envisioned a decentralized system in which academic and industrial scientists remained in their home laboratories. As the war effort expanded, it became necessary to create large central laboratories with the help of universities, such as the Radio Research Laboratory at Harvard with 600 people or the Radiation Laboratory at MIT, with 4,000 employees.

The physics research laboratory set up at Los Alamos (New Mexico) was even larger, a small city that was part of the Manhattan District Project along with plutonium-generating reactors in Hanford (Washington) and a gaseous-diffusion facility at Oak Ridge (Tennessee). At Los Alamos, scientists and engineers were gathered to design and build nuclear bombs using the materials produced in Hanford (plutonium) and Oak Ridge (uranium). Supplies also came from Canadian locations, such as Trail (heavy water) and Port Radium (fissile ores), while Canada hosted its own research laboratories, mostly in Montreal and in Chalk River.

Set up in 1942–1943, the Manhattan District Project was sufficiently autonomous that atomic research ceased being a concern of the OSRD, which was free to focus on conventional research. This work led to improvements in radar, sonar, proximity fuses, and the electronic computer, among others.

The institutional arrangements (agencies, independent institutes, funding bodies) set up to carry out these tasks often remained in place after the war. In 1945, in *Science—The Endless Frontier* (United States Government Printing Office), Vannevar Bush pushed for the creation of a permanent government body (a National Research Foundation) able to fund and manage research in the national interest. His argument articulated what is sometimes called the "linear model" of innovation, where research flows into development, development leads to production, and production then allows the marketing of the resulting product. Therefore, in order for the United States to enjoy a continuous stream of new products and an expanding economy, research, both basic and applied, needed to be funded.

Though Vannevar Bush did not get his wish right away, medical research, especially at universities, quickly obtained funding from the government, mainly through the National Institutes of Health. Other research programs received help from the Office of Naval Research (ONR) created in 1946. By 1948, the ONR was funding 40 percent of all basic research in the United States, and its presence was particularly pronounced in the physical sciences, where nearly half of doctoral students in 1950 enjoyed its support. In the computing field, ONR funds supported some important early projects, such as Project Whirlwind (based at MIT), the Hurricane machine at Raytheon, and Harvard's Mark III.

In the United States, therefore, the military came to oversee (and control) a significant fraction of directed research. In addition, military procurement contracts could prove extremely profitable for private companies bidding for tenders, and these might also fund R&D accordingly (whether in-house or in partnership with university-based research).

One of the main organizers of this alliance, Vannevar Bush was an academic, engineer, and entrepreneur who saw little that was wrong with such relationships. Yet, by 1961, when former military man Dwight D. Eisenhower stepped down as president, Eisenhower sounded a note of worry about the "military-industrial complex" in his farewell address. The scale and profitability of military industries bought them unheard-of influence. At the very least, they would exert that influence to defend their reasons for existing at all, by supporting more alarming assessments of enemy threats, for instance. Others might also intervene to preserve the complex because it was beneficial to them. (In other words, Eisenhower feared that military industries were in a position to lobby effectively for expensive, high-tech weaponry and a permanently high level of preparedness for war.)

The military itself had also become a major political player in a way that it had never been before, especially in the United States. During the First World War, the German enemy had been denounced for subordinating science to militarism (**Box 1**). Others criticized the military-industrial-academic "iron triangle" for its consumption of resources better used elsewhere, its bending of research to its own needs, its creation of supportive political constituencies, and its enrolling of academic legitimacy to endorse its ends. Military contracts bought some of the professors' time, attention to problems selected for their military relevance, control of the publication of

> **BOX 1 ▶ Document: Prussian Militarism**
>
> *"But Prussia not merely was not a democracy, Prussia was not a state; Prussia was an army. It had its great institutions, it had its great universities, it had developed its science. All these were subordinate to the one predominant purpose of an all-conquering army to enslave the world. The army was the spear point of Prussia—the rest was the gilded haft."*
>
> During the First World War, British Prime Minister Lloyd George condemned Germany's subordination of science to the needs of military supremacy.
>
> (*Source:* Morning Chronicle, *Halifax, 13 April 1917, p. 2.*)

research results, and ownership of any new product yielded by such work. Obvious consequences include the relative neglect of problems with no military relevance, the smaller share of the faculty's attention devoted to students, the work of graduate students on projects predetermined by funding, and the worrisome fact that some worthwhile results might remain secret (classified) for years. In short, universities delivered research, products (inventions), and trained personnel (students who graduate as engineers or scientists).

The United States government also encouraged contacts between research universities and industry, leading to a constant flow back and forth between the laboratories of Stanford and MIT, and the factories of General Electric and Boeing. The federal contracts signed with universities varied, but in most cases the universities provided laboratory space, management, and some scientific personnel for large, multi-disciplinary efforts.

The rise of organized research did not only involve the military. The National Science Foundation was finally established in 1950 to support basic research in universities. The monetary amounts that flowed to support research were disconcerting to some and others openly doubted that it fostered the resourcefulness that is the mark of the truly ingenious mind (**Box 2**). By 1960, federal funding of academic research accounted for over 60 percent of the total funds devoted to university research. In 2010, the National Science Foundation was able to point to its part in helping develop such innovations as magnetic resonance imaging, fibre optics, and supercomputers.

Though the National Science Foundation was dedicated to the support of basic research which was expected to yield practical benefits, it accounted for less than 20 percent of federal support for university research after World War II. Another third came from the Department of Defense and two allied agencies, NASA and the

> **BOX 2 ▶ Document: A Sceptic Speaks Out**
>
> *"Without any doubt, we possess the world's most highly developed technique of combining the efforts of large numbers of scientists and large quantities of money toward the realization of a single project. This should not lead us to any undue complacency concerning our scientific position, for it is equally clear that we are bringing up a generation of young men who cannot think of any scientific project except in terms of large numbers of men and large quantities of money. The skill by which the French and English do great amounts of work with apparatus which an American high-school teacher would scorn as a casual stick-and-string job, is not to be found among any but a vanishingly small minority of our young men. The present vogue of the big laboratory is a new thing in science. There are those of us who wish to think that it may never last to be an old thing, for when the scientific ideas of this generation are exhausted, or at least reveal vastly diminishing returns on their intellectual investment, I do not foresee that the next generation will be able to furnish the colossal ideas on which colossal projects naturally rest."*
>
> (Source: Norbert Wiener, The Human Use of Human Beings: Cybernetics and Society, 1954, p. 126.)

Department of Energy (earlier known as the Atomic Energy Commission). Most of the remainder came from the National Institutes of Health.

In the field of leading-edge ("bleeding-edge") applied research, the United States set up ARPA (Advanced Research Projects Agency) in 1958 after Sputnik. Though it was always meant to support research for military purposes, first in space and then in most fields except space, this was made explicit in 1972 when it became DARPA (Defense Advanced Research Projects Agency).

By then, the "iron triangle" of the military-industrial-university complex was an established subset of government-funded and -organized research. The military funding of industrial activity and academic investigation created political constituencies favourable to the continuance of projects and programs with military ends. At the same time, the military ended up furthering industrial and academic ends (more profit, more fully-funded research) while industry and universities furthered military ends (developing technologies of military use, through applied research in industry and more basic research in universities). This led to questions of the independence of the researchers. This is not only an issue for social scientists. For example, professional ethics of the sort that allow engineers to stand up and state that a bridge design is defective are predicated on the independence of professionals (*i.e.*, doctors, engineers, climate scientists, and the like). If that independence is compromised, can they still be considered to be genuine professionals?

The rise in importance of government grants to fund basic research, military research, and medical research changed research in universities after World War II.

Industry researchers were left to specialize in work that improved existing products and processes, while also coming up with the next generation of products and processes. University researchers, on the other hand, specialized in the investigation of phenomena in order to achieve better understanding of their most basic nature. A characteristic of such basic research is that any publication of results allows others to benefit. Universities were also funded to tackle more practical problems associated with health and defense, but it should be noted that this left relatively few academic researchers to work with the problems of purely commercial businesses.

Consider that, in the United States as late as 1992, 69 percent of aerospace engineers, 34 percent of physicists, 32 percent of electrical and electronic engineers, half of all aircraft assemblers, and 20 percent of machinists were funded directly or indirectly by the US Defense Department. If scientists, engineers, and technicians tasked with basic and medical research were added to these totals, not much was left for the development of commercial products. Indeed, US spending on non-military research and development was lower (as a percentage of GNP) than in Japan and Germany throughout the 1970s.

And it must be emphasized that money spent on military research does not necessarily translate into commercial products, even as remote spin-offs. In Canada, government funding of Avro to build military jets (including the Arrow) did not allow it to build a jet passenger plane because Avro did not enjoy access to the markets that would have justified production. In the United States, plane-makers benefited from the combination of government funding and of access to a large potential market. Military funding is not a necessity—Japan has developed a large and sophisticated manufacturing sector without large amounts of spending on military research and development.

Since the end of the Cold War around 1990, government funding has not kept pace with the private funding of research and development.

As a result, the academic research establishment has struggled. Funding growth no longer kept up with the growth of research costs, while federal and state governments pressured universities to produce more research with commercial pay-offs (going back to the Bayh-Dole Act of 1980). Therefore, universities have turned back to industries and paid more attention to industrial needs. Funding from the private sector has increased, though it remains a relatively small share of the overall outside support.

The scale of government support for research and development in the United States is unique, but most other industrialized countries have taken steps during the

United States: R&D Funding

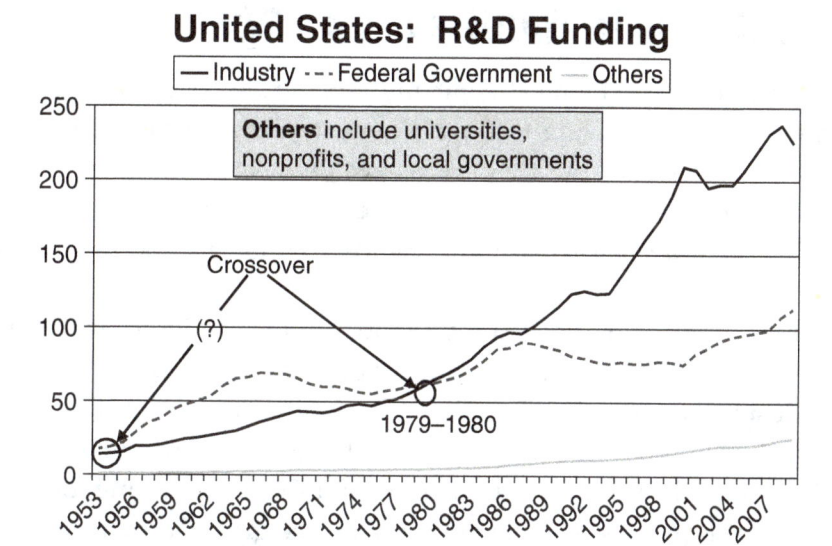

FIGURE 2 ▶ The relative importance of funding sources for research and development in the United States has shifted at least a couple of times since 1953. The amounts are given in billions of constant 2005 dollars, between 1953 and 2009. *(Data source:* Science and Engineering Indicators, *2012.)*

last half-century to organize research. While public funding has been a bounty, it has meant more paperwork and bureaucracy for researchers, and insistent requests for more accountability. Many scientists and engineers of the nineteenth century were only accountable to their families, their direct employers, or their investors for the use of their time and money. Modern investigators must justify their work repeatedly to juries of their peers and to funding authorities. Though modern researchers have much greater means at their disposal, they may not have greater freedom.

In the twenty-first century, the increased privatization of research, the global internet, and opportunities abroad have led a number of North American companies and multinationals to take advantage of the skilled workforce in countries like China. While some corporate laboratories have been shut down in North America, research and development centers in China, for instance, have generated a growing number of patents (over 2,000 in 2010). While some were claimed by Chinese researchers and assigned to their employers, others were granted to teams based partly in China and partly elsewhere. Globalization has made it possible to implement an international division of labour that combines engineers and scientists in emerging economies with the organizational and technological know-how of multinational companies.

FROM COAL TAR TO MODERN PLASTICS

In the 1930s, the famous chemical company DuPont de Nemours used the slogan "Better Things for Better Living through Chemistry." Chemicals have become fearsome or at least worrisome, but they were once the wave of the future. By the time the DuPont de Nemours slogan was coined, chemists and chemical engineers had become the white-coated incarnation of science, technology, and progress all rolled into one.

Whether it is distrust or just healthy skepticism that underlies modern reactions to chemistry, it remains one of the lynchpins of modern civilization. In Europe, the chemical industries account for 1.7 million jobs, while another 3 million people work for subcontractors or other jobs dependent on chemical manufacturing.

It all had started humbly enough back in 1856 when young British chemist William Henry Perkin (1838–1907), working with the great German chemist August Wilhelm von Hoffman, discovered that a chemical synthesized from coal residues was able to impart to pieces of clothing a beautiful soft shade of purple, soon called mauve in France. It became so popular in the following years it was known to some as the Mauve Decade.

This dye was known as aniline. Other artificial dyes were soon discovered (synthetic indigo, alizarine), but only some were able to compete with natural products given the primitive production methods of the time. Nevertheless, chemical firms based in Germany and Switzerland developed many dyestuffs and other organic compounds from coal tar, nurturing a profitable industry by the end of the nineteenth century.

The progress of organic chemistry led to the determination of the structure of more and more compounds: chlorophyll, steroids, and terpenes, among others. By the turn of the twentieth century, the attention of chemists focused more and more on the synthesis of drugs, both old and new. Aspirin relied on the active ingredient (ASA) of an old remedy, willow bark. While synthetic morphine relieved pain, chemotherapy was pioneered by such scientists as German bacteriologist Paul Ehrlich (1854–1915) who synthesized *arsphenamine* for use against syphilis. Before the discovery and application of antibiotics, German chemist Gerhard Domagk determined in 1932 that *sulfanilamide* and certain related compounds (known at the time as "sulfa drugs") could be used to fight a number of infectious diseases.

Chemistry also led to better explosives. As far back as 1845, a lucky accident led chemist Christian Friedrich Schönbein (1799–1868) to discover nitrocellulose, an efficient and relatively smokeless explosive. Named "guncotton," it was eventually made a part of cordite. Another component of cordite was *nitroglycerine*, discovered in 1847 by Italian chemist Ascanio Sobrero. Though powerful, it was too sensitive for safe use by itself. In 1866, Alfred B. Nobel (1833–1896) found an absorbent earth (*kieselguhr*); combined with nitroglycerine, it yielded essentially what is now known as dynamite, much safer to handle on worksites though still tremendously powerful.

While fully nitrated cellulose was an explosive, partially nitrated cellulose (*pyroxylin*) had other uses. When US inventor John Wesley Hyatt came up with a substitute for ivory (to be used in the manufacture of billiard balls) in 1866, he combined dissolved pyroxylin with camphor to produce *celluloid*, the first synthetic plastic. Celluloid was later applied in 1884 by George Eastman, the founder of Kodak, to the fabrication of thin films for photography. Also in 1884, French chemist Louis Bernigaud produced fibers from pyroxylin that could be woven into a new synthetic material that was called *rayon* (or *rayonne* in French, from the verb *rayonner*, "to radiate," because he found the material surprisingly bright and reflective).

The science of artificial materials took a giant step with chemist Leo Hendrik Baekeland who produced a polymer for which he could not find a solvent. When he noted that it could also be moulded into a material that was hard, water-resistant, solvent-resistant, and a non-conductor of electricity, he realized that he had a useful product. Known as *Bakelite*, it soon became in its black and shiny form, an iconic material of the early twentieth century.

The success of these early synthetics encouraged a century-old company, Du Pont de Nemours, to diversify. Founded in 1802 as a gunpowder manufacturer, it had come to control almost all of the US market by the end of the nineteenth century. To escape possible sales downturns and antitrust legal suits, it established an industrial research laboratory in 1903, purchased foreign patents, and sought to develop new products. In 1924, it acquired the US rights to a French invention, cellophane, and turned out a moisture-proof variety that enjoyed increasing popularity as a wrap used by commercial facilities. Other synthetic polymers, such as neoprene, an important synthetic rubber first produced in 1932, and nylon, followed. The increasing quantity and variety of these artificial substances have completely altered the look and feel of our artificial environments. Rock, wood, ivory, bone, and natural textiles can all be replaced with artificial substitutes, and nowadays they often are.

Yet, in the end, the most important result of chemical science in the twentieth century may have been the discovery of the Haber-Bosch process for the easy, inorganic synthesis of ammonia, a key ingredient of fertilizers. Developed by Fritz Haber and Karl Bosch of Germany before World War I, the process turned out ammonia. While it was of military importance during the First World War because ammonia can be turned into nitrates and then into explosives, easy access to fertilizers has led to a multiplication of agricultural yields. In the world's wealthier countries, agricultural yields have been enhanced by fertilizers to the point where the only way to burst through the "yield ceiling" involves tinkering with crop genetics and improving management techniques. In other parts of the world (Africa, Central America, and eastern Europe), a sizable "yield gap" separates the current levels of food production from the levels that could be achieved using better practices. Much of the gap could be filled by using improved seeds, more effective use of fertilizers, smarter irrigation methods, reduced tillage (which spares the topsoil), and various organic ways of replenishing the soil's nutrient content.

By relying on the Haber-Bosch process, artificial nitrates, including ammonium nitrate (NH_4NO_3), have replaced such natural sources as the Chilean nitrates ($NaNO_3$) that were mined and exported worldwide through the end of the nineteenth century and the beginning of the twentieth.

Nitrogen is one of the basic building blocks of life. While it is abundant in the atmosphere, its molecular form (N_2) is relatively inert, chemically speaking. For nitrogen to become part of a more reactive compound such as nitrate or ammonium (better suited to life's biochemical needs), it must be "fixed." In nature, this conversion is done either by bacteria associated with plants or the soil, or by lightning. (A thunderbolt will dissociate a nitrogen molecule, allowing one nitrogen atom to react with the free oxygen formed at the same time and produce nitric oxide. Nitric oxide gives rise to nitrogen dioxide, which combines with water to form dilute nitric acid. Falling to the earth as rain, the acid reacts with minerals in the soil to form nitrates then taken up by life forms.)

However, starting with Haber, scientists have found more and more ways to "fix" nitrogen artificially. (The original Haber-Bosch process used methane as a feedstock, while the current version relies on petroleum.) This was a boon for the production of both munitions (high explosives) and fertilizers. The large-scale munitions plant set up during World War II in the United States led to a long-lasting decline in the real price of fertilizer after the war, as much had been learned about maximizing production of the raw material for both. Yet, as fertilizers became cheaper than ever, there were consequences downstream.

Since many plant species are adapted to and function best in soils and waters containing low levels of available nitrogen, not all nitrates provided by fertilizers are taken up and the excess is often washed into waterways. Excess nitrates in the soil may be converted with the assistance of bacteria into the greenhouse gas nitrous oxide (N$_2$O).

In rivers, lakes, and seas, these nitrates often end up fertilizing marine plants and blue-green algae (cyanobacteria), resulting in summertime growth explosions that produce *blooms*. At very high levels in drinking water, nitrates may also threaten human health by blocking the blood's ability to carry oxygen. Exposure to nitrates in drinking water has also been linked to thyroid cancer, respiratory tract infections, and birth defects. One toxic by-product of cyanobacteria known as beta-methylamino-L-alanin (BMA), has been fingered as one possible contributor to neurological disorders such as Alzheimer's and amyotrophic lateral sclerosis.

The over enrichment of the sea or of any aquatic environment by nutrients, mainly nitrogen and phosphorus, is known as *eutrophication*. Sources of these nutrients include fertilizers and agricultural run-off incorporating animal excrement, as well as industrial and urban waste discharges accounting for much of the phosphorus—in the form of polyphosphate detergents, at one point. Ideally, the amounts of both nitrogen and phosphorus thus delivered should be reduced in order to reduce eutrophication.

In the ocean, fertilizer-driven blooms block the light required by bottom-dwelling photosynthesizers, envelop coral reefs, produce large quantities of toxins, and then decompose, falling to the bottom. They also perturb the food chain, especially if top predator species are being overfished, opening it to invasive species.

The decay processes of the falling organic matter of a bloom consume oxygen dissolved in the water as bacteria feast on the remains and multiply, sucking vital oxygen from the surrounding seawater. When oxygen levels fall below a certain point, fish and other marine life (such as shrimp) will suffocate and so blooms are associated with massive fish kills in addition to biochemical pollution. Therefore, blooms often precede the formation of *dead zones*, devoid of most species except jellyfish and other highly-tolerant invaders, as in the Gulf of Mexico, the Baltic Sea, or the Black Sea. In 2007 and 2008, the extent of the Gulf of Mexico dead zone topped 20,000 square kilometres—the increase of this dead zone explains in large part the steady decline in the landings of brown shrimp by Louisiana shrimpers since 1990. In China, which registers some of the world's greatest overuse of synthetic fertilizers, massive algae blooms in places like the city of Qingdao and Lake Taihu are becoming yearly occurrences.

By some counts, nitrogen contamination of lakes, rivers, and bays is already the single greatest source of water pollution in the world, and it is expected to triple over the next 50 years.

CONCLUSION

The gradual nature of increasing chemical loads in rivers, lakes, and seas has attracted fluctuating levels of attention since World War II. Concern rose to a peak in the 1960s as the United States passed the Water Quality Act in 1965. Through the Western world, obvious sources of mainly industrial pollution were circumscribed, reduced, or eliminated during the following decades. Less obvious sources, such as agricultural run-off, were ignored to some extent. The Walkerton, Ontario crisis in 2000 where farm run-off contaminated local drinking water, killing seven people and sickening 2,500 others, was primarily understood as a failure of water monitoring, not as a pollution problem.

Less easy to overlook was the shift to an automobile-centered society as cities sprawled and the air grew hazy with smog. Parkways, freeways, and then divided highways facilitated movement within cities, between cities, and also between city centres and suburbs. Yet, perhaps the most significant consequence of fossil fuel burning by the transportation sector in North America long went unnoticed. The carbon dioxide produced by internal combustion engines added to the increasing overhang of greenhouse gases in the atmosphere, almost certainly driving global warming.

If technology raised unsustainable expectations by the second half of the twentieth century, a sense of disappointment loomed as early as the First World War in many of the world's most developed countries outside the United States. The 1960s proved to be a pivotal decade during hope clashed with mistrust. On the one hand, the first men on the Moon in 1969 realized an age-old dream articulated in early science fiction and they lent credence to the century's futuristic visions. On the other hand, environmental scandals and accidents ranging from radioactive fallout and mercury poisoning in Japan, to oil spills at sea sharpened a new generation's distrust of authority. In 1962, Rachel Carson's *Silent Spring* crystallized these doubts and created in large part the modern environmental consciousness.

CHAPTER 11

Remote Control: The Information Revolution

▶▶▶▶▶▶▶▶▶▶▶▶▶▶▶▶▶▶▶▶▶▶▶▶▶▶▶▶▶▶▶

Modern electronic computers were conceived during the fever years of World War II. The first expensive computers inspired as many hopes as fears due to their control by governments and large corporations at a time when some thinkers were growing afraid of the power of new technologies. The invention of the Internet was very much a Cold War story, part and parcel of the rise of the "military-industrial-university complex" in the wake of nuclear weapons research, though it has only been adopted by the wider public within the last couple of decades. As a result of the ongoing miniaturization of computing power and internet access, the effects of the information revolution are still being measured. Instead of transforming the broader environment, it is affecting the structure of our daily lives.

THE ORIGINS OF COMPUTING

The first computers were humans, long before there were electronic or even mechanical machines. The *computus* was the calculation by European monks of the date for Easter, according to a fairly complex algorithm. The people who performed such intricate calculations, usually calendrical or astronomical, became known as computers.

Up to the 18th century, computationally challenging problems often arose from astronomy, whether they concerned dating, time-keeping, or navigation. Such a problem could either be complex (requiring numerous operations to obtain a single result) or it could be massive (requiring numerous repetitions of a few operations to generate a large number of results). In either case, a single individual was easily overwhelmed. The calculation of a new date for the return of Halley's Comet required nearly 18 months of work by two men and a woman. The reduction of census data or of surveying data was mathematically simpler, but the sheer amount of data equally demanded a huge effort.

By the end of the 18th century, it became commonplace for skilled mathematicians to break down a problem into a series of simpler steps, ideally limited to just the four ordinary operations of arithmetic (addition, subtraction, multiplication, and division). The problems would be entrusted to computers or calculators, equipped with instructions, paper and ink, logarithmic and trigonometric tables, and even mechanical adding machines during the early decades of the twentieth century. These human computers were often poorly paid and came from varied backgrounds (ex-wigmakers' apprentices in Revolutionary France, street urchins in Victorian England, convicts in the Netherlands); by the turn of the twentieth century, many were women for reasons similar to their predominance as telephone operators.

There were definite limits to the performance of human computers. Using a mechanical adding machine, an experienced calculator might multiply two ten-digit numbers in 10 or 12 seconds, but time was also required to write and copy results, or consult tables. Therefore, a single operator was only expected to perform 400 such operations in a single day, for an average elapsed time of 72 seconds. The very earliest electronic computers could multiply two 10-digit numbers in about 0.003 seconds; a twenty-thousand fold improvement. Thus, even though the most primitive electronic computers broke down fairly often, the work they could do between breakdowns was far greater than what human computers had achieved.

About 50 years ago, when electronic computers were still novelties, the University of Toronto designated Calvin "Kelly" Gotlieb as its "chief computer" when it made him the head of the new department that was to be responsible for building, developing, and operating electronic computers.

FROM MECHANICAL TO ELECTRONIC COMPUTERS: CALCULATORS

Not counting the abacus and similar counting aids, or the slide rules made possible by the development of logarithms by John Napier in 1614, the first calculating machines were built in the 17th century. One of them was designed by French mathematician Blaise Pascal (1623–1662). While his machine could add and subtract, the machine designed by G. W. Leibniz (1646–1716) could also multiply and divide. Leibniz believed in the importance of mechanizing calculation; in 1674, he described a machine that could solve algebraic equations.

Leibniz also pioneered the modern notation used for calculus and developed the study of series, two advances that proved crucial. With the rules in hand for integration and differentiation, many mathematical operations became reducible to simpler ones.

Inventors continued to improve simple calculating machines throughout the eighteenth and nineteenth centuries. For instance, using the design pioneered by Leibniz, the French mechanic Charles X. Thomas built an *arithmometer* for the 1855 World Fair that was capable of multiplying two 15-digit numbers, the culmination of a life's work on calculating machines stretching back to his first attempt in 1820 (a machine that could only yield products of six digits or less). One of the immediate predecessors of the 1855 machine could multiply two 8-digit numbers together in 18 seconds, divide a 15-digit number by an 8-digit one in 24 seconds, and extract the square root of a 15-digit number in about 75 seconds.

The *arithmometer* gave rise to commercially useful calculators, if only by showing the way. In Europe, the Thomas machines sold very well in France, while the machines built by imitators in other countries also did well.

In the United States, during the late nineteenth century, several inventors raced to patent various improvements on calculating machines. The ancestor of the Burroughs Adding Machine Company, which flourished during the first half of the twentieth century and later got into computers, was known until 1905 as the American Arithmometer Company, founded by William S. Burroughs around 1886. (By merging with Sperry in 1986, Burroughs became part of Unisys.)

Working with a different mechanical paradigm, engineer Herman Hollerith (1860–1929) invented a census tabulator in 1884. By then, the hand tallying of the 1880 census of the United States had been going on for years (it would not be finished until 1889 or so), and it was feared that the results of the 1890 census might not be known until the following census in 1900. The 1880 headcount alone had taken a few months and processing the rest of the data to generate useful statistics was painfully slow and error-prone when done manually by clerks.

Hollerith won a government competition with a machine that dropped pins through holes in punched cards, touching individual cups of mercury to complete electrical circuits that spun the counting dials. The government ordered 56 census tabulators. In the end, these rented machines processed 62 million cards at a rate of 1,000 cards an hour per machine. The headcount was finished in 6 weeks.

Interestingly, processing all of the data took seven years (as opposed to nine for the previous, hand-tallied census) and cost $11.5 million (as opposed to $5.8 million). This was $5 million below the amount forecasted, but the rather modest gain in processing time appears to reflect the fact that the census staff took advantage of the new technology to conduct a more detailed and thorough analysis of the raw data. Crowding the technological envelope is nothing new.

Hollerith's Tabulating Machine Company merged with the International Time Recording Company, Bundy Manufacturing, and Computing Scale of America in 1911. The four companies formed the Computing-Tabulating-Recording Company. In 1924, the company changed its name to become the International Business Machines Corporation—IBM.

The census tabulator designed by Hollerith was an extraordinary device for sorting through vast quantities of cards, but, mathematically-speaking, it did little except add.

MECHANICAL COMPUTERS

The way forward to the modern computer was pointed by Charles Babbage (1792–1871) in the early nineteenth century. His Difference Engine was designed to produce tables of numbers and typeset them to reduce the risks of errors both in calculation and copying.

A dispute with the machinist working on the production of the engine led to Babbage losing control over the existing parts and specially-designed tools used in their construction. Babbage went on to envision a new sort of calculating machine that he called an Analytical Engine. His machines incorporated for the first time key elements of the architecture of programmable computers: (i) an input device, (ii) a processor or number calculator, (iii) a control unit built to direct the assigned task and the sequence of calculations, (iv) a storage unit to hold the number in wait for processing, and (v) an output device.

Unfortunately, Babbage was unable to finance the building of his Analytical Engine. The government lost interest in funding it, and Babbage's fortune had been gravely depleted by the money spent on the Difference Engine.

Meanwhile, a Swedish printer by the name of George Scheutz teamed up with his son to build an engine modeled after Babbage's description of his Difference Engine. In 1855, it was exhibited at the Royal Society in London. It tabulated values corresponding to a general law up to sixteen digits, but it only printed out eight digits and was capable of increasing the eighth digit by one if the ninth digit was greater than five. It computed and typeset with a speed of 25 digits per minute, though it was able to go faster. In 1856, the machine was bought by the US astronomer Gould, then director of the Dudley Observatory, to produce astronomical tables. A similar machine was ordered from a British machinist to produce statistical tables using data collected in Great Britain.

One contemporary typesetter calculated that the Scheutz machine might save 18 pounds 4 shillings per page of logarithmic tables, and nearly 60 hours of work for the same page. The bulk of the savings could be attributed to the replacement by the gears of the machine of the highly-skilled computers who pulled together the calculations performed by all the other computers; the savings earned by the automated typesetting were not as great, if only because the work of typesetters was not as highly paid as that of the top computers. Though the niche was too small for the Scheutz machine to be a breakthrough invention, it clearly showed what was possible.

THE ROAD TO ELECTRONIC COMPUTERS

While working on the light bulb, Thomas Edison discovered that if an evacuated bulb contained a filament *and* a metal plate, the current circulated through the filament would pass to the plate and be carried out of the bulb if the plate was attached to its own circuit.

Some years later, John Ambrose Fleming, a physicist working for the British Marconi company, discovered that if an alternating current was applied to the filament, a direct current would emerge from the plate. Fleming called it a diode (since it held two electrodes).

When US radio inventor Lee DeForest took up the diode, he discovered that if a third element (a small conducting wire grid fed its own current) was introduced, the bulb would function as a very sensitive radio wave detector. This was a triode, in effect, but DeForest called it an *audion*, for marketing reasons. Since it could detect a continuous electromagnetic wave, it could function as a wireless telephony receiver and amplifier.

In 1912, a young US student and amateur radio operator, Edwin H. Armstrong, started to experiment with the audion for his senior thesis at the engineering college of Columbia University. He discovered that if the current produced by the plate was fed back into the grid, the signal was greatly amplified. A few months later, he discovered that it was even possible to turn a vacuum tube into a transmitter. Armstrong patented his discoveries, and by 1915, vacuum tube technology started to dominate radio manufacturing. After World War I, radio took off as a commercial medium. Within 20 years, many homes had a radio, creating a large industry based on vacuum tubes and fostering a growing familiarity with electronic technology.

By this time, professional chemists, electrical engineers, and physicists in industrialized countries were faced with dealing with increasingly complex mathematics as part of their work. Some, including astronomers, artillery men, and surveyors, were able to make do with the improved slide rule developed by André Mannheim after 1850. The use of slide rules became ever more widespread among engineers and scientists; during World War II, navigators aboard US bombers used specialized slide rules to calculate their positions or to prepare bombing runs. Slide rules were used by Albert Einstein, by the engineers of Hoover Dam, by the inventors of transistor radio, and by the designers of the V-2 rocket, Sputnik, the Vostok, and the Saturn 5 moon rocket.

Nicknamed "slipsticks," slide rules were more portable than the gear-driven mechanical calculators descended from the machines of Leibniz, Thomas, and Burroughs. However, they could not be used to add or subtract straightforwardly, and their precision was limited.

From 1947 onward, one expensive option was available: the Curta pocket mechanical calculator, invented by Austrian businessman Curt Herzstark (1902–1988) while an inmate in the Buchenwald concentration camp. The family business up to World War II had made and sold Remington and Burroughs office machines, but Herzstark felt the need for a truly portable calculator. Before WWII, a "portable" calculating machine might weigh 14 kilos and come equipped with cranks large enough to start an old automobile. While the Curta could be held in the palm of one's hand and could yield 11- and 15-digit numbers, it was expensive ($125 in 1969). Only 150,000 were ever made.

For the next step up in computational complexity, something else was needed. More power was needed for many problems, but engineers could also see the need on the horizon for something that would combine the convenience of slide rules and the precision of mechanical calculators. Those concerned with the challenge started to turn to electronics for an answer after World War I, even though it involved a huge jump in the level of expense.

As a result, modern electronic computers were only born during World War II, when cost was no longer an object. It drew on mechanical and conceptual ancestors that went back to the counting machines of the 17th century, the analytical engine of

Babbage, and the census counter of Hollerith. More immediately, the way had been paved by the work of Vannevar Bush, at M.I.T., and of his collaborators starting in 1925. Their differential analyzer was inspired by the machines of Babbage. Though they experimented with making the machine electrical, the working models were purely mechanical.

During World War II, the needs of cryptography for code-breaking and of the cutting-edge physics involved in the design of the first atomic bomb outpaced the computational performances possible with all current machines. The wartime sense of urgency meant that sufficient funding was made available to explore new technology. The first electronic computers developed to do better used vacuum tubes. In fact, the 1945–1946 ENIAC built by John Mauchly and J. Presper Eckert at the Moore School of Engineering of the University of Pennsylvania (to calculate ballistic trajectories for artillery tables) used 17,000 vacuum tubes.

Meanwhile, IBM had backed the construction by Howard Aiken in 1944 of the pioneering Harvard Mark I, which was not electronic but did feature automatic operational sequences. Not unlike Babbage's planned Analytical Engine, the Mark I used paper tape punched with holes to code both the instructions and the data. However, Aiken's machine also used electromechanical switches that were slower and more cumbersome than the all-electronic switching provided by vacuum tubes.

A number of other advanced computing engines were also designed or built, during or before the war years, in the United States (by John Vincent Atanasoff), in Germany (by Konrad Zuse), and in Great Britain (under the direction of Alan Turing). However, the ENIAC proved to be a breakthrough as a practical computing device that could be applied to a number of different problems. In other countries, such as the Soviet Union, the public unveiling of the ENIAC after the war stimulated work on advanced digital computing. Indeed, the Soviet Union always remained behind the United States, either reverse engineering early commercial US models or taking advantage of computing research conducted in associated countries such as Hungary or Czechoslovakia.

The invention of the Internet was very much a Cold War story, though it has only come to prominence in the last couple of decades. Originally, the Advanced Research Projects Agency (ARPA) wished to connect the computing centres that it was funding across the United States in order to maximize their effectiveness. While academics and scientists were involved in the genesis of the Internet, ARPA contracted with the Cambridge (Massachusetts) company Bolt, Beranek & Newman (BBN) to launch the network then known as ARPANET. As part of its work, the company introduced the @ sign. (It was later acquired by another company in 1997, ending up as part of

Verizon, a Bell System company. However, it was sold off to a group of private investors in 2004.)

ELECTRONIC COMPUTERS IN CANADA

The first electronic computers had been designed for large-scale computations. In Canada, this could only be of interest to scientists and a few engineers working with ballistics or nuclear technology. In 1946, a group of University of Toronto professors and NRC representatives traveled to the United States to find out more about the new machines.

In 1947, the resulting report proposed that a national computing centre be created at the University of Toronto to answer the needs of scientists and engineers.

Originally, the University of Toronto Computation Centre was small. It was managed by Calvin C. Gotlieb, a physics PhD graduate from the University of Toronto, who was assisted by J. Perham Stanley and Beatrice Worsley (1921–1972), a mathematics and physics MSc graduate of M.I.T. Worsley would later write what is believed to be the first PhD dissertation involving modern computers at the University of Cambridge by 1952. In 1948, the centre owned a couple of IBM punch card calculators, but it was agreed that the centre would build a licenced copy of the Bell Laboratories Model VI electromechanical relay-based computer before moving on to designing and building its own modern electronic computer.

However, the Bell licence fee was so expensive that the NRC refused to put up the money. With electronic computers on the horizon, this was considered an effective but obsolescent machine. Instead, the University of Toronto was encouraged to move ahead with the University of Toronto Electronic Computer (UTEC).

However, only a small-scale prototype of UTEC was ever built. By 1951, a Mark I Ferranti computer had become available (ordered by the British Atomic Energy Authority, it was built but left without an owner when a new government cancelled the order) and the NRC pressured the University of Toronto to buy it instead of building a full-scale UTEC. The Computation Centre was reluctant; it was in contact with John von Neumann's group in the United States and it felt that the serial design of the Ferranti Mark I was more limited than the parallel design planned for the future UTEC. Nevertheless, the NRC controlled the funding and it had the last word.

The new machine was called Ferut (Ferranti at the University of Toronto), pronounced "ferret." It arrived in Toronto in 1952 and the Computation Centre staff soon discovered the challenges of programming and maintaining a high-performance machine with thousands of vacuum tubes, gaining valuable experience as they did so. As project assistant, Worsley collaborated with a young physics professor, J. N. Patterson Hume, on the creation of software known as Transcode. Students learned to work with it and transferred their knowledge to other sites. Since Ferut remained the only machine available, other researchers needed to connect with Toronto. In 1955, a pioneering teletypewriter hookup was set up between the University of Saskatchewan and the University of Toronto. Initially, local operators would feed the computer with the punched tape produced by the teleprinter and send the output tapes back to Saskatchewan. Other universities followed suit, leading to successful attempts to create a live remote connection to Ferut by simply running a very long tape down the hall from the teletypewriter into the computer tape reader.

For a few years, Ferut was Canada's most powerful computer and it was used for a variety of jobs, including the design of the Avro Arrow jet fighter. It was also used to develop Toronto's traffic control system (perhaps the world's first computer-controlled city system) as well as a flight reservation system for Air Canada. It more importantly was used for Ontario Hydro "backwater" calculations that were essential for the planning of the St. Lawrence Seaway. Indeed, as the corresponding US authorities did not control the computing power required to check these computations, they were forced to accept the Canadian plans for the seaway route.

The speed of computing developments may be judged from the fact that, in 1958, Ferut was replaced by an IBM 650, a standard make that had already been bought by over a dozen customers in Canada. The IBM 650 was roughly as powerful as Ferut, but it came with an enormous library of ready-made software. Ferut was shipped to Ottawa where it was used for a few more years doing calculations for the NRC Mechanical Engineering Section. The IBM 650 served as a stopgap for the Computation Centre until it could acquire an IBM 7090 in 1962, the top of the line commercial model of the time.

Calvin Gotlieb, who had become the director of the University of Toronto's Institute of Computer Science in 1961, oversaw the creation of a graduate Department of Computer Science in 1964, the first in Canada. J. N. Patterson Hume was the chair of the computer science department from 1975 to 1980, and he collaborated with Gotlieb on a number of works dealing with the new subject, coining up to eleven new words now found in the *Oxford English Dictionary*.

During WWII, Gotlieb had worked on proximity fuses, developing the oscillators installed in the nose cones of shells, and on trajectory calculations. He joined the University of Toronto in 1946–1947 where he worked for the electronic section of the Computation Centre. There, he was initially in charge of punched cards.

FROM VIRTUAL SPACE TO CYBERSPACE

The concept of virtual reality can be traced back to a philosophical reflection by Suzanne K. Langer in the United States. In her 1957 book, *Problems of Art* (Charles Scribner's Sons), she suggested that an artwork should be seen as the result of an objective translation of the inner life, associating emotions and intimate experiences. This translation results in an image, dynamic or not, that is a virtual object, but not an unreal one:

> "Anything that exists only for perception, and plays no ordinary, passive part in nature as common objects do, is a virtual entity. It is not unreal; where it confronts you, you really perceive it, you don't dream or imagine that you do. The image in a mirror is a virtual image."[1]

Dance created a dynamic virtual image by materializing the interplay of primal Forces. Painting presented a static virtual image, which contained a space and objects, both of which existed only for the sense of sight. Langer therefore applied the same adjective—virtual—to the apparent space visible in a painting.

> "There are certain merely apparent objects in nature: rainbows, mirages, and simple reflections in still water or on other shiny surfaces. The most familiar instances are images, in mirrors which we construct for the purpose of getting reflections. It is the mirror that has made physicists recognize and describe this sort of space, which by the usual standard of practical experience is illusory; they call it virtual space. Let us borrow that technical term, 'virtual'."[2]

A few years later, this concept of virtual space is said to have inspired young computer scientist Ivan Sutherland who used it to set a goal for his colleagues—the use of computers to create a virtual world, distinct from our world but endowed with an illusory reality. In 1965, Sutherland hoped that computers would open a window onto the world built within the computer's electronic circuits and he drew one obvious conclusion:

---

[1] Suzanne Langer, *Problems of Art: The Philosophical Lectures* (New York: Charles Scribner's Sons, 1957), p. 5.
[2] *Ibid.*, p. 29.

> *"If the task of the display is to serve as a looking-glass into the mathematical wonderland constructed in computer memory, it should serve as many senses as possible."* [3]

Assuming it was possible (at least in theory) to come up with a variety of devices capable of creating the illusion of interaction with a real world, Sutherland set as a goal the creation of a virtual world entirely controlled by the computer so that a *total experience* of utterly distinct realities would become possible.

He called the *ultimate display* a room inside which the computer would appear to control material existence:

> *"A chair displayed in such a room would be good enough to sit in. Handcuffs displayed in such a room would be confining, and a bullet displayed in such a room would be fatal. With appropriate programming such a display could literally be the Wonderland into which Alice walked."*[4]

In practice, Sutherland had already created a computer program known as Sketchpad as part of his PhD work in 1963. The program allowed the user to draw forms memorized by the computer that could then be handled in symbolic form, either through software commands or through new actions by the user. What is now elementary was then revolutionary. Modern engineering has come to depend heavily on computer-aided design (CAD) software and many more people use programs along the same lines to manipulate pictures and graphics. By 1965, Sutherland was aiming for the integration of all possible interfaces to create a virtual world so perfect that it would only lack reality. He moved on to the development of head-mounted displays (or virtual reality goggles), which culminated with a prototype in 1970. It was the starting point of a series of developments that included the ancestors of modern flight simulators.

The reality of a virtual reality is located in its effects and not its substance. The virtual space identified by Langer in the case of paintings showing a place produces the same effects on a viewer as the sight of a real place. The gaze wanders within it and the brain models it. However, the virtual place does not exist. In 1984, Canadian

---

[3] Ivan Sutherland, "The Ultimate Display," in *Information Processing 1965: Proceedings of IFIP Congress 65. Volume 2*, Wayne A. Kalenich, ed. (Washington: Spartan Books / London: Macmillan and Co., 1965), p. 507.
[4] *Ibid.*, p. 508.

science fiction author William Gibson called it *cyberspace* in his novel *Neuromancer* (Ace).

FROM MAINFRAMES TO THE INTERNET

The history of electronic computers may be divided in three historical phases.

From the end of World War II to the beginning of the 1970s, computers were mainframes—huge machines with extremely modest computing power in spite of their sheer size (they filled entire rooms) and their cutting-edge technology, so expensive they could only be built and run by governments or major corporations. The operating manuals alone could fill a cabinet or two. Thus, the 1954 SAGE (Semi-Automatic Ground Environment) computer incorporated 55,000 vacuum tubes and linked hundreds of radar stations to coordinate the air defenses of the United States. It is said that some of the maintenance technicians used roller skates to carry replacement tubes to keep the machine humming.

The replacement of vacuum tubes by solid state transistors allowed mainframes to be designed on a smaller scale and even commercialized. Bell used many vacuum-tube triodes for long-distance telephony, but these triodes had a high failure rate, were expensive, and required large amounts of power. As early as 1939, Bell Laboratories researchers Walter Brattain and William Shockley attempted to replicate a triode using a semiconductor. Work was suspended during the war; afterwards, Brattain, Shockley, and John Bardeen returned to the problem. In December 1947, they demonstrated a point-contact transistor using germanium doped with impurities. In 1951, Shockley's subsequent research led to the junction transistor.

Shockley left Bell Laboratories to set up his own transistor company in 1955. Eight of his employees, led by Robert Noyce, left him in 1957 to set up their own spin-off company, Fairchild Electronics, with the support of the pre-existing Fairchild Camera Company. Noyce soon patented his ideas for ways to connect separate transistors with photoetched copper wires on a single silicon crystal chip. By 1968, he moved on to create, with colleague Gordon Moore, a new company called Intel to manufacture integrated circuits, also known as *microchips*.

Meanwhile, Texas Instruments had gone into the manufacture of transistors and convinced a small company, Regency, to build transistor radios by Christmas 1954. Radios had already become more or less portable, but transistor radios were truly pocket-sized. One member of the Texas Instruments team, Jack Kilby, then realized that silicon, doped and undoped, could not only be used to make transistors, but also resistors and capacitors, thus making it possible to place a complete electrical circuit on a single silicon crystal, one that would be fast and require little power. The technology was demonstrated in December 1958. The work of Kilby and Noyce, taken as a whole, turned the *integrated circuit* into a reality.

In 1963, Robert Ragen developed one of the first transistorized electronic calculators (the Friden EC-130), taking advantage of the compactness of solid-state transistors to build a desktop machine equipped with four functions that could calculate to 12 digits of precision. It was not a mass market product, but it was a harbinger of things to come. It was designed with the help of a slide rule, but its successors would bring about the complete replacement of slide rules. By the late 1960s, the EC-130 was remade with integrated circuits; this smaller and lighter version showed the way. Electronics was headed for yet more miniaturization.

Early on, NASA and the military were major clients for integrated circuits because of the high penalties associated with older technologies that were much more massive for an equivalent performance when it was necessary to send them into space. Computer makers were next to accept integrated circuits. By 1964, RCA could boast that its computers were equipped with fully-integrated circuits. In 1972, Hewlett-Packard offered the first pocket scientific calculator, the HP-35, packed with six integrated circuits and using a light-emitting diode display. Though pricey, it was as portable as a slide rule, and much more capable.

The next step involved Japanese firms hiring Intel engineers to create a microchip for better portable electronic calculators. The Intel 4004 was a general purpose chip that packed as much power as the room-sized ENIAC in a speck measuring roughly 3 by 4 millimetres. In November 1971, it was recognized as a breakthrough and announced as "a microprogrammable computer on a chip." As it was still limited, Intel required a few more generations of development to put out the 8080 in 1974, the first true general-purpose *microprocessor* for commercial use. It could handle 8 bits (binary digits) and contained nearly 5,000 transistors.

The invention of microprocessors allowed a generation of entrepreneurs in the 1970s to offer the first personal computers (also known as minicomputers or microcomputers). In 1974, a company known as MITS created the Altair 8800, the first microcomputer kit. It inspired others. The Apple I (1975) was a do-it-yourself computer. For $666.66, the retail buyer did not get a finished machine. Instead, he or she received a circuit board and a 16-page assembly manual. Supplying a keyboard, a monitor, and even a casing (often made out of plywood) was his or her responsibility. By 1981, however, the market had grown enough to justify the interest of IBM; it contracted with Microsoft for an operating system of its "PC." Within a few years, Microsoft-based technology (if not IBM itself) pulled away from all its rivals.

Since the early 1990s, the Internet that had been until then the almost exclusive preserve of academics, computer professionals, and government users opened up to the owners of personal computers. The invention of graphic browsers (such as the Netscape Navigator and the Microsoft Explorer) unleashed a wave of innovation, accompanied by a level of stock speculation that became known as the information technology bubble (or "dot-com bubble") when it burst and deflated in 2000–2001 after four years of irrational exuberance.

CHAPTER 12

Modern Technology and the Ecological Threshold

▶▶▶▶▶▶▶▶▶▶▶▶▶▶▶▶▶▶▶▶▶▶▶▶▶▶▶▶

THE RISE OF AN ENVIRONMENTAL SENSIBILITY

The history of the environmental movement is rooted in a Western conception of the natural world that some argue springs out of the Biblical statements that made humans the stewards of the Earth. While this could easily be interpreted as a divine mandate that allowed humans to use all of the fruits and resources of Nature, it also entailed a feeling of responsibility. Throughout much of European history, population pressure and expanding settled areas crowded out wildlife. By the 17th century, the only forests to survive were designated as hunting reserves for the aristocracy, standing timber reserves for the long-term needs of the state or other institutions, or communal woods tended in order to supply villagers with firewood and construction materials.

Europe's kings and nobles enjoyed ever more elaborate gardens as domesticated enclaves of an almost vanished wilderness. By the 17th century, the French school of garden design disciplined vegetation, creating straight rows of trees, carefully shaped bushes, and ornate flowerbeds. Such gardens embodied an attention to symmetry and an eye for geometrical patterns that proclaimed nature's subservience to the human mind.

The English school of garden design developed in the course of the 18th century, influenced by landscape painters and descriptions of Chinese gardens. Often comprising artificial lakes or ponds, sculpted meadows, and precisely spotted groves of trees, English landscape gardens embodied an idealized view of nature. The inclusion of picturesque ruins such as the ones visited by young English nobles undertaking Grand Tours of Europe for their edification pointed to nature's power over human artifice. Nevertheless, at a time when European explorers had run into hostile forests and jungles all around the globe, English gardens offered a hopeful view of nature, one that could be reconciled to human needs and one that announced a profound change in Western views of nature.

In England, poets such as William Wordsworth (1723–1850) and Samuel Taylor Coleridge (1772–1834) launched the Romantic Age in 1798. The movement that they fostered celebrated the beauties of the natural landscape, broadly conceived. Whereas the wilderness had long been an object of fear so that people shrank from venturing into trackless woods bristling with savage animals or mountain country where a misstep could result in a deadly fall, a new generation discovered the appeal of grand, inhuman landscapes. Towering mountains, valley vistas, and snowy polar expanses were described as sublime, inspiring a species of sacred terror. The cozy fields, pastures, and coppiced woods of the English countryside were no longer the supreme standard of natural beauty, nor the calculated pleasures of French or English gardens.

The conservation movement grew out of a wish to broaden the possibility of enjoyment of natural settings so that it would no longer be restricted to monarchs and landowners. Railways, canals, and turnpikes made it possible to reach areas that had once been remote from population centres. Wordsworth articulated the case for saving from industrial development the beloved uplands around his northern England birthplace by celebrating such a protected region as "a sort of national property, in which every man has a right and interest who has an eye to perceive, and a heart to enjoy."[1] The Romantics were politically liberal and the goal of setting aside unique landscapes for all suited their democratic instincts.

Wordsworth's native region, the Lake District in northern England, an area of picturesque lakes, hills, forests, and mountains, became an early focus for preserva-

---

[1] William Wordsworth, "Description of the scenery of the lakes," in *A Complete Guide to the Lakes* (J. Hudson, 1843), p. 170.

tion. When the National Trust was established in 1895, it was one of the first areas that it sought to protect by acquiring lands and gaining control over their use. Held to be especially beautiful by Romantic poets, the landscape owed part of its beauty to herds of sheep that nibbled and uprooted most edible plants. While some hillsides were stripped bare by such herds, the lakes and woods of the region reproduced on a larger scale the modest attractions of an English garden. Railways allowed sightseers to flock to the area while they also threatened its preservation by fostering industrial activity.

In the United States too, attitudes changed throughout the nineteenth century. The first waves of European settlers were repelled by the wilderness they encountered. The thick woods may in fact have developed as a result of the retreat or extinction of native populations who had maintained them as game reserves by burning the underbrush or who had cleared them periodically to cultivate the soil. Nevertheless, to wrest harvests from the soil, pioneers would first have to venture into the woods to bring down tree after tree, if only to heat their homes and cook their food. Wood also served as a construction material, as fuel for steam engines, and as the basis for charcoal in iron furnaces. While Great Britain relied on coal for its steam engines and ironmaking, US wood consumption was five times greater per capita than in England in 1860.

As an added incentive to cut down forests and replace them with fields or pastures, European philosophers of the 17th and 18th centuries entertained the idea that forests cooled the local climate. The first Europeans were struck by the climatic divergence between Western Europe and Northern America. From one side of the Atlantic to the other, winter was dramatically different along the same line of latitude. Well into the nineteenth century, some geographers and scientists believed that forests captured the cold of winter and kept the sun from warming the land. Clearing forests would both warm the climate and feed the colonial population. The US forestry industry relentlessly marched westwards as the railways penetrated into the deepest recesses of the continent. By 1859, half of US lumber was cut west of the Appalachians. In most cases outside of Eastern forests, US forests from the Great Lakes states to the Deep South and the Pacific Northwest were razed to the ground, leaving no trees to supply the required reseeding. The cleared land was sold to farmers, though it often proved to be of marginal interest for agriculture. In 1890, US botanist Charles Mohr advocated reforestation instead with fast-growing pine. The first tree farm followed in 1914.

Doubts about the wisdom of clear-cutting were expressed as early as 1847 by US naturalist George Marsh who recognized the consequences for soil erosion and increased run-off. Others lamented the loss of pristine landscapes. Echoing the English Romantics, Scottish-born John Muir (1838–1914) celebrated the mystic beauty of the forests of California's Sierra Nevada mountains. The closing of the American frontier in 1890 lent new impetus to the movement to preserve untouched nature within legally-protected parks.

The US Congress created Forest Reserves safe from unrestrained exploitation in 1891 with an eye to preserving a key resource over the long run. Gifford Pinchot (1865–1946), the heir to a US lumbering fortune, took the lead in promoting sustainable forestry practices based on the conservation of standing forests and a concern for long-term yield rather than short-term returns. Trained at the French National School of Forestry, he was named the first chief of the US Forest Service when it was created in 1905. Since he believed in the commercial exploitation of the resource, at least on a small scale, he clashed with strict conservationists like Muir. On the other hand, his stance in favour of forest renewal led him to oppose business interests hoping for bulk timber sales. After he was fired in 1910, the Forest Service survived and popularized firefighting, selective cutting, and forest thinning practices to optimize individual tree growth.

Another prosperous and influential businessman, Stephen Mather (1867–1930), led the fight to establish parks that would answer the hopes of strict conservationists. In 1917, he was named the first director of the US National Park Service charged with the park system established the previous year. The protection of scenic landscapes and wildlife habitats was the main purpose of his work.

In Canada too, the railway played a part in the creation of a network of parks, but it was because the new Canadian Pacific Railway line through the western mountain ranges enabled visitors to discover the beauty of the area around Banff. The Rocky Mountains (now Banff) Park was created in 1885 and more park or scenic reserves were added during the following decades. In 1911, the existing holdings were placed under the single authority of the Dominion Parks Branch, headed by Commissioner James Harkin until his retirement in 1936. The ancestor of today's Parks Canada, it is counted by some as the world's first agency dedicated to managing a parks system in the national interest.

While parks had been associated until then with forest reserves, Harkin realized that untouched nature would be judged to hold a value all its own if Canadians could appreciate the soothing and even restorative character of a park visit. Furthermore, tourism would help finance the parks themselves. As a result, access to Canada's parks was improved by the building of roads and hotels. By the time of the First World War, Harkin was calling for a combination of scenic parks, wildlife sanctuaries, historic sites, and parks located to cater to population concentrations. Logging, mining, and hunting were controlled but allowed until 1930, when a new law advanced conservation as a priority. The new science of ecology initially justified human interference to restore the balance of nature disturbed by decades of hunting predators. The resulting slaughter of "surplus" animal populations finally led to a hands-off policy by the 1960s to let predators and prey find their own balance. Since then, the parks have increasingly been run so as to preserve nature inviolate, but each generation has needed to stand firm against attempted encroachments and inroads.

DEATH AND DESTRUCTION

The power of technology to threaten life first came into focus in times of war.

The war of 1812 between the United States and Great Britain was fought with the conventional armies and navies of the day. The weaponry used on both sides was mostly unchanged since the 18th century. During the earlier War of Independence of the United States, American inventor David Bushnell had tried using a small submarine to sink British ships. In Europe, the revolutionary armies of France had developed a corps of balloonists to provide its officers with a broader view of the battlefield, until Napoleon abolished it. Even though Robert Fulton proposed such novel weapons as torpedoes and great armoured ships equipped with steam cannons, the war of 1812 featured few military innovations. One exception was the British use of rockets against Fort McHenry near Baltimore in 1814, a weapon developed by a British officer, William Congreve, and first used on a significant scale during the battle of Copenhagen in 1807. The "rockets' red glare" were immortalized in the US patriotic hymn, "The Star Spangled Banner" (1814).

The American Civil War (1861–1865) was a harbinger of things to come in the military domain. The troops on both sides were still equipped at the outset with a number of flintlock, smooth-bore muskets with only short-range accuracy. Yet, long guns available to civilians were known to be superior. In 1814, Joshua Shaw had replaced flint with the percussion cap, which increased the likelihood of setting off the main powder charge inside the bore when the trigger was pulled. Rifling became easier to justify once the round ball was replaced by the modern bullet. The familiar pointed cylinder was provided with a hollow base that expanded when the gun was fired. The bullet's expansion insured a tight fit, but the unexpanded size facilitated loading from the muzzle end. It was no longer necessary to tamp down the ball and the bullet also responded well to the rifling. The additional spin increased the range and the Springfield rifles eventually provided to Northern soldiers in the Civil War were effective to at least 350 metres. Breechloaders and repeaters were manufactured during the last two years of the war.

The new effectiveness of the infantryman's gun resulted in murderous battles. The war's human toll approached 620,000 dead, mostly among the armies on both sides. The cavalry charge became pointless while the infantry charging alone, without supporting artillery fire, faced withering rifle fire from defenders sheltering in trenches or foxholes, or behind earthworks. The stalemate on land led to innovation elsewhere.

Balloons were used in the air. At sea and along major rivers, armoured steamboats and ironclad ships were deployed in a limited number of encounters. On the other hand, trains were used extensively to supply armies in the field and move troops rapidly. Railway hubs were the focus of some campaigns, while the telegraph kept commanders and politicians in the loop.

The mechanization of war fully prevailed during the First World War (1914–1918). Canada was at war from the first, though it took time to enrol, train, and ship the massive numbers of troops required for a new kind of warfare overseas.

The first contingent of the Canadian expeditionary force shipped out with some 7,600 horses. By the final year of the war, the Canadian army still relied on 23,000 horses mostly used as draft and pack animals, though a small number served as parade mounts for officers as well. While the war did feature a few cavalry charges or engagements, the killing power of modern artillery, reloadable rifles, and machine guns quickly convinced the generals that cavalry no longer had much of a role on the battlefield. Horses remained important for logistics near the front. In 1918, the Canadian army backed animal horsepower with mechanical horsepower: 1,009 truck, 223 cars, 84 ambulances, and 2,327 bicycles.

The death toll of a massive land war fought with rifles, machine guns, steel cannons, bombs from the air, and poison gases was breathtaking. By the end of the First World War, millions of men had died in the mud of Western trenches or the woods of Eastern Europe, on the mountain slopes of Italy or on the beaches of Turkey. After the war, the view of technology shifted to take into account its destructive potential.

THE VANISHING SUBSTANCE OF TECHNOLOGIES

The sheer increase in human numbers over the course of the twentieth century has granted enormous power to the most basic human activities. Indeed, in Canada, the Syncrude mine tapping the Athabasca tar sands is the world's largest mine (by surface area) and it is expected to move over its lifetime a total of 30 gigatonnes of earth, an amount comparable to the sediment carried yearly by all of the world's rivers. Geomorphologist Roger Hooke of the University of Maine recently estimated that humans now move more of the planet's crustal material (earth, sand, rock) than any other single known process. Using such common machines as bulldozers, humans shift over 40 gigatonnes of Earth's dry surface every year (on average).

This compares to 30 gigatonnes of bedrock shifted by oceanic mountain building, between 23 and 37 gigatonnes of silt carried downstream by the world's rivers, 13 gigatonnes pushed up by continental mountain building, 4.1 gigatonnes displaced by glaciers, and 1.9 gigatonnes attributable to ocean waves and winds. (Even the yearly influx of extraterrestrial dust falling to earth through the planet's atmosphere is no more than 38 gigatonnes.) Yet, this prodigious feat of earth-moving by human technologies goes essentially unnoticed because it happens one little bit at a time.

The same is true of global warming. The human release of carbon dioxide into the atmosphere is still only a tenth or so of the natural flows of carbon in the global environment (even though humanity has released in only a couple of centuries carbon stored over hundreds of millions of years), but it is a net increment which natural processes cannot entirely compensate for in the short term. The additional warmth attributed to the results of human activity amounts to just about 2 watts per square meter of the Earth's surface; this is the equivalent of the energy dissipated by two miniature Christmas tree bulbs. It is a tiny amount, but scientists predict that its steady accumulation over time will produce huge effects by the end of this century (climate change, ocean warming, glacier melt, ice shelf melting in the Antarctic, sea ice melting in the Arctic, and ocean level rise). Thus, human intervention has built up a significant additional presence of atmospheric carbon dioxide, some of which is expected to be part of the air for at least 800 years, or longer if we continue to add carbon dioxide to the atmosphere.

Furthermore, with the world's human population now over seven billion, there is less and less room left for wildlife. It is estimated the quantity of biomass made up of humans and their livestock is greater than the total comprised by all other large animals. Estimates of the percentage of plant life found in ecosystems affected in some way by human activity run as high as 90 percent. Human tampering with natural cycles has easily doubled the transfer of nitrogen from the atmosphere to the biomass and the soil, yet most of it goes to individual farms and fields in small, apparently unimpressive quantities.

As a result of all of the above, Paul Crutzen and Eugene Stoermer have proposed that humanity has initiated a new geological era, one in which it is the principal force shaping the future of the Earth's biosphere, so that it should be known as the "Anthropocene."

The twentieth century may have been characterized by the elusiveness of its new technologies, their operation often ghostly or invisible while their effects have been anything but. The technologies of the nineteenth century were obvious. Canals and railroads carved up the landscape. Wires (used by telegraphs, telephones, and the electrical system) filled the skies above city streets, stretched alongside railroads, and carried power from distant hydroelectric dams to the bustling cities served by underground subways, ground-level streetcars, and even a few elevated railways. If the car is identified as a technology of the late nineteenth century, even the highways of the twentieth century and the urban sprawl they fostered could be seen as late-blooming consequences of nineteenth-century technologies.

In the medical field, where the microbiological revolution led by Pasteur did start to introduce invisible entities (germ theory of disease, new vaccines), it should not be ignored that most of the health advances of the nineteenth century relied on improvements in hygiene (through the provision of sewers and running water), often justified by the erroneous *miasma* theory of disease. The *miasma* theory essentially blamed disease on agents that were invisible perhaps, but that could be smelled. The principles of asepsis and antisepsis were not imposed without a hard-fought battle, since they posited causative agents of infection and disease that were at best invisible to the unaided eye (bacteria) and sometimes utterly undetectable with contemporaneous technology (viruses). (Viruses were not actually observed until the twentieth century.)

However, the most distinctive technologies of the twentieth century were much less visible. Taylorism and Fordism did not rely solely on new and obvious inventions; they often made use of existing technologies and organized daily work in new manners. The result of these innovations was obvious in the vastly increased output, but it could be hard to place one's finger on a specific device responsible for the increased productivity.

Radio was even more elusive. The fact it was known as the wireless reveals how striking it was to communicate with the help of invisible waves. Radar, television broadcasts, and microwave ovens only added to the power of the unseen. The intangible nature of such technologies may be pointed to by French filmmaker Jacques Tati's movie *Playtime* (1967), which emphasizes the vanishing substance of technologies. The hapless hero is a visitor from the countryside to Paris buildings that were slightly ahead of their time in 1967, but that became tangible realities during the following decades. The movie's main character is bemused by doors and walls made of glass. They become too hard to see, they play tricks on the senses (by showing him objects where they aren't or by distorting their appearance), they reveal everything without telling him anything (by allowing light but not sound to pass through) and yet they remain unyielding.

Beyond nineteenth-century chemistry, whose fundamental units (molecules) were individually invisible to the naked eye or even to the best microscopes, twentieth-century electronics relied on the impalpable electron. Easily visible in some circumstances, impinging on phosphor screens at high velocities, electrons receded into the depths of matter as solid state electronics evolved after World War II. The invention of the transistor, which replaced the vacuum tube, led to the modern state of affairs where electronic computing, the most powerful technological driver of the last few decades, happens out of sight and hearing, only betrayed by waste heat.

This common invisibility is also obvious in other fields. Biologists were only able to discover the structure of DNA with the help of clues provided by X-ray crystallography. Research then focused on the genome that was thought to contain the secrets of life. Radioactivity was another scientific phenomenon that eluded the senses and that was nevertheless harnessed to technological ends. It could not be seen (without instruments) and it could not be felt, even as it killed. So, the fallout from nuclear bomb tests would escape notice, even as it contaminated drinking water, soil, plants, and the animals part of the food chain.

ELUSIVE TECHNOLOGIES AND DISILLUSIONMENT

One consequence of this elusiveness of new technologies was a growing estrangement between technologies and their users. Mechanical inventions such as the steam engine, the locomotive, the automobile, and the bicycle could not always be repaired by their operators or owners, but their inner workings could be grasped without special instruments. And the risks they posed were immediate and tangible—being run over by a car or blasted by the exploding boiler of a steam engine needed no explanations.

On the other hand, as technologies have become harder to grasp, their risks have also become harder to grasp. Users have been forced to rely on the explanations and the assurances of engineers and other experts. They have been forced to trust them more and more. It is easy to know, for instance, when a bicycle is in good working order or what is wrong with a car motor whose crankshaft is broken. However, one must trust that a vaccine is working since the only proof of its efficacy will be negative, if the person given a dose does *not* fall sick. And pinpointing the trouble with a faulty microprocessor may require such specialized equipment that it will be easier to build in fault tolerance beforehand or just junk it when it develops a problem; in any event, it is rarely the user who will be able to identify the trouble with solid state electronics.

As for the risks posed by radioactivity, pesticides, and biotechnological innovations, they are often *delayed* and *indirect,* and result from mechanisms operating below the threshold of human perception. Users cannot judge them personally; again, they must trust engineers and other experts.

All of this has fed a growing disillusionment with technology in the course of the twentieth century.

Partly, this disillusionment was fostered by the demonstration that new technologies could be turned to destructive ends, especially during the two world wars. During the Second Battle of Ypres (April 22 to May 25, 1915) in Belgium, future Nobel Prize-winner and German scientist Fritz Jacob Haber directed the use of chlorine as a battlefield weapon, collapsing the left side of the Ypres Salient and putting Canadian troops under heavy (and murderous) pressure, leading to thousands of casualties—and to a chemical arms race that was fought till the end of the war. As a consequence, the Great War was known to some as the chemists' war; when chlorine was used, it was soon discovered that a dampened cloth held against the face would help since chlorine is water-soluble. A Canadian medical officer and chemistry student suggested the use of urine-soaked cloth, thinking the chlorine would react with the ammonia or uric acid.

During World War II, rockets and atomic bombs were only the most innovative instances of technologies deployed to lethal purposes.

Partly, it was fostered by the discovery of risks posed even by the normal, everyday use of some new technologies. Technological innovation had social and environmental consequences long before the twentieth century, but the pace of technological development after the Second World War made them more and more visible, while the recollection of the destructive applications of technology and science in war always loomed in the background of the public's expectations.

THE ROAD TO TECHNOSCIENCE

The ever finer manipulation of natural entities would be impossible without the reliance on scientific results by inventors, engineers, and technicians. Increased funding made it increasingly possible for researchers to explore fields that might yield practical results. The increasing number of engineers and technicians to have graduated with diplomas was another factor. Higher education exposed them to the methods and results of scientists. All that was left to do was to forge alliances.

As scientific know-how became more complex, leading to the mastery of increasingly narrow specialties by each scientist, it became necessary to gather ever larger groups of researchers to tackle a major problem. To build a nuclear bomb, the United States practically created the city of Los Alamos. Large-scale projects (space exploration, high energy physics, genome sequencing) would be unthinkable without teamwork. The specialists who interact will often come from extremely varied backgrounds.

This is what is called Big Science. As an enterprise, it requires a great deal of funding and logistical support, the cooperation of scientists, engineers, technicians, and other support staff, and the collaboration of different institutions in the public sector (foundations, universities, government agencies either civilian or military) and in the private sector (companies).

The coordination of large numbers of professionals, each one with his or her own requirements for labour and material, demands in turn a higher level of management. So does the combination of entirely distinct professionals, such as scientists and engineers.

Therefore, research drawing upon both engineers and scientists can only proceed as part of fairly elaborate institutional arrangements. Government agencies, independent institutes, and funding bodies are often involved. The military-industrial-academic "iron triangle" relies on the collaboration of research universities, industrial concerns, and even military organizations.

PESTICIDES: HISTORICAL CONTEXT

The debate over pesticides also drew upon commonly invisible entities. At one end, the chemical products used as pesticides (insecticides, herbicides, and fungicides) are entirely visible and material. However, by the time they are diluted in groundwater or accumulated inside living cells, they are quite ungraspable.

The use of technology had environmental consequences long before the twentieth century, but the accelerated pace of technological development after World War II made these consequences more and more visible. Furthermore, with the development of effective chemical poisons, it became possible to envision the "eradication" of unwanted species. If the reshaping of nature in North America had been less than deliberate when European settlers had brought over new species or exterminated existing ones, such goals were openly declared as desirable after World War II.

Environmental consequences (though conceived narrowly) were among the principal objectives of such campaigns. In some cases, ironically, the "enemy" was itself an invader of more or less recent vintage (the imported red fire ant, or *Solenopsis invicta* for instance).

Several factors played a part in the use and abuse of chemical products whose possible effects were wilfully ignored. First and foremost, the need for herbicides became dramatic in the specific context of North American farming. The farming practiced by European settlers in North America was highly vulnerable to weeds. It was characterized by (i) monoculture ("specialization" in the modern jargon), and (ii) a lack of rigorous crop rotations.

In the British Isles, farmers had also been afflicted with weeds, and some of the worst ones made the trip across the Atlantic, including wild oats and wild mustard. Later, new weeds from Eurasia, such as Russian thistle and Russian knapweed, joined the older ones to complicate the job of farming in North America. What European settlers often didn't bring over were the methods used to control weeds in Europe, methods which made up what was called "good husbandry." Over the centuries, European farmers had learned various ways of keeping weeds in check. Techniques such as crop rotation, row cropping, and weeding of field margins were essential to the *control* of weeds. They could not eliminate weeds, however, and so farmers were taught that weeds were troublesome but inevitable.

However, good husbandry did not take root in North America, even though educators, the farm press, and agricultural scientists kept underlining its merits until the mid-twentieth century. There were various reasons for this. Crop rotation was hindered by the lack of markets for products other than wheat. Careful weeding was often impossible due to the general scarcity of labour in North American colonies, and to the high cost of available labour. Even where weeding could be mechanized, it still depended on a very specific knowledge of the soil. Other remedial practices were abandoned as farmers struggled to maximize their incomes in order to cover their original investments in land and tools. The basic measure taken to push back weed was summertime fallowing, but, by the early 1940s, weeds had become the leading cause of reduced wheat yields throughout the Canadian Prairies.

PESTICIDES: THE ROAD TO SYNTHETICS

As long as farming methods and goals remained unchanged, it was fairly clear that fields would remain open to weeds. This fostered the search for a different kind of solution. In 1945, that solution was the selective herbicide 2,4-D. It was cheap, easily applied, selective in its ability to destroy only broadleaf weeds in grain fields, and perfectly compatible with existing practices. Today, the solution is often identified with the broad-spectrum herbicide glyphosate (which genetically-modified crops such as Monsanto's Roundup Ready wheat are engineered to resist). In between, a number of different herbicides have been experimented and touted.

Unwanted insect species and fungi also prompted the development of new chemical poisons (insecticides and fungicides) during the twentieth century. Invasive species from outside North America without local natural enemies caused enormous damage, prompting the search for any solution, whether biological or chemical. By 1945, the solution was thought to be DDT (dichlorodiphenyltrichloroethane), the obvious successor to earlier insecticides. During the Second World War, DDT had been deployed as an insecticide against the mosquitoes responsible for malaria and the lice responsible for typhus in the war-ravaged cities of Europe.

Contributing factors to the postwar over-reliance on chemical means include:

▶ ignorance: the persistence of such substances as DDT in fatty tissues so that they not only accumulated but were concentrated up the food chain was relatively new (previous pesticides had been either biodegradable or insoluble).

▶ the wartime context in the case of DDT: (1) the sheer urgency of reducing the risks associated with malaria and typhus allowed the usual standards for innocuousness to be set aside and led to a focus on acute, short-term effects on humans to the detriment of possible long-term effects and of consequences for other animals; (2) the government was able to mobilize researchers and private companies to accelerate testing, development, and production in ways that would have been impossible in peacetime; (3) part of the research was classified or only divulged on a piecemeal basis so that known risks were revealed later than known benefits—or not at all.

▶ the use of chemical pesticides was thought to be cheap, in part because the cost for a single application (to be repeated yearly, and ignoring environmental consequences) was compared with (1) the cost for a one-time treatment that might last twenty years, or (2) labour-intensive measures that spared other animals and plants (thereby ignoring environmental benefits).

▶ the academic-industrial complex: protecting harvests through the eradication of pests was a cause that seemed worthwhile to scientists and that was well-funded by industry; the resulting synergy left little room for dissenting voices. This was part of Big Science—the more people and resources committed, the harder it was to admit error or change course.

Yet, other methods were known. Before Carl Djerassi's efforts to develop the control of pests using their biological enemies, French-Canadian biologist Félix d'Hérelle (1873–1949) had been inspired by the work of nineteenth-century zoologist Elie Metchnikoff, who envisioned the use of microorganisms deadly to insects. As an employee of the Institut Pasteur in the field (Argentina, Mexico, north Africa; between 1907 and 1921), Félix d'Hérelle investigated the diseases of pests. Insect pathogens are highly selective and apparently harmless to all but their intended targets. Félix d'Hérelle isolated the bacterium responsible for locust enteritis. In 1917, as World War I was raging, he rediscovered bacterial viruses—bacteriophages—and his later work on parasites of unicellular organisms attracted much attention before the discovery of antibiotics. During the first half of the century, in fact, many biologists like d'Hérelle worked to discover new strains of insect pathogens and to determine the best way of using them.

Others focused on the natural enemies of insect pests. As early as 1888, Albert Koebele brought back from Australia to the United States a natural enemy of one pest, the cottony cushion scale, that threatened the California citrus industry. The vedalia beetle proved quite effective at controlling the infestation. In the United States, by the time of Rachel Carson's *Silent Spring* (Houghton Mifflin, 1962), about 100 species of imported predators and parasites of insect pests had become established. The success stories included a wasp imported from Japan to control an insect attacking eastern apple orchards and several enemies of the spotted alfalfa aphid from the Middle East, which had been proving ruinous for alfalfa crops.

Some attempts were less successful, or backfired, devastating not only the pests but associated species. The tachinid fly imported long ago to fight the gypsy moth has reduced the population of harmless moth species. The worst effects were observed on islands (such as Hawaii) where a new species could run wild and, as is generally the case, could not be extirpated if the cure was worse than the disease. Defenders of biological control methods note that they should be compared to the environmental costs of using synthetic pesticides or introducing genetic modifications, not to a policy of inaction. While adding new species to an ecosystem can have undesirable effects, they are dwarfed by the impact of converting natural habitats or even cultivated fields into land for roads, buildings, and urban sprawl. On balance, the biological control of pests is still judged to be a worthy alternative though it may demand as thorough an investigation as chemical or biotechnological solutions.

By 1953, A. D. Pickett, an entomologist who had been working for 35 years in the apple orchards of Nova Scotia, had given up on the indiscriminate use of chemical pesticides, whether inorganic like *lead arsenate* before World War II, or drawn from the new post-war generation that included DDT. A pioneer in taking full advantage of the predatory and parasitic species, Pickett finally started experimenting with a combination of natural controls and insecticides—using as much as possible of the former and as little as possible of the latter. Minimum dosages of insecticides were applied, to control the pest without harming the beneficial species. Important predators were spared by carefully choosing times when they were yet unborn. And broad-spectrum pesticides were replaced by selective insecticides.

Nevertheless, by 1960, it was reported that only 2 percent of all the economic entomologists in the United States worked in the field of biological controls; most of the rest were engaged in research on chemical insecticides.

PESTICIDES: THE GLORY DAYS OF DDT

After the war, a worldwide campaign to eradicate malaria relied on DDT.

Malaria is a disease that results from a parasite infecting humans. Four species of the genus *Plasmodium* can target humans. The most lethal is known as *Plasmodium falciparum*. By the turn of this century, this species caused up to 500 million infections in Africa and took a toll of one to two million dead, mostly children. Since 2005, the number of cases has decreased to less than 300 million, of which more than 80 percent are identified in Africa. Since 2000, the death toll has decreased from about a million a year to 781,000 in 2009, nearly 90 percent of which take place in Africa. The associated economic toll is grievous—while estimates are imprecise, experts suspect that the combination of unnecessary deaths and time lost to bouts of sickness may cost up to one percent of the gross national product in many African countries.

Once upon a time, malaria plagued much of Europe (as far north as Scandinavia) and of North America (including parts of the US Midwest), as well as some of the temperate zones of Asia and South America. Malaria only kills a small fraction of those infected, but infections are debilitating. The development of infected children suffers and the ill-health of such a fraction of the population translates into major economic losses.

During the first half of the twentieth century, it was often eliminated in the more prosperous countries by the draining of wetlands, the use of quinine (made from cinchona bark), and the adoption of mosquito screens for doors and windows.

After World War II, DDT was introduced as a weapon against malaria in addition to its role as a pesticide for both food (maize) and non-food crops (cotton). Against malaria, DDT helped by targeting the insect vector of the malaria parasite. Mosquito nets and hammocks were dipped in DDT, mosquito breeding sites and house walls were sprayed with DDT, and public works cleaned out stagnant pools, all of which freed millions from the malaria threat. (In India, when the effectiveness of these measures peaked, the yearly death toll from malaria fell from 800,000 to almost zero.) In the very poorest countries, mainly in sub-Saharan Africa, the distribution of chloroquine tablets (a cheap synthetic relative of quinine) reduced the incidence of malaria in the 1960s and the 1970s.

However, as the *Plasmodium* parasites became resistant to quinine and chloroquine, while DDT was banned by several industrialized countries for crop-spraying after 1972, malaria made a comeback.

The ban on DDT was only made total in a few cases; most countries allowed its use for public health, especially to combat malaria. However, in the poorest countries, the use of DDT can only be funded by donor organizations from wealthier nations which are often reticent to finance a pesticide with such a bad reputation. Yet, in many locations where the target species have not developed a resistance to the pesticide, DDT remains effective (in association with therapeutic drugs for infected patients), lasts twice as long as alternatives when it is sprayed inside a home, and costs a quarter as much as the next cheaper option.

One recent test case of the usefulness of DDT was provided by South Africa when it set aside DDT as a pesticide for synthetic pyrethroids in 1996. Malaria cases and deaths increased rapidly, though other factors were present. The areas affected by the upsurge also experienced heavy rains after years of drought, expanding the breeding grounds of malaria-bearing mosquitoes. At the same time, refugees from Mozambique, Zimbabwe, and Botswana moved in, many of them malaria carriers. Finally, the *Plasmodium* parasite was proving resistant to anti-malarial drugs, including chloroquine, and mosquitoes demonstrated resistance to the pyrethroids.

The burst of new cases was brought under control by the return to DDT and the adoption of a new anti-malarial drug, artemisin, as part of multi-drug treatments. In fact, an upsurge in anti-malarial funding from international donors made it possible to address the scourge of malaria in the rest of Africa during the early years of the twenty-first century. In the fight to defeat malaria, the United States and Canada provided, in 2012, more than half of the global budget of 2.5 billion dollars.

By 2011, about 60 percent of all African sufferers of malaria were being treated with artemisin-based drugs. Two other significant remedies have been deployed in recent years throughout much of sub-Saharan Africa. The distribution of mostly free mosquito nets and screens, usually impregnated with an insecticide, was financed by donors on such a scale that, starting in 2006, more than 40 million a year were handed out. By 2012, over half a billion had been distributed and the death rate was cut by a third.

More surprisingly, the mobile phone has also played an impressive part in the new war on malaria. One free texting service allows would-be buyers of anti-malarial drugs to check the identification number in order to know that they are buying a genuine batch instead of a cheap knock-off or wholly fraudulent product. In Cameroun, Chad, Senegal, and Tanzania, a non-governmental organisation offers free advice to people who sign up for a text messaging service that will provide reminders about sleeping under a mosquito net, for instance. Elsewhere, text messaging has made it easier to restock clinics and small dispensaries in the countryside with both anti-malarial drugs and malaria tests. The new malaria tests almost qualify as a key breakthrough as well since testing technology multiplies the effectiveness of the existing stocks of anti-malarial drugs by allowing medical personnel to distinguish malarial fevers from other infections. As a result, the new drugs need not be administered to people who aren't suffering from malaria on the off-chance that they might be. Mobile phones are also used to track cases of the disease and collect real-time information on the epidemic. Since mobile phones have achieved market penetration rates in many African countries of about 70 percent, they are expected to play a lasting role in helping to control the disease, even if funding slackens off.

Meanwhile, current research is starting to target the real culprits in malaria transmission—the older female mosquitoes that are most likely to transmit the malaria parasite. (Younger mosquitoes may not have been infected yet or, if infected, are less likely to transmit the parasite.) A highly-targeted pesticide (or another means of eliminating mosquitoes that have completed at least four cycles of parasite egg production) would not only halt the transmission of the parasite, but also avoid fostering mosquito resistance to that pesticide since many of the older females are past their most fertile life stage. Survivors would therefore be unable to pass on any resistance genes. The authors of one recent essay on this topic expressed the hope that "late-life-acting insecticides would never be undermined by mosquito evolution" and that

"Done right, a one-off investment in a single insecticide would solve the problem of mosquito resistance forever."[2] Future research will show if that optimism is justified. Meanwhile, the control of ponds and wetlands to minimize the breeding of mosquitoes continues to prove effective, as in the Mexican state of Oaxaca that recently reported a one-third reduction of malaria cases without any use of DDT.

Other means of controlling insect populations include the sterilization (with radiation) of large numbers of male insects that are then released to mate with females—since the mating does not produce offspring, population growth is sharply reduced. However, this method does not work with mosquitoes. Recently, geneticists have attempted to breed populations of mosquitoes endowed with a gene that selectively harms females, so that they do not live long enough to reproduce. For now, they are targeting the single mosquito species (*A. aegypti*) that carries the dengue virus instead of the 30 to 40 mosquito species able to pass on the malaria parasite, but work is ongoing to extend the technique to mosquito vectors of malaria. An alternative strategy involves spreading dengue resistance genes within a given mosquito population in order to block the replication of the dengue virus inside the mosquito's body. Yet another method involves vaccinating mosquitoes against the *Plasmodium* parasite in order to interrupt its life cycle. In this case, humans are inoculated with the antibodies that bind to a mosquito protein that is needed by the parasite and the mosquito's bite transfers the vaccine to its own body.

PESTICIDES: THE OPPOSITION GATHERS

In 1962, more than a decade of data enabled Rachel Carson to identify in *Silent Spring* the disastrous—and entirely unheralded—side-effects of widely used pesticides. She was not the first to warn that DDT might drive fish, frogs, and birds extinct. As early as 1945, researchers such as Richard Pough (1904–2003) pointed to the possibility. Nor was she the first to identify DDT as a dangerous nerve poison for humans if it was mishandled and as the forerunner of chemicals that proved lethal not only for pests but for many other species in the environment. Many of the same risks had already been noted during World War II. However, she combined a masterful grasp of the scientific facts with the eloquence of an experienced science writer.

The modern environmental movement crystallized in the wake of Carson's book, especially in North America. She dramatized the disappearance of species affected

---

[2] Andrew F. Read, Penelope A. Lynch, and Matthew B. Thomas, "How to Make Evolution-Proof Insecticides for Malaria Control," *PLoS Biology*, **7**, Number 4 (2009), p. 1.

by pesticides by invoking the pastoral ideal of the traditional village, suddenly bereft of bird songs. And she deployed to great effect the old, pre-WWII nightmare of the poison gas attack of a city by rewriting it as a bombardment targeting all animal life, not just pests.

Indeed, the use of DDT had progressively brought it closer and closer to people's daily life. As a weapon against malaria, DDT could be applied to mosquito breeding sites as well as to walls, windows, and furniture. People might come into contact with those, but only occasionally. As a weapon against typhus, DDT would be sprayed in the form of delousing powder on the surface of skin or clothing. So, it stayed on the outside of the body.

As a weapon against agricultural pests, on the other hand, DDT would be applied to crops, leading to the contamination of the food eaten by people. (Even when it was used to treat cotton fields, such was its persistence in the environment that it often ended up contaminating food crops.) Therefore, DDT was ingested, and Carson's readers, being told that DDT was most probably a part of them, were that much more sensitive to her message.

DDT was finally banned when it was shown to cause cancer in laboratory settings. The ecological crisis brought about by the use of pesticides has only been corrected partially, despite the creation of the Environmental Protection Agency (EPA) in the United States (1970), followed by the creation of the Congressional Office of Technology Assessment (1972–1995). That same year, after studies suggesting that it caused cancer, DDT was banned in the United States, sparking a greater consciousness worldwide of the health effects of such products. By shifting the task of pesticide oversight and the Food Safety Inspection Service to the Environmental Protection Agency from the Department of Agriculture, the US government recognized that it was more prudent to beware the risks of chemical crop treatments than to assume they were wholly beneficial.

While the more dangerous pesticides were banned in North America, they have often continued to be used (and abused) in developing countries, often with a lesser degree of regulation and oversight. Pesticide burns and pesticide-linked ailments (sometimes due to suicide attempts using easily available pesticide stocks) are often part of the caseloads of rural hospitals.

The effects of pesticides were (and are) complex.

Biologically, they wiped out insect pests, but also ravaged other animal and insect populations within reach of pesticide applications. In time, the selective pressure they applied on species resulted in the rise of pesticide resistance. This had a real impact on the local ecology, though the creation of local refuges has mitigated the consequences of pesticide use on local fauna and flora.

Indeed, modern seed and pesticide companies frequently make the creation of a refuge or of a land parcel planted with untreated or genetically unmodified plants a condition of the use of their products as this slows or even stops the development of genetic resistance. This has led in some cases to the paradoxical situation where the farmers who do not use genetically modified crops reap greater financial rewards from the introduction of genetically modified crops in the local environment than farmers who do use genetically modified crops because the former benefit from the reduced pest populations brought about by the modified crops without having to pay for the genetically modified seeds; on the other hand, the fields of the former are essentially large-scale refuges harbouring pests that do not need to develop resistance, thus extending the usefulness of genetically modified crops by the latter farmers. Still, it is feared that the development of genetically-modified organisms might similarly alter the local ecology if the altered organisms spread in the wild.

Economically, pesticides were from the first one more *input* that farmers needed to buy to produce commercial crops. However, unlike farm machinery, farmers had to restock regularly—every year or more. In this respect, pesticides resembled chemical fertilizers or hybrid corn. Furthermore, the operation of the treadmill effect forced the improvident farmers either to increase the quantities they bought or to switch to new chemical compounds every so often.

With genetically-modified organisms, the dependence of farmers on outside suppliers is extended one more step since they are now obligated to buy seeds as well. It is not entirely new, as this was pioneered with the creation before World War II of hybrid corn that did not breed true, but genetic engineering has expanded the requirement to new crops. And regulatory systems in North America have often come down on the side of the seed sellers, by supporting the patenting of single genes and public breeding rights.

With respect to human health, the persistence of organic pesticides and their ability to penetrate organic tissues magnified their toxicity, and the novelty of these properties delayed proper research into their effects. Studies cited in 1997 showed that, more than a decade after the ban of DDT, 99.5 percent of the US population still had a detectable level of DDT or a DDT metabolite in their blood.

Animal studies of the effects of DDT on species often accepted as close to humans (primates, rats or mice) have indicated that DDT might be dangerously carcinogenic. Studies of human health effects as a result of background exposure are sparse, but they suggest an increased risk of pancreatic cancer and non-Hodgkin's lymphoma, while links with other cancers (including breast cancer) are inconclusive. Impaired lactation in women and effects on the male reproductive system are possible consequences of low-level exposure, though unproven. In short, the Longnecker, Rogan, and Lucier study in 1997 concluded that, "Other than the long-recognized neurologic toxicity associated with DDT poisoning, and laboratory abnormalities in DDT-exposed workers, human health effects of DDT exposure are not established."

By the 1970s, after decades of single-minded reliance on synthetic pesticides, popular opposition and renewed scientific doubts led to new investments in the development of integrated pest management (IPM), using a combination of techniques to control pest populations to levels below the threshold for economic damage. These techniques include biological control by natural predators, parasites, or diseases; plant breeding for pest resistance; better tracking of pest populations in the field to optimize and minimize pesticide applications; and the exploitation of the pest's own chemical signals (hormones, etc.) to interfere with its reproduction. They are still used today, for instance, as part of efforts to control the enemies of cacao crops in Southeast Asia.

While organic farming eschewed chemicals and took off, industrial agriculture in North America continues to rely on industrially-produced herbicides, fungicides, and insecticides that are generally accepted as safe. Ongoing work by Tyrone Hayes of the University of California, Rick Relyea of the University of Pittsburgh, and others indicates that, while each chemical taken alone may not pose a risk, the combination of chemicals introduced in the environment may have a grievous synergistic effect on the health of some animals (frogs, rats).

PESTICIDES: SUMMING UP

The yearly tests conducted up to 2008 by the Food and Drug Administration (FDA) in the United States revealed that a significant fraction of food products still harboured pesticide residues. In 2003 and 2008, the six pesticides most often found in food were:

- **DDT** (organochlorine present in 23% and 22% of the food products sampled in 2003 and in 2008 respectively): even though it was banned in 1972 because of its persistence in the environment, DDT still shows up because of accumulated soil residues in North America and because it is still used on crops from other countries. (Levels: 0.0001–0.031 ppm and 0.0001–0.090 ppm)

- **Endosulfan** (organochlorine present in 18% and 11% of the food products sampled in 2003 and 2008 respectively): introduced in 1954 and recently restricted to agricultural and commercial uses. (Levels: 0.0001–0.266 ppm and 0.0001–0.0645 ppm)

- **Malathion** (organophosphate present in 16% and 12% of the food products sampled in 2003 and 2008 respectively): introduced in 1950. (Levels: 0.0007–0.080 ppm and 0.0003–0.031 ppm)

- **Dieldrin** (organochlorine present in 15% and 11% of the food products sampled in 2003 and 2008 respectively): between 1950 and 1970, it was only second to DDT in usage and it was banned in 1974 for use on crops. (Levels: 0.0001–0.020 ppm and 0.0001–0.011 ppm)

- **Chlorpyrifos-methyl** (organophosphate present in 20% and 9% of the food products sampled in 2003 and 2008 respectively): used on stored grain since 1985; as it is moderately persistent in the soil, most applications have been voluntarily curtailed; between 2003 and 2008 it fell out of the top five. (Levels: 0.0001–0.573 ppm and 0.0001–0.025 ppm)

- **Quintozene** (organochlorine present in 10% of the food products sampled in 2008): used as a fungicide with cotton, rice, and seed grains, but restricted in the United States in 2006, so that its use on crops was limited or ended; in 2008, it rose to become one of the top five. (Levels: 0.0001–0.0217 ppm)

The data do not necessarily reveal health dangers. Allowable limits for pesticide residues were only exceeded in about 2% of food products sampled in the United States in 2003. In 2008, 0.9% of domestically produced food and 4.7% of food imports in the United States contained pesticide residues in excess of regulatory limits. Most pesticide residues are therefore thought to be well below the amount that would affect people's health, though Carson herself wondered in 1962 about the possible synergistic effects of pesticide combinations present in the human body. What it certainly illustrates is the long-term persistence of some pesticides in the environment.

According to Edward O. Wilson, chemical pollution remains today the third-ranking cause of species extinction in the United States, after habitat destruction and "biological pollution—the influx of alien species that outcompete and push back natives ones."[3] It should be emphasized that neither *pesticide resistance* nor the *pesticide treadmill* negate the productivity gains associated with pesticide use, which is why pesticides continue to be used. However, these gains are obtained at a cost to the environment (local eradications of various species), at the risk of long-term effects, and at a higher expense than expected for farmers, all of which has consequences for both the farming sector and the environment.

Of course, chemical pollution includes more than pesticides. Though laws have become stricter, both groundwater and running water are still contaminated by effluent from factories (by-products of manufacturing processes), by run-off from farms (animal waste, fertilizers, pesticides), by untreated effluent from sewer systems, by leachates from dumps both legal and illegal, and by tailings or other by-products of mines and oil/gas wells. (Though modern dumps are often better insulated by layers of clay and other liners, the drilling of nearby test wells as a matter of course indicates there is no confidence in their absolute effectiveness.) The air is also polluted on a continual basis by the exhaust from cars, factories, and power plants.

Seen from another angle, the ability of the chemical industries to promote their pesticides and herbicides over the objections of many may result from the power of the new alliance of science and technology, sometimes designated as *technoscience*.

Worldwide, the use of pesticides took off in concert with the "Green Revolution" attributed to work pioneered by biologist Norman Borlaug (1914–2009). At a time when the population of poorer countries was exploding as a result of public health and sanitation improvements, he showed that conventional breeding could lead not only to greater yields and efficiencies, as with the hybrid corn, but also to greater food availability in poorer countries. Borlaug achieved his most convincing successes in Mexico where his modified wheat boosted the productivity of farmers six-fold. Other agronomists went on to replicate his breakthrough with other crops, including rice.

The general drawback of the new crop strains was their dependence on pesticides, fertilizers, controlled irrigation, and mechanization. As with hybrid corn, several varieties did not breed true, so that seeds had to be purchased anew every year to achieve the highest possible productivity. This contributed to the market stranglehold of an increasingly small number of US and European seed companies that turned into global behemoths.

---

[3] Edward O. Wilson, "Afterword," *Silent Spring* (Houghton Mifflin, 2002), p. 361.

FROM PESTICIDES TO GMOs

After the ban in many Western countries of the most dangerous pesticides, the use of replacement pesticides while respecting the new safety regulations proved expensive. By then, scientists were seeking to invent safer methods to control pests and weeds hampering agricultural productivity. They were driven in part by the need to reduce the collateral damage produced by broad-spectrum pesticides, but also by the awareness that the evolution of pesticide resistance in pests could no longer be addressed only by increasing doses or switching to another pesticide in the same chemical family. One of their goals was to target pests as selectively as possible; another was to maximize the usefulness of the remaining pesticides. It is ironic that this led to genetically-modified organisms (GMOs) endowed with precisely those qualities but which have roused sometimes fierce opposition.

After all, if plants are incorporating in their genomes the ability to express chemicals that would be used externally otherwise, it is not clear that such genetically-modified plants should be less safe than traditional plants grown in a chemically-sprayed field. Defenders of genetically-modified crops also point out that there are other environmental benefits to their use such as the anticipated decrease of pesticide use and the reduction of soil disturbance (tillage) which leads to erosion and soil loss. Increasing harvest yields would also go some way towards meeting food demand resulting from population growth.

On the other hand, the potential effects on the environment (through genetic contamination) are unknowable and the control gained by the companies responsible, such as Monsanto, over individual farmers is highly debatable—though it is not new, having been pioneered by the inventors of hybrid corn, for instance. Thus, the exploration of alternatives to synthetic pesticides has led, somewhat paradoxically, to the creation of genetically-modified plants whose benefits are perhaps even more controversial.

CONSTRUCTING SUPPER (OR LUNCH)

Between 1950 and 1999, the US production of broiler chicken meat increased on average 7 percent per annum, to a total of 40 billion pounds (or 16 million tonnes). During the same time, real prices declined by about a third. This tremendous increase was achieved through the application of both science and technology to the raising of poultry, along with legislative measures and increased investment.

Some technologies were developed specifically to assist in perfecting the art of raising chickens, but many were simply applied as they became available for general purposes. Electric power was only brought to the countryside in the United States after the First World War. Once electricity reached farms, it became possible to power incubators and to drive the machinery that controlled temperature and ventilation for the enclosures used to house chickens. This control of temperature, ventilation, and sanitation was the main advantage of raising poultry indoors, sparing them the harsher conditions outdoors.

Yet, chickens raised indoors were soon discovered to exhibit weakness that resulted in losses. Ongoing research by biologists led to the discovery that this was probably due to a lack of vitamin D from the lack of sunshine; once vitamin D was added to the diet of the chickens, research moved on to optimizing other aspects of their feed.

Corn, a low fiber, high-energy cereal, became a major part of their diet. For essential amino acids, soybeans were combined with the corn. This move turned chickens into a convenient way of converting major US crops into a compact consumer product—broiler chicken meat.

After World War II, it was discovered that administering subtherapeutic doses of antibiotics to chickens helped them to grow faster while improving their health. In 1951, the US Food and Drug Administration approved the use of penicillin and chlortetracycline as chicken feed additives. By the late 1990s, poultry producers used more antimicrobials than were used for either cattle or hogs. Yet, as far back as 1959, Japanese scientists had discovered that there existed a mechanism for the transmission of resistance traits in bacteria via the transfer of plasmids (DNA fragments) from one bacterium to another, thus accelerating the spread of resistant bacteria.

Finally, chickens were bred intensively to acquire the desired traits. In 1948 and 1951, nationwide competitions were held to find the "Chicken of Tomorrow." Breeders submitted their best animals. Soon, companies applied to chickens the lessons learned in developed hybrid corn. Pure inbred lines were crossed to produce high-quality hybrids. These commercial chicken lines were characterized by the "biological lock of hybridization." They could not be bred, for breeding hybrids produced highly variable results. Poultry producers therefore became dependent on the companies that controlled the pure inbred lines.

All of the strategies used to increase poultry production (directed breeding, intensive confinement, improved nutrition, and antibiotics as well as other drugs) favored industry concentration.

DIRECT GENETIC MODIFICATION

The power of conventional, or traditional, breeding is clearly shown by the forced evolution of chickens over the last hundred years, aided by better feed and cooping. Yet, the process can be a slow one since each successive generation must be allowed to mature and demonstrate the sought-for characteristics, or not, before a new set of breeding choices is made.

In theory, genetic engineering should be much faster. In principle, scientists only need to identify the relevant sequence of a genome and transfer it into the genome of the target species. The history of the use of bacterium *Bacillus thuringiensis* (Bt) in agriculture illustrates this best-case scenario. Originally, researchers realized, by the early twentieth century, that some strains of this soil-dwelling microbe produced a protein that was deadly to only certain insects, which happened to include several agricultural pests, but not desirable ones, such as bees. Farmers initially spread the bacteria proper in their fields. After the Second World War, scientists isolated the toxic protein. Once it was synthesized, it could be sold as a spray-on insecticide and many organic farmers still use the crystallized protein or the spores that can produce viable bacteria.

As scientists decoded the genetic basis of all life during the same period, it became possible to identify which stretches of DNA accounted for the synthesis of given proteins. The genes that coded for the production by the bacillus of the key protein were eventually identified.

The methods of recombinant DNA developed after 1970 to make it possible to permanently transfer such genes between organisms. At the DNA level, the genetic code is the same so that it is feasible to transfer genes between fish and mammals, between plants and animals, or between microbes and plants. A gene transfer technique pioneered by Belgian biologist Marc van Montagu was first used to transfer the key Bt genes in 1983 into tobacco plants to endow them with the same defense against insects as *Bacillus thuringiensis*. Similar transfers were later carried out with the Bt genes to breed transgenic potatoes, corn, soybeans, and cotton. The Environmental Protection Agency approved the Bt tuber in 1995, but Bt corn and other crops have enjoyed greater success since then.

The public reaction to genetically modified organisms has been mixed. In Europe, it has been largely hostile and the cultivation of transgenic crops is broadly restricted in countries such as Austria, Hungary, France, Luxembourg, and Germany. Twenty-first century activists have invaded plots and fields planted with genetically modified plants, often to uproot them and sometimes to plant instead organic varieties.

In the United States, the initial reaction to the Flavr Savr tomato approved for human consumption in 1994 was sufficiently controversial to make it into a flop. Like conventional tomatoes, it was harvested in an unripened state, but it enjoyed a longer shelf-life. It was sold until 1997 only and the producer was later acquired by Monsanto. However, industrial crops used to make processed foods (soybeans, maize, and canola) took off, as well as one non-food crop (cotton). Between 1996 and 2010, the acreage of land planted with GMOs went from basically nothing to about 10 percent of the world's croplands.

Total Area of Biotech Crops Cultivated Worldwide
(In Millions of Hectares)

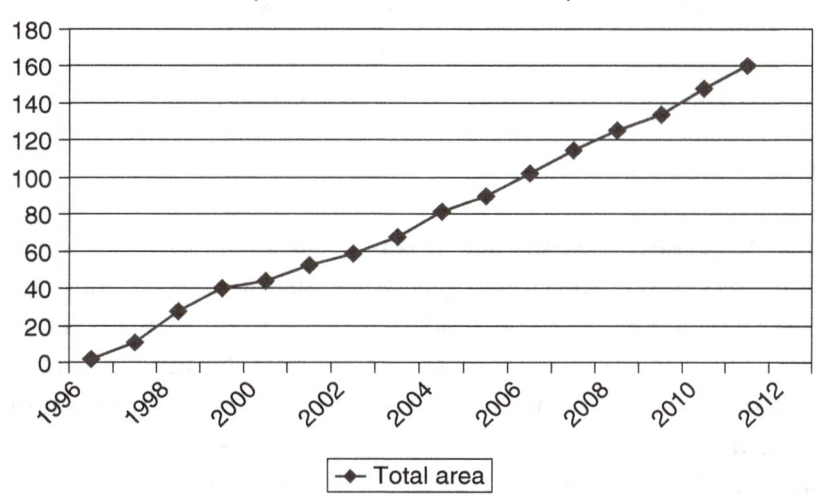

FIGURE 1 ▶ The total area (in millions of hectares) of biotech crops cultivated worldwide has never stopped growing since the first genetically modified crops were introduced. *(Data source: ISAAA reports.)*

Until 2010, North America produced the clear majority of the world's genetically-modified crops, but Brazilian harvests have increased rapidly in recent years.

Transgenic Crops, 2006–2012
(Percentage of the World's Total Transgenic Crop Area by Country)

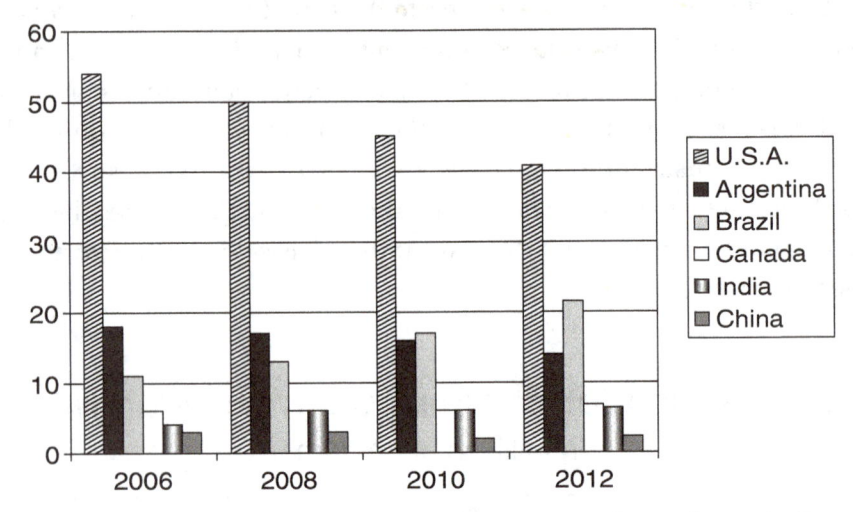

FIGURE 2 ▶ While the United States remains the dominant producer of genetically-modified crops, Brazil has nearly doubled its share of the world's total transgenic crop area since 2006. The percentage of the worldwide area is given here for six of the seven top producers of such crops. *(Data source: ISAAA reports.)*

Currently, most genetically-modified crops are bred for herbicide tolerance alone, with only a minority favouring insect resistance instead. The second most common GMOs are those which combine herbicide tolerance and insect resistance. All other possible traits, such as virus resistance, enrichment in vitamin A, drought resistance or more efficient nitrogen absorption, account for less than one percent of the crops grown worldwide.

Arguments as to the safety and advantages of genetically-modified organisms have been put forward by proponents and opponents. The objections fall into three main categories:

With respect to human health, critics point out that few targeted studies have been undertaken to systematically examine the effects of consuming transgenic food products, even though genetically-modified corn, soybeans, and canola are all part of the food chain in North America. Not only are they fed to cows, pigs, and chickens, but they are also used to make corn syrup, a staple of many processed foods, corn oil, canola oil, and tortillas. Yet, the suspect proteins may not even survive the processing required to extract oil. Some of the studies that have been conducted and reviewed did conclude that transgenic crops did not pose any health hazards for rats, mice, or other animals. On the other hand, while conventional breeding works with the existing store of plant genes plus a few mutants and interlopers, genetic engineering can bring in genes that have never been part of the human food supply and cannot be assumed to be wholly safe. Geneticists also note that the genome is a dynamic entity that actually reacts over time to the introduction of new genes, with unforeseen long-term consequences. Opponents suggest that every single combination of a crop, a recombinant gene, and a given habitat should be tested to determine possible consequences. The fact remains that genetically-modified crop plants are not tested for safety in the same way new drugs are tested by the FDA in the United States.

With respect to environmental impacts, the unrestrained use of herbicides on herbicide-tolerant crops has led to the development of herbicide-resistant weeds. As a result, in a classic example of the pesticide treadmill, herbicide doses have been increased even as they start to prove ineffective. The control enjoyed by the seed companies over their market has also led to fears that they might encourage wholesale adoption of such a small number of crop strains that it would lead to an effective monoculture, reducing agricultural diversity and ultimately even genetic diversity in the wild if domesticated plants crossbreed with relatives or spread their modified genes. A monoculture would be uniquely exposed to collapse if any new pest or hazard threatened it without the existence of potentially unaffected strains as a back-up and insurance policy.

With respect to economic impact, opponents have pointed to the control gained by the seed companies as biotechnology practically guarantees them a monopoly and the rents that can be derived from market control. Furthermore, the higher cost of genetically-modified seed looms as a possible threat to smaller farmers who might be, especially in poorer countries, unable to afford them. As for the monetary benefits, they seem to flow mostly to corporations while neither farmers nor consumers enjoy significant relief from the new technology.

The hostile reception to transgenic crops was also shaped, at least in Europe, by the cultural climate. Within the space of a few years, Western Europe was hit by fears over the safety of its food supply as the 1996 mad cow crisis, which involved the transmission of a form of bovine spongiform encephalopathy from cows to humans, was followed by an epidemic of hoof and mouth disease in the United Kingdom in 2001.

With pesticides as with genetically-modified crops, the nature of the product is clearly part and parcel of the public reaction. Pesticide residues in food have been conflated with intrusive genes in crops as undesirable additions to mealtimes. The idea that consumers might be unaware of the potentially toxic ingredients of their food has proven to be more worrisome, at least to a vocal minority, than the use of similar biotechnologies to synthesize insulin, vaccines, new pharmaceuticals, plastics, or biofuels.

BASIC DEFINITIONS OF PESTICIDE TECHNOLOGY

Fertilizer: a product intended to enhance the soil's fertility, therefore increasing the crop's yield (the size of the harvest per unit of cultivated area).

Pesticide: a product intended to combat crop pests (*i.e.*, the smaller life forms that feed off crops thus reducing the yield at the expense of the farmer); a pesticide targeting insects is an *insecticide*, a pesticide targeting weeds is a *herbicide*, and a pesticide targeting fungi is a *fungicide*, but all are pesticides.

Broad-spectrum agent (or pesticide): when a broad-spectrum agent is applied to a field, it will kill all or a large number of the species present; such a pesticide is not specific to any given species; it is broadly toxic.

Pesticide resistance: when a pesticide is applied, a small number of pests may happen to be endowed with some form of resistance to that pesticide; as long as these survive and are able to reproduce, further applications of the pesticide will only set the table for uncontrolled reproduction of the strain endowed with resistance; in California, the multiplication of insects impervious to spraying was observed as early as the time of World War I; by 1958, when Canadian entomologist A. W. A. Brown was engaged by the World Health Organization to prepare a comprehensive survey of the resistance problem, it was realized that even the new synthetic pesticides were meeting with resistance and, indeed, fostering it. In essence, pesticide use *selects* for resistant insects and favours their takeover to an astonishing degree.

Pesticide treadmill: a broad-spectrum pesticide typically wipes out a variety of species, including the targeted pest but also beneficial species; as a result, other species—previously known as secondary pests—whose natural enemies or superior competitors have been decimated are now free to move in and may prove just as devastating for a crop as the original pest. As a result, it becomes necessary to apply yet more pesticides. This vicious circle of pesticide use leading to more pesticide use is known as the pesticide treadmill (in the sense that, on a treadmill, however hard you run, you cannot get ahead—you stay in place). Another form of the treadmill is associated with pesticide resistance: as it develops, new or different pesticides must be used to overcome the pests that have developed immunity.

Nota Bene: *Fertilizers* should not be confused with *pesticides*. Fertilizers are products that promote plant growth and improve the yield of the desired product, whether grain, fruit, or vegetable. Pesticides are designed to kill pests (insects, fungi, weeds) that either feed off cultivated plants or invade their habitat, competing for resources that might have gone into yields instead.

CHAPTER 13

Biotechnology: Old and New

▶▶▶▶▶▶▶▶▶▶▶▶▶▶▶▶▶▶▶▶▶▶▶▶▶▶▶▶▶

HISTORICAL BACKGROUND

Agriculture was one of the earliest technological systems. Indeed, considering the variety of crops, it would be more accurate to call it a complex of technological systems (one geared to grow wheat, another to grow oats, another to grow olives, etc.). It built upon an existing foundation—the human adaptations to the use of fire. According to Harvard University anthropologist Richard Wrangham, cooking with fire may go as far back as 1.8 million years ago, when the hominid species *Homo erectus* appeared in the fossil records with smaller teeth, larger skulls, and bones suggesting smaller torsos and abdomens. This could be a consequence of cooked food being easier to chew and digest, and more nutritious.

One Paleolithic site (Ohalo II) found near the Sea of Galilee includes the remains of wild grains including barley, grinding equipment, and a stone oven. It has been dated to 23,000 years before the present, proving that ancient humans had already added wild cereals to the fruits and nuts they gathered, and ground them into rough seed cakes. Even older archaeological sites in Italy, Russia, and the Czech Republic have yielded bits of plants, such as cattail-like roots, on grindstones going back 30,000 years. True agriculture goes as far back as 11,000 years in the Mediterranean

Fertile Crescent (wheat), 9,000 years in Mesoamerica (corn), 8,000 years in South America (quinoa, squash, peanut, and cotton), and 8,000 years in China (rice).

The environmental consequences of agriculture would be profound, even if they were limited to the modification of the plants cultivated for food and of the natural landscape cleared for cultivation. The research team led by Jonathan A. Foley (University of Minnesota) estimated in 2011 that agriculture has cleared or significantly transformed 70 percent of the planet's grasslands compared to what they were in prehistoric times, 50 percent of the savannas, 45 percent of the temperate deciduous forests, and 25 percent of the tropical forests.

Evidence gathered from ice cores drilled from the Antarctic and Greenland ice sheets actually suggests that deforestation and irrigation associated with agriculture led to ancient increases of atmospheric carbon dioxide (8,000 years ago) and methane (5,000 years ago). These increases may have counteracted the natural decreases of the same gases that would have been expected as a result of the Milankovich cycles (driven by pure orbital mechanics) that govern the amount of sunshine received at the Earth's surface. By augmenting the greenhouse effect, these increases would have postponed the glacial period that should have started thousands of years ago, according to William Ruddiman (University of Virginia). The increasing levels of carbon dioxide seem to be associated with the spread of wheat cultivation to parts of Europe and China where it was necessary to clear fields by cutting down or burning down forests (which led to the release of the carbon locked inside the wood's cellulose). Elsewhere, forests may have been burned on a regular basis by hunters and other farmers maintaining a preferred forest state. The increase in methane seems to be associated with the start of the irrigation of human-made rice paddies in southern Asia, the decomposition of vegetation in standing water producing methane. While this theory is disputed, it points to the powerful effects of everyday technologies that are readily overlooked in spite of their broad transformation of the planet's landscape.

Beyond the atmosphere's composition, the transition to agriculture has affected the local *albedo* (a measure of the amount of light reflected by the Earth's surface). Replacing forests with croplands increases how much sunlight the land reflects. And modern agriculture often pumps water out of the ground (from *aquifers*) or uses river water for irrigation, both of which change how much water rivers carry to the ocean.

Even the most primitive forms of agriculture required granaries, implements to aid with the harvesting, and the development of special skills to keep watch over fields, separate the wheat from the chaff, and recover the grain. (Sowing came later.) About 10,000 years ago, mice moved in to take advantage of human stores of grain in

Israel. As early as 9,500 years ago in Cyprus, cats had become *commensals* of farmers, helping them to control the mice population around granaries in exchange for food and shelter. Over the following thousands of years, farmers kept an eye out for plants that stood up to bad weather, diseases, or pests, and were prolific. They soon started not only selecting such plants, but also trying to capture those traits by crossbreeding them into other plants.

Without the development of new wheat varieties, the settlement of parts of Canada would have been far more difficult. Even earlier, the discovery of the Americas led to numerous biotechnology transfers resulting in the worldwide spread of many crops once native to the Americas such as maize, tobacco, the tomato, and the potato, as well as the reverse.

FROM TRADITIONAL BIOTECHNOLOGY TO MODERN AGRICULTURE

Medicine is one of the oldest scientific disciplines. The Hippocratic corpus of Greek texts in Antiquity already points to a concern for determining the efficacy of various treatments and products. The *materia medica* known to Greek doctors comprised a vast array of plant-based remedies. Arab practitioners perfected distillation as a way to achieve new levels of purity and Renaissance alchemists such as Paracelsus experimented with the use of inorganic substances, including arsenic and mercury, as possible cures in small doses. Folk medicine pointed the more attentive researchers like Edward Jenner towards new avenues, leading to the development of a vaccination for smallpox in 1798. The chemical revolution wrought by Lavoisier and other 18th-century chemists led to a systematic inventory of new elements and compounds, some of which proved of medical interest.

In biotechnology, the late nineteenth century and early twentieth century saw many breakthroughs, such as the development of new vaccines (against rabies, diphtheria, and tuberculosis) as part of the Pasteurian revolution, the elucidation of diseases and parasitic relationships, the isolation of some biologically active substances (hormones, vitamins, antihistamines), and the definition of the laws of genetics by Mendel (unbeknownst to most at the time).

Applications of these discoveries awaited the twentieth century however, during which further discoveries were made, especially in the field of genetics. Antibiotics and vaccines combined to stifle the spread of some infectious diseases, even eliminating smallpox. Insulin was isolated by Canadian researchers at the University of

Toronto and applied to the treatment of diabetes. (Insulin is a hormone; hormones are chemical messengers and were so named in 1905.) As the importance of trace elements in the diet was recognized, nutrition improved. As part of the Pasteurian revolution, cleanliness and public sanitation were prized, and the new emphasis on hygiene paid off. Epidemics were curtailed, freeing women from the duties of home care, reducing mortality, and increasing the general population.

By the second half of the twentieth century, the genetic code was decoded and new classes of drugs were discovered. Building upon the breakthrough of British doctor Alexander Fleming in recognizing the antibiotic action of penicillin in 1922, post-war researchers added a number of compounds to the arsenal of drugs able to combat hostile microorganisms in the body. By the 1950s, psychoactive chemicals were discovered and the first benzodiazepines were marketed in the 1960s. Librium (launched in 1960) and more famous Valium (launched in 1963) were psychotropic drugs that could treat anxiety and alcohol withdrawal. Librium was also prescribed for insomnia, one of many drugs sold for sleep disorders such as barbiturates. As a mood-altering drug that might be taken for prolonged periods of time to relieve anxiety, Librium was subjected to extensive testing by the standards of the period. While news reports claimed that 2,000 physicians had used the drug on 20,000 patients in the course of 1959, the actual total of patients reported as test subjects to the US Food and Drug Administration (FDA) was 1163. Since Librium was tested on more than one condition, only 570 of these patients suffered from the psychiatric disorders that Librium would be used to address.

The success of penicillin raised hopes of drugs that would be "magic bullets" capable of utterly vanquishing a disease time after time without fail. Yet, drugs can be ineffective at best. At worst, they can have serious side effects that may kill patients in the worst cases. In the United States, drug approval was up to the FDA, but in 1958, it only had three full-time physicians and four part-time doctors finishing their residency training to deal with a flood of submissions, about 400 new drug applications per year on average between 1952 and 1962, and about 3,000 supplemental applications a year (requesting permission to use an approved drug for a different condition) between 1957 and 1962.

In 1961 and 1962, the Thalidomide scandal dominated the medical news. A drug prescribed to expectant mothers both as a sedative and in order to alleviate the severity of morning sickness, Thalidomide was used in Canada and in much of Western Europe, though it was not approved in the United States. It turned out to be responsible for an international epidemic of birth defects and miscarriages accounting for over 10,000 victims. As a result, US laws were tightened and imposed more stringent reporting guidelines on drug manufacturers so that they would provide information on any problems arising after a drug was marketed. Procedures for the approval of new drugs were relaxed somewhat in the 1980s in the name of encouraging innovation.

While modern biochemistry has turned the human body into a technological arena, it is not the only modern development that raises hard questions about risks, as we now live in a society dominated by risk assessment and the need to make decisions about environmental threats on the basis of limited information.

By 1970, scientists had translated the discoveries of scientists such as Watson and Crick (the double helix of DNA) into means for the manipulation of the genetic code. (This was demonstrated by the insertion of three E. coli genes into the genome of a monkey virus in 1972.) As genetic engineering became possible at a time when other technological innovations (synthetic pesticides, the birth control pill) had proven to be less than unalloyed goods, the public was bombarded with fearsome scenarios and so 140 of the world's top biologists met in the historic 1975 Asilomar conference in California's Monterey Peninsula. Over four days, they hammered out a set of rules to govern future research, define containment procedures, and determine safety regulations. Many biologists still adhere to this code, though genetic engineering has now progressed to the point where it is feasible to build gene by gene the code for living organisms. Synthetic biology, which makes it possible to build a functional virus from scratch in a few weeks, now appears to be where recombinant DNA technology was in the early 1970s. It was the techniques of recombinant DNA engineering that made it possible both to turn out cheap insulin by adding human genes to bacteria and to create plants modified to resist an industry-standard herbicide.

As a consequence, the final frontier of technology is life itself. Earlier technological changes affected such things as the bases of production and distribution: transportation, agricultural productivity, and power sources such as steam and electricity. The natural environment often bore the brunt of their needs and impacts. Later technological changes transformed social relationships: new means of communications and information processing (telegraphs, telephones, and computers), the increasing scale of manufacturing and distribution, and the management of work itself. All aspects of personal and public life were affected, especially in the direction of greater *enmeshment* of people's lives, at farther and farther removes.

When we come to biotechnology, we find a technology that is even more fundamental. It is no longer productivity nor relationships that are altered, but the objects themselves: the plants, the animals, the microbes . . . More than that, the *subjects* are.

As people benefit from new drugs, remedies, and implants, they are now finding themselves on that frontier.

TECHNOSCIENCE

Today, at least 95 percent of the world's agricultural production depends on only 24 different domesticated plant species. Of those, wheat, corn, and rice make up a majority of humanity's caloric intake.

Top Crops (by acreage) in 2012

Crop	Fraction of World's Harvested Croplands
Wheat	18.3%
Maize (corn)	15.4%
Rice	14.2%
Soybeans	9.3%
Barley	4.3%
Sorghum	3.3%
Seed cotton	3.0%
Rapeseed	3.0%
Millet	2.7%
Dry beans	2.5%

(Source: FAO)

The artificial selection of crops by pre-modern plant breeders has given us much of our food. Modern biotechnology started with systematic attempts to improve crops, using proven methods such as artificial selection and cross-breeding. In Canada, research of this kind was conducted at Ottawa's Experimental Farm, funded by the federal Ministry of Agriculture at a time when it was one of the government's major ministries.

In the United States, botanist Luther Burbank became known as the "Wizard of Horticulture" for his breeding of new flowers and fruits. By the time of his death in 1926, he had developed over 800 strains and varieties of plants. A natural genetic variant of his Burbank potato now known as the Russet Burbank is probably the world's dominant potato variety in food processing. Burbank's empirical breeding methods epitomized the trial-and-error methods that still prevailed during his lifetime, though a more scientific approach was already beginning to preside over the research that would lead to the development of high-yielding double-cross hybrid corn by 1935.

US geneticist George Harrison Shull formulated the principles behind the production of hybrid corn as early as 1908. Its ability to resist drought encouraged its adoption by farmers during the drought-ravaged 1930s even though it would force them to buy seed every year from the seed companies producing the hybrid corn. Manpower shortages during World War II, corporate advertising, and a strong push from the United States Department of Agriculture (USDA) led to an increasing complete switch to hybrid corn. Within thirty years, the scientific work of Shull had led to the development of an effective biotechnological innovation.

After the Second World War, a renewed stress on selection over the last century led to what was called the Green Revolution of the 1960s. Crops were selected by scientists such as Norman Borlaug for larger seed-bearing heads to increase yields. Since the larger heads were heavier, shorter plant heights were bred into rice and wheat to prevent the plants from bending too close to the ground. More breeding was done to engineer disease resistance, environmental stress tolerance, and a more efficient utilization of nitrogen fertilizers. Additional investments in irrigation and the supplying of fertilizers to poor farmers helped multiply agricultural yields (by a factor of three in India over thirty years).

Desirable Traits

Growth	Maturation	Grain Size/Number	Seed-head Size		
Architecture	Height	Branching	Flowering		
Stress tolerance	Drought	Pests	Diseases	Herbicides	Intensive fertilization
Nutrients	Starch	Proteins	Lipids	Vitamins	

(Source: Jerry D. Glober, Cindy M. Cox, and John P. Reganold, "Future Farming: A Return to Roots?", Scientific American, August 2007, p. 82–89.)

However, the new methods of biotechnological giants are not limited to the plant kingdom. The investigation of genes and genomes may be extended to animals and people. In plants, it allows genes from other plants to be identified and tested in crop species even though their beneficial effects on desirable traits are not evident from the original plant's appearance or properties. Focusing on the presence of the chosen gene instead of the appearance of the adult plant (which may or may not have incorporated the gene) also helps accelerate the breeding of better plants. This may be seen as one example of a new alliance of science and technology sometimes designated as *technoscience*.

Ruth Schwartz Cowan suggests that technoscience is the outcome of the blurring of distinctions along the spectrum that goes from pure science to pure technology. Yet, science is rarely pure, while technology as far back as the 18th century has often owed a debt to scientific investigations. After all, Copernicus never lost sight of calendrical problems when he worked out a heliocentric system. Galileo's work on falling objects was of interest to artillery men and Galileo himself developed the theory of statics as a result of observations made in the shipbuilding yards of Venice.

The absence of discontinuities or sharp distinctions along a spectrum does not mean that sharply different entities stop existing. The electromagnetic spectrum is essentially continuous, but blue is not the same as red. Even though the qualities we call blue and red are mental entities, the corresponding physical realities cannot be confused just because they lie on a continuous spectrum. Philosophers thus speak of *differences in degree* that can become *differences in kind*.

If there is something new about technoscience, it is not so much the existence of a relationship between science and application as the tightness, mutuality, and complexity of that relationship. There is little new about "enterprises in which people seek the truth about nature in order to transform it,"[1] or manage it better, or anticipate its phenomena. There is even less that is new about "enterprises in which some truths about nature have been uncovered in the practice of trying to transform it."[2] This is what German philosopher Martin Heidegger suggested was the essence of technology itself. Science may be producing pure truths about isolated systems, but technological enterprises often reveal surprising new facts about the interactions of nature, artifacts, and people.

Technoscience is probably best defined sociologically. It is characterized by large teams of collaborators from several disciplines and occupations: administrators, accountants, scientists from various fields, engineers, technicians, etc. It is goal-oriented and it may involve cross-institutional collaborations: university professors, industrial and consulting engineers, government specialists, and venture capitalists all coming together. It often features international collaborations due to the increasingly

---

[1] Ruth Schwartz Cowan, *A Social History of American Technology* (Oxford University Press, 1997), p. 308.
[2] *Ibid.*

specialized nature of science and technology, to the point where few countries can count on specialists in all the fields of knowledge. For similar reasons, the number of geographical locations involved in technoscientific developments has often increased, as diverse facilities, sources of raw materials, and human workers must be pressed into service to come up with innovative products. All of this makes what Cowan defines as technoscience a close relative of "Big Science." As technoscience has grown, so have the risks associated with its implementation.

RISKS AND THEIR PERCEPTION

When discussed in the context of major technological failures or accidents, the concept of risk may seem straightforward. Risk is the chance of danger to life or limb. Loss of life is the ultimate standard.

Yet, even the definition of risk is trickier than it seems. First, a technology may present risks without being really dangerous; the possibility of danger should not be confused with the probability of danger.

Second, danger can arise through the failure of a technology or through its regular operation. The risk of failure may be low, and the danger high, as when a steam boiler explodes with lethal consequences. On the other hand, the regular disposal of effluent in a river may be a near certainty while the danger it poses to people's health is harder to evaluate.

Train crashes and bridge collapses kill directly. There is no question of cause and effect. However, exposure to a noxious chemical or the accumulation of chemical residues in the body may only lead to a statistically higher than normal risk of disease (cancer) and death. Since there are normal levels, somebody who has not been exposed to radiation or synthetic pesticides may sicken and die just like somebody who has been exposed. Alternatively, someone who has been exposed may not get sick and may die of completely unrelated causes. While the elevation of the risk is real, the chain of cause and effect is no longer absolute.

Furthermore, there are different levels of risks that may be weighed against each other. GMOs pose a credible risk to the integrity of ecological systems, if only through an additional reduction of biodiversity. Such an impoverishment of the natural environment may eventually impair the *carrying capacity* of the land (the land's ability to produce resources, such as crops, that humans and other animals need to live). But any effect on human health is far less certain than the effects on the environment. Therefore, different people may assess their importance differently.

These differing assessments may also owe something to the general social context. As living standards rise, the risks associated with the use of a given technology may be seen differently even if they haven't changed materially. A wealthy society characterized by greater comfort than ever before and longer lifespans may be more sensitive to the loss of life and limb than one where accidents are more common and living conditions are worse.

Finally, in the real world, different sorts of risks may be considered at the same time. These include not only health risks and ecological risks, but legal risks. (Will an operator or manufacturer be sued? Will the inventor's intellectual property be compromised and counterfeited?) There are also commercial risks. (Will the seller fail to make a profit?) Issues of (national) prestige and philanthropy may also be implicated. Nazi Germany continued to fly hydrogen-filled zeppelins not only because they carried passengers, but also because they were a great advertisement for German technological prowess. And the inventors of the Pill believed so much in the benefits of easy contraception that they were willing to ignore possible health risks of the Pill in order to ensure that it would always work as advertised, and that it would not fall under suspicion as just another chancy means of contraception that worked half the time.

It is perhaps easy to say no technology should bring about loss of life or limb, but the fundamental concept of *accident* suggests that complete control is impossible. Therefore, "zero risk" might be unattainable even if a technology was improbably safe and all the operators present were diligent in applying all the necessary precautions. Though the building of Hoover Dam would be considered extremely unsafe nowadays, major construction projects still entail today the *risk* of workplace death (even a thorough and careful worker can slip in the way of a machine at the wrong time). If zero risk were to be taken literally, no building project would ever be started. And nobody would get out of bed—though the bed is statistically a very risky place since most people die in a bed.

THE ELUSIVENESS OF NEW RISKS

On the other hand, the rise of technoscience makes the risks associated with new technologies harder to understand insofar as they require a greater knowledge of science to be understood. The explosion of boilers on steamboats or in stationary steam engine installations was an easily grasped kind of risk. The risks associated with nuclear power or pesticides or genetically-modified organisms are less clear-cut. The list of modern hazards includes chemical products, radioactive substances, climate change, and the potential risks associated with novel technologies such as bio- and nanotechnology. Judging risks has clearly become more complicated.

Furthermore, the increasing scale of technological systems has resulted in greater scope for unforeseen interactions of the components of those systems. While modern technologies are designed to unprecedented standards and subjected to exacting tests and demands for accuracy, not all circumstances or combinations of circumstances can be prepared for.

In the case of the British Comet airliner, a pioneering jet-propelled airliner of the late 1940s, the effects of dynamic stresses and pressurisation in large planes were underestimated. Metal fatigue was known to the designers and the plane was carefully tested. However, a minor design choice was overlooked. The use of square windows, hatches, and doorways with sharp corners instead of rounded ones seems to have fostered cracks in the metal, along with the use of punched rivets to install the windows. The cracks only became serious after the testing, however, leading to catastrophic crashes—in part because the test flights had been made at low internal pressure. Once the cabin was fully pressurized for commercial flights, the combination led to disaster over time.

What has developed, however, is an increasingly intricate system designed to handle risks. As they become known (sometimes through catastrophic failures), the risks of existing technologies are identified and eliminated or minimized. Engineering or scientific studies, incident reports by users, and inquiries after major failures all contribute to the identification of risks. Incremental design changes, major modifications recommended by coroners or safety boards, and even outright bans may then be implemented to reduce or eliminate the risks identified as such.

Mature technologies, such as automobiles and jet airliners, have often solved many of the problems associated with their operation. When used within the appropriate performance envelope, they may be very safe, but this level of safety will not always carry over to a new design.

In such cases, the major remaining risk factor is the human one. Lack of foresight and short-term thinking favouring immediate gains over long-term pay-offs often lead to the underestimation of risks and, consequently, a lack of preparation for a chance mishap. The people at the controls of a technological system will often test their luck, relying on past performance as a predictor of future performance. In 2003, the *Columbia* space shuttle disintegrated in the atmosphere as a result of missing heat shield tiles, which had been knocked off during the launch by falling debris from the booster rocket struts. The fragility of the heat tiles had been known since the very first shuttle flights, leading to the routine testing and replacement of tiles after each shuttle flight. The flaking-off of insulation from the booster system had been observed before. Yet, because nothing catastrophic had ever developed as a result of either problem, management pushed for the return of the shuttle as scheduled even though NASA engineers wanted more time to assess possible damage and its consequences.

Finally, the societal consequences of new technologies have become clearer through repeated experience. Innovators may promise wealth and prosperity, but it is also well-known that new technologies challenge social routines, threaten the prevailing social order, force the reallocation of resources, accelerate the redistribution of wealth, and modify the established balance of power. These are not the direct result of a given machine's operation, but of the way they are *made, distributed* (sold), and *used*. Thus, new technologies will kindle both enthusiasm and reticence.

All of this (elusiveness, scale, complexity, downstream impacts) tends to shift the public's attention from the technologies or the risks themselves to the people speaking for these technologies, so that the credibility of technological advocates becomes crucial. At the same time, public opinion has become more powerful with the help of various modern media. It is no longer enough for a technology to answer to official rules and regulations. In the past, property rights protected technology from public scrutiny. The person or corporation that owned a machine or a technological system enjoyed great freedom when it came to deciding how to operate it. Nowadays, though laws and penalties remain as a last resort, the owners and creators of new technologies must be aware of public opinion and of generally accepted standards of ethical behaviour.

EXTERNALITIES

In free-market societies, property rights still protect some deleterious uses of common technologies. In the jargon of economists, an *externality* is a cost or benefit that cannot be allocated to a given technology user *alone*. It can include the cost of outside effects resulting from the use of a technology. Burning oil or coal to produce electricity, for instance, has detrimental health effects (through air pollution) and environmental effects (the global greenhouse effect, the strip mining of entire mountains for coal extraction that has led to 47 percent of all streams and rivers in Kentucky being too polluted for drinking, swimming or fishing, etc.). These detrimental effects are shouldered by everybody (whether through taxes that pay for mitigation or through health outcomes).

In this sense, externalities are a form of subsidy insofar as the producers or the users are not paying all of the costs associated with a technology. More precisely, when somebody does not assume the entire cost of their actions or transactions, there is a *negative externality*. When somebody does not enjoy the full benefit of their actions or transactions, there is a *positive externality*.

Car drivers, for instance, do not bear (or do not bear alone) all the costs of their use of a car. They do pay for the car itself, the tires, the fuel, the oil changes, the repairs, and so on. Some fees (for the registration of a plate or the renewal of a driver's licence) also help pay for the upkeep of roads. If they drive their car till they junk it, the cost of disposal or recycling will be borne by the scrap dealer (who may even make a profit).

However, the pollution produced by the car is a cost borne by the entire population of a city, a country, or even the planet (depending on the molecular species at fault). Measures taken to scrub the air or to curb the production of pollutants elsewhere to compensate will be paid for by the taxes of others—who may not even be drivers.

Similarly, the congestion produced by many drivers taking their cars into a city is an externality. Each driver suffers a bit, but the commuters using buses and even the pedestrians in the city are also affected by the clogging of the city's streets.

One externality is the exploitation of a common resource (pure air, road space) by some people at the expense of others. Often, the risks associated with technologies are externalities. As a result, debates about risks may oppose those who bear the full brunt of pollution, for instance, without benefiting from the technology responsible (*e.g.*, the car) to those who consider the cost of pollution to be negligible relative to the benefits they draw from their use of the technology responsible. (This is most clearly seen in the case of second-hand smoke. While inhaling second-hand smoke is probably less harmful than the act of smoking is to the smoker, the "second-hand smoker" bears all the risks of tobacco smoke inhalation while enjoying none of the "benefits" of smoking, however subjective.)

The problem, therefore, is that risks are not always judged in isolation.

IN BAD COMPANY

Beyond objectively measurable benefits and costs, risks are also evaluated in broader contexts.

When an outcome is sufficiently worrisome, studies suggest people do not weigh the odds even when the odds are known. There is an emotional reaction (otherwise known as fear) that leads people to avoid mortal risks whether the likelihood of such risks is one in a million or one in ten million. Thus, plane accidents lead to a fear of flying, however low the likelihood.

Studies have shown that people are sensitive to novelty (and its unknowns) and more tolerant of known risks, especially if they enjoy a sense of control over their exposure to these risks (when riding a bicycle or driving a car in heavy traffic, for instance). Risks that are *chosen* in some sense are treated differently. As in the case of DDT (used in North America to increase food and cotton production, with disputed consequences for human health), we may wish to regulate low-probability risks rather than high-probability ones when we consider that the low-probability risk is an unnecessary one (Is cheaper food a *necessity*? Is cheaper cotton?), while the high-probability risk (the health consequences of eating too much or exercising too little) is one that is *chosen*, and necessary to our sense of individual freedom.

As a consequence, relative to existing measures of risk significance, people have been shown to significantly underrate everyday risks and overrate new ones. In the absence of accumulated experience with a risk factor, people are forced to evaluate risks on other bases. The *associations* of a risk factor are among these other bases used for informal risk assessment.

Nuclear power proved to be not only worrisome for the public, but even fearsome and hateful. The strength of the backlash may be explained by the fact that its benefits were oversold ("too cheap to meter") and yet that it could not be detached from the specter of the Bomb and mutually assured destruction (MAD). The Cold War linked it with the Bomb with such force that an overestimation of its dangers was probably unavoidable. The nuclear accidents of the 1980s only reinforced this tendency and the Fukushima reactor breakdowns will probably affect public attitudes in the same way even though their consequences have proven manageable so far, albeit at significant human cost.

Pesticides were oversold in a very similar fashion. As opposition mounted, a link was also sought with the poison gases used during both World Wars, though the molecular family relationship did not prove as convincing to the public as the link forged between nuclear power and nuclear destruction.

Overselling new technologies has come to generate almost automatic mistrust, independently of their merits. Attempts to avoid suspicion can breed suspicion. (When companies refuse to label foods containing GMOs, people ask instead what the companies have to hide.)

Suspicion is likely fostered by the fact that the companies most liable to have to defend themselves publicly are often the ones in real trouble. Furthermore, companies that cannot ameliorate their product (asbestos, cigarettes) may have to choose between continued denial and going under. The result of excessive spin and outright denial of the facts can only be generalized distrust.

Linkages remain powerful. When they were first marketed, microwave ovens were sometimes disparaged as a dangerous piece of new technology. Even though microwave radiation is very different from nuclear radiation, people made a connection that became manifest when they spoke of *"nuking"* the food placed in a microwave oven. (Unsurprisingly, a technology that is much more closely related to nuclear technology, such as food irradiation by gamma rays, generates even more intense opposition.)

Genetically-modified organisms (GMOs) came to the public's attention as a product of agribusiness and the food processing industry. They also came to the fore at the time of the mad cow scare in Europe, just as the issue of healthy eating was being raised more and more in connection with serious ailments including cancer, heart disease, and obesity. Though GMOs were touted for their potential health benefits, since they made it possible to use lesser amounts of broad-spectrum insecticides and less toxic herbicides (though in greater quantities), their application to increased production was quickly linked with the emphasis on mass production that had led to herbivores eating the remains of other herbivores, thereby fostering the spread of BSE (bovine spongiform encephalopathy) among the cow herds of Great Britain.

Though the risks of some technologies are real, there does seem to be an additional psychological or historical component to their perception. Insofar as the known risks of death and injury are concerned, we accept a much higher level of risk when we drive a car (or ride in one) than the overall levels associated with nuclear power or pesticide use. (Of course, long-term uncertainties associated with low-dose radioactivity and cumulative pesticide residues—with possible synergistic effects—loom large, but these uncertainties may also turn out to be negligible.) Car accidents kill and injure thousands of drivers, passengers, and pedestrians every year in North America. The sensation of control and the benefits of personal mobility clearly lead us to downgrade the risks.

The historian's task is to understand the disconnect between the reality, the perception, and the estimation. The estimation is what the experts will determine the risks to be ahead of time (and the experts have been wrong before). The perception is what the users and the broader public judge, *collectively*, to be the case (whether their judgment is shaped by the unequal assumption of risks, the association with other factors, etc.). The reality is what will turn out to *be* the case—but it can only be known after the debate, and sometimes only long after.

In turn, the historian's understanding should help us to understand the reception of genetically-modified organisms, and new biotechnologies in general.

OLD TACTICS AND NEW STRATEGIES

If the health risks of the Pill are undeniable, the ecological (uncontrolled spread of designer genes) and socio-economic (shift of the balance of power between farmer and seed merchant) dangers of GMOs still seem to outweigh their direct health risks. No toxic effect produced in humans by the consumption of transgenic food has been verified anywhere in the world. Direct effects of GMOs on wildlife (mammals, birds, and insects) other than those targeted by the added genes have only been demonstrated in restricted circumstances (when crop pollination coincides with the larval stage of Monarch butterflies, for instance). Furthermore, it should be noted that the use of GMOs in the field has spared the environment the application of large amounts of pesticides, thus reducing the potential impact of industrial agriculture on insect populations. The expected increase in yields has been obtained for corn, cotton, and soy.

What seems clear is that the genetic engineering of herbicide-resistant crops (corn, cotton, and soybeans) in the mid-1990s fostered the development of herbicide-resistant weeds. By 2003, statistics gathered in the United States showed that 34 percent of corn acreage (the land used to grow corn), 71 percent of cotton acreage, and 75 percent of soybean acreage were given over to genetically-modified varieties. It is perhaps unsurprising then that the International Survey for Herbicide Resistant Weeds in Corvallis (Oregon, USA) later found that since 1995, more than 50 species of herbicide-tolerant weeds had evolved. At least twelve weed species no longer respond to glyphosate (Roundup). It is estimated that nearly a billion tonnes of herbicides is spread by farmers on their crops every year, and that many US soy and corn farmers rely almost exclusively on a single weed-killer (Roundup). This is another illustration of pesticide resistance, apparently encouraged by the belief in magic bullets (GMOs + Roundup). So far, it has been possible to control herbicide-resistant weeds with alternate herbicides and the industry plans to introduce crops able to withstand more than one herbicide. New strategies (combining multiple herbicides; applying them before and after weeds sprout and grow) are also being investigated, along with a possible return to older ways of fighting weeds, such as tilling and crop rotation.

The pesticide treadmill effect has also been observed to affect genetically-modified cotton in China, as reported in 2006. This "Bt cotton" carries a gene from the *Bacillus thuringiensis* (Bt) bacterium that allows it to produce a protein that is toxic to the bollworm, the main cotton pest. Over the span of seven years of cultivation in China, "Bt cotton" was found to require much less pesticide for the bollworm, but the near elimination of the bollworm allowed secondary pests to move in. Within a few years, the farmers buying the more expensive "Bt cotton" were no longer saving money on pesticides because they needed just as much as before to control the secondary pests. Pesticide resistance to a genetically-modified cotton sold by Monsanto was also reported recently in India, forcing the adoption of a new version incorporating two genes from the *Bacillus thuringiensis* instead of only one.

In North America, farmers using GMOs are often required to maintain a refuge that is pesticide-free and/or planted with non-GM crops so that neither pesticide resistance nor secondary pests are able to develop.

On the other hand, it has been argued that, even before the use of synthetic pesticides and GMOs, farmers needed to deal with evolving crop diseases and parasites. In the nineteenth and early twentieth centuries, solving potato and grape blights in Europe often required modifying the predominant agricultural variety of the day. Conventional plant breeding methods continue to be used to respond to new diseases. However, the ability to introduce new genes taken from other varieties or wild relatives of a domesticated crop relies on the maintenance of biodiversity, both in cultivated strains and in the wild.

Furthermore, credible studies show that, in the short term at least, farmers in the developing world have benefited from genetically-modified crops. The money earned by spending less on pesticides and selling more abundant crops was more than enough to offset the higher cost of transgenic seeds. In some cases but not all, smaller farms benefited more than large farms. The general environment benefits from the reduced use of pesticides and a concomitant decrease in greenhouse gas emissions. Manufacturing a pesticide like Monsanto's glyphosate generates four tons of slag as a by-product for each ton of the herbicide.

Agricultural output worldwide has risen, though some have argued that more conventional means of increasing agricultural productivity (better irrigation, selective breeding, increased fertilizer use), at least in poorer countries where the necessary investments have eluded the farming sector.

The fact remains, however, that most GMO research is conducted by multinational corporations, whereas the "Green Revolution" that boosted food production worldwide 40 years ago was the result of work by public-sector researchers. The corporations hold patents on their transgenic crops and they market them on a for-profit basis, whereas the public institutions behind the Green Revolution freely disseminated the new breeds and methods found by their researchers. (In Argentina, where transgenic soybeans were not patented, farmers have adopted the new crops and increased both yields and profits.) As a result, China is the only developing country where farmers are using transgenic crops not invented by multinational corporations. And since the Monsanto transgenic cotton must compete with the Chinese-developed transgenic varieties, prices are lower than elsewhere.

And the only country cultivating "Bt rice" on a commercial basis in 2006 was Iran, even though rice is a major food crop such that any improvement to rice would benefit a major part of the world's population.

Yet, the combination of fears has made it possible to check Big Science in the case of some genetically-modified crops such as Roundup Ready wheat. Canadian farmers were concerned that genetically-modified cereals would be harder to market and might even make it harder to sell their unmodified crops if grain from both was mixed so that consumers abroad would be unable to distinguish them. They were also worried by the high level of corporate control associated with producing genetically-modified crops. Meanwhile, agricultural scientists warned that herbicide-resistant wheat might become a superweed, just like genetically-modified canola had already proven able to escape the confines of the fields first planted with it. (The purported solution is the so-called Terminator gene, which makes the genetically-modified plants effectively sterile. They produce seeds, but the seeds will not grow. However, the gene reinforces the control of the seed companies.)

Organic farmers argued (and proved) that older methods ("good husbandry") could keep weeds at bay in a sustainable fashion without requiring herbicides, though at a higher cost in time and effort. Weeding with a hoe is highly labour-intensive. (Mechanical weeding is said to be technically feasible as long as the moment is judged carefully as a function of soil moistness, depth of plowing, and soil type, among other factors.) The coalition opposed to Roundup Ready wheat grew as consumer and environmental groups expressed alarm over the possibilities of consequences for human health and environmental integrity, and the resulting alliance was enough to force a change of course.

Thus, the problem is found not only in the interaction of a specific technology (genetic modification) and of the existing environment, but also in the *technological system* that it requires. To transfer genetically-modified organisms to new locales means transferring the institutions also (intellectual property regimes, multinational companies, yearly seed sales) that made them possible. As a consequence, the opposition may target less a given technology and its measurable risks than the power sought for a technological system including people ranging from seed vendors to shareholders.

THE PILL, ITS EFFECTS, AND THE BEGINNINGS OF REGULATION

The Pill is often considered a modern medical miracle. The current version of the Pill has been optimized by reducing the content of progestin to between one-tenth and one-twentieth of the original dosage, and that of estrogen to between one-third to one-sixth. (Early dosages were 100 microgrammes or more, compared to 20, 30, or 35 microgrammes today.) The descendent of the original Enovid remains the contraceptive of choice of women in the United States. Of the women not controlling their fertility through surgical means, about 44% took the Pill in 1995, while 51% of the 15- to 24-year-olds used it as a contraceptive. Almost 80% of women now between 45 and 55 years old have taken the Pill at some point.

The story of the Pill is that of an effort paved with good intentions (empowering women by giving them a measure of control over reproduction), tinged with some less praiseworthy worries (about the poor and the "inferior" races outbreeding the First World). Its invention drew upon many strands: the extraction of progesterone from a wild yam by the company Syntex (founded by Russell Marker who had found a way of making steroids from plants); the 1951 synthesis of a plant-derived progestin for oral use by Syntex chemist Carl Djerassi; the direction and financing provided by Margaret Sanger and Katharine Dexter McCormick; the work done by steroid researcher Gregory Pincus at the Worcester Foundation for Experimental Biology in Massachusetts (who had already demonstrated the in-vitro fertilization of rabbits); and the replacement of progesterone by progestins under the supervision of infertility doctor John Rock in a 1954 trial conducted with 50 women.

Yet, the story of the Pill is also the story of the quest of a magic bullet, not unlike the new synthetic pesticides. It was marketed at a time when abortion was still illegal, in most cases, in North America, so that, in the view of some contemporaries, people were left with little choice but to try a "super-potent birth control pill" even if it caused "undesirable and sometimes fatal side effects."

Disappointment was all the greater when oral contraceptives turned out to be not quite magic. Between 1961 and 1968, it became clear that the Pill multiplied the (originally small) risk of fatal thrombotic disorders, as well as less serious complications, among women who took it. By 1969, Barbara Seaman complained in *The Doctors' Case*

Against the Pill that: "To put it in plain English, medicine's knowledge about the pill is still so vague that no doctor can answer the following crucial question with any degree of precision: for which women is the pill merely risky, and for which women is it very dangerous?" Part of the answer had to wait until 1995, when it was determined that a genetic mutation (factor V Leiden) increased the risk of thrombotic complications for some women, which meant the risk was correspondingly lower for others.

Back in that first decade of use, even doctors were in the dark, and everybody faced the problem of weighing costs and benefits (**Box 1**). Seaman quotes Dr. Louis Hellman, head of a department of obstetrics and gynecology at a New York university and chairman of the FDA Advisory Committee for Obstetrics and Gynecology, as asking: "Suppose that the oral contraceptives add one case in a hundred, one case in a thousand, one case in ten thousand to the known cancers of the cervix. Where does the judgment come in to remove these drugs from the market? Where is the safety balanced against the benefits derived?"

BOX 1 ▶ Document: One Woman's Reaction to the Pill's Dangers

"When Mrs. Sandra T. arrived for her semi-annual checkup in her Vermont physician's office in the spring of 1969 and asked for a refill of her pill prescription, the doctor urged her to give the pill up. He told her that her varicose veins were looking worse, and explained that this might mean she was in danger of developing a clotting disorder. He explained that the incidence of clotting disorders in pill-users was proving to be much higher than originally suspected. He showed Mrs. T. several popular articles which he considered well documented and, as he explained, were in line with reports he'd been reading in 'practically every issue' of the medical journals he received. One was a clipping from Newsweek of May, 1969, quoting Dr. Roy Hertz of the National Institutes of Health as suggesting that by 1971 breast cancer may start to occur increasingly among the women who take oral contraceptives.

"Some women would decline to take the pill, based on the possibility that it might cause cancer. Mrs. T. read the article quickly and tossed it back on her doctor's desk.

" 'Look,' she said, 'I don't care if you *promise* me cancer in five years, I'm staying on the pill. At least I'll enjoy the five years I have left. For the first time in eighteen years of married life I can put my feet up for an hour and read a magazine. I can watch my favorite TV program without having to catch up on my ironing at the same time. I can usually get a full night's sleep because there's no baby to feed or toddler to take to the toilet. If you refuse to give me the pill, I'll go get it from someone else.' "

(Source: Barbara Seaman, The Doctors' Case Against the Pill, 1969, pp. 14–15.)

The husband of one woman who died of "a thrombus in the right ovarian vein, which caused an embolus which eventually caused the pulmonary embolism" sued the manufacturer of the birth control pill she was taking at the time. Though he lost in court, the jury recommended that the manufacturers provide a more explicit warning of the dangers associated with the Pill. But the widower is also quoted by Seaman as insisting that his wife's death should not be treated as a mere statistical exception: "She was a real person, the mother of five, not a statistic."

Yet, the story of oral contraceptives has often been one of statistics. Numbers have been used to measure both the risks and the social effects.

Great consequences are ascribed to the invention of the Pill: the resurgence of feminism in the 1960s, as well as the social and sexual revolutions of the 1970s. Yet, those phenomena were associated with other social forces at play in the United States of that era. The civil rights movement, initially focused on segregation and discrimination in the United States South, was easily extended to "women's liberation." The war in Vietnam similarly stimulated calls for a loosening of former rules and expectations.

At a more concrete level, it is undeniable that the aspirations and career choices of women changed in the late 1960s. It is not only that they were more present in the paid workforce—though numbers increased—since women had been working for generations. The most groundbreaking change was their entry into the professions on an equal footing with men. While their numbers in engineering remained low, there was a sharp uptick around 1970 in the percentage of women among first-year students in medical, law, dentistry, and MBA programs in the United States. Until then, fewer than 10 percent of medical students were women, and the comparable figures were even more dismal for law (4 percent), business (3 percent), and dentistry (one percent). In little more than a decade, their representation reached over one-third in law, passed one-third in medicine and business, and registered around one-fifth in dentistry. By the early 1990s, after another decade, women accounted for more than 40 percent of all first-year medical and law students, and more than 35 percent of all first year MBA and dentistry students in the United States. Nowadays, in professional faculties such as law, women sometimes outnumber men.

Over the decades, the result has been a transformed workforce in such professional fields. By the end of the twentieth century, 27 percent of all US physicians were women, as well as 29 percent of all lawyers and judges.

While the Pill was not the only driver of this epochal shift, it was certainly a factor. In theory, it facilitated the management of sexual life, marriage, and education.

Without the Pill, or so the story goes, women stayed away from higher education, especially in professional fields, because financial costs were compounded by the potential complications from a pregnancy or an early marriage, leaving them with stark choices: abstinence, out-of-wedlock pregnancy, or the juggling of marriage (with its attendant duties) and professional studies (that were more demanding than other college degrees). And if they graduated at an age when most of their cohort had already married, they would find fewer potential spouses.

The Pill obviously helped with the first conundrum. Yet, it should be underlined that the State laws derived from legislation introduced by Comstock in the United States discouraged or outlawed all forms of abortion and contraception. Once these laws were struck down, all of these became legitimate. The Pill was only the most effective and *convenient* form of contraception; other means of contraception were available, not even mentioning abortion. Also, it should be noted that it was partly the cultural context that meant marriage or out-of-wedlock pregnancy unduly hindered women—through legislative or social measures such as maternity leave and daycare, other countries had women professionals (such as doctors in Soviet Russia) long before oral contraceptives were invented and brought over.

It is also less than obvious that the Pill was responsible for the rising age of marriage that solved the second conundrum. Was that a cause or a consequence of the increasing numbers of women opting for higher education?

THE PILL AND OTHER TURNING POINTS

Beyond its social consequences, the early Pill known as Enovid turned out to have significant impacts on women's health. The management of these impacts showed the way in matters of regulating and controlling new technologies through laws or government agencies. By the early 1970s, worries over the health effects of the Pill combined with the accumulating evidence of the undesirable side-effects of pesticides to spur a rethinking of management policies in the case of science and technology.

Opposition to new technologies dates back to the nineteenth century. Workers protested the introduction of new machines and worsening working conditions, while others defended the natural environment as well as the artistic and historical heritage endangered by technological progress (as in the case of railways cutting through cities and wilderness that provoked opposition in England). However, opposition was assuaged by legislation to improve safety and ensure the protection of threatened natural settings (national parks were created in various countries).

Genetic engineering may have started like an extension of the quest for an alternative to pesticides, but it is also part of the drive to reduce costs. Cheap food may have greater health effects than the accumulation of pesticides and toxins, but the drive itself to have cheap food has social and environmental effects. Overproduction leads to low prices; in the past, value-added processing of grain might mean the distilling of rotgut whiskey for export from west of the Appalachians to east of the Appalachians. Today, adding value means processing food in other ways (turning corn into cheap corn syrup that makes it easier to sweeten processed foods).

Back in the early nineteenth century, the newly invented steamboat occasioned the first legislation by the United States federal government that regulated an industry in the name of public safety. In the first decades of steamboating, many lives were lost because of such accidents. In 1824, one killed thirteen people and maimed several dozen, leading to a congressional inquiry. A law to ban the use of high-pressure steam engines was unsuccessfully proposed. However, accidents kept happening: between 1825 and 1830, forty-two explosions killed 273 people and a particularly severe explosion near Memphis killed 50 to 60 persons in 1830. A law requiring the inspection of steamboat boilers failed for constitutional reasons.

A new type of argument was provided by the Franklin Institute of Philadelphia—a recent association formed to promote the "mechanical arts and applied sciences"—which in 1831 undertook a series of studies to ascertain the cause of boiler explosions. Its report was presented to Congress in 1836 along with suggestions for appropriate legislation. After a boiler explosion killed 140 people in Charleston, a law was passed in 1838 providing for boiler inspectors. The law did not necessarily reduce accidents in absolute terms, though it was strengthened in 1852. The great *Sultana* disaster of 1865 was still in the future.

However, the law set an important precedent in the field of regulation. Until then, most Americans had believed the government should not interfere with the rights of personal property; however, the boiler explosions had apparently convinced a majority that property rights must give way at some point to civil rights.

It was a first swing of the pendulum away from granting private interests complete control of the use of powerful new technologies. At the same time, it also reflected a change in what was judged to be an acceptable balance between their advantages and disadvantages.

Consider the first Victoria Bridge in Montréal, built during the late 1850s on the model of the tubular bridge of Robert Stephenson over Menai Straits on the Irish Sea in Great Britain (finished in 1850). Wooden covered bridges had been built in wooded countries (Scandinavia, Switzerland, Canada, and the United States) for over a century by then. Though the cast-iron rectangular tube helped protect the roadway, its main goal was to achieve sufficient stiffness to span the distance between piles and sustain the weight of heavy trains (suspension bridges of the time were more subject to twisting). Yet, the enclosed tube trapped the smoke from the locomotive and funnelled it into the cars behind. As coal replaced wood as a fuel for the locomotives and as the power of the engines increased, the smoke became sufficiently bothersome to require cutting a wide slit in the tube's upper side. A few years later, the tubular bridge was replaced by a steel latticework bridge.

Since then, have we learned to change course more rapidly; or to consider that technologies are not set in concrete and can be corrected or managed? The side-effects of new technologies, the accidents they cause, and the risks they pose are part of Heidegger's thesis that technology reveals the deepest nature of things by attempting to requisition them and make use of them.

Numerous train accidents (Tay Bridge), the collapses of bridges (Quebec City), and the spectacular failures of monumental technologies (the sinking of the *Titanic*, the burning of the *Hindenburg*) have often brought about new safety measures as we learned more about the corresponding technologies. Each accident teaches lessons, sometimes unheeded.

The same is seen in the story of the Pill. Around 1970, it was only one of several issues—atmospheric nuclear bomb tests, the abuse of synthetic pesticides, the extension of the interstate highway network—that led to the creation of the Environmental Protection Agency (1970) and of the Congressional Office of Technology Assessment (1972), which were part of a broader movement in industrialized countries.

Yet, the more recent involvement of government in the introduction and application of powerful new technologies—as with the United States Department of Agriculture endorsing and overseeing the sometimes hasty and overenthusiastic use of synthetic pesticides—has led to a new search for alternatives. If private interests and government agencies cannot be trusted, who can? The military? Academic scientists? Is the answer to trust no one?

Or is it to trust, but verify? While verification does not let the masters of new technologies get away with keeping their risks secret, it does not solve the problem of social valuation. In some cases, a new technology will have environmental consequences that are largely accepted because they are deemed of little value to the society at large. The extermination of the Plains bison was in no way a secret, but it did not matter because bison were of little value to the settlers and ranchers coming to the Prairies. In the same way, traditional seeds are of little value to many seed companies because they cannot be "owned."

THE ECONOMICS OF ENERGY

The oil and gas industry is at the heart of most modern industrialized economies, whether as a mere provider of fuel and raw materials for petrochemicals, or as a major economic actor engaging in extraction and refining.

In Europe, many countries import fossil fuels. In North America, both Canada and the United States have had major oil and gas industries since the middle of the nineteenth century. Until recently, oil production had declined in the United States since the 1970s while it had risen in Canada, in part as a result of new methods for extracting oil from the Alberta tar sands. However, the use of hydraulic fracturing has recently modified the long-established trend in the United States, leading to renewed questions about the outlook for greenhouse gas emissions and global warming.

Hydraulic fracturing, also known as fracking, is a new drilling technique with a long history. Perfected by a Houston company in the late 1940s, it involves pumping water laced with sand and chemical additives into natural gas- or oil-bearing shale layers to saturate rocky fissures. The pressures generated helped to shatter the stone and release the resident hydrocarbons. As long as vertical drilling dominated, this method released too little gas or oil to be economical. However, by the late twentieth century, it became possible to drill horizontally and crack shale layers over a much greater area.

The resulting fracking boom has increased the production of oil and natural gas in the United States after years of decline and stagnation. It has also led to complaints of air and water pollution near drilling sites. Defenders of fracking argue that natural gas generates lower greenhouse gas emissions when burned, though critics point to the additional greenhouse gas emissions incurred during the fracking process. Ongoing research may reduce the environmental impacts of fracking, but increased oil and natural gas production will continue to underpin an industrial economy based on fossil fuel consumption.

TOMORROW: REGULATION AND REMEDIATION

Early technological systems modified the environment directly. The American axe felled whole forests, canals connected rivers with different fish populations, guns wielded by hunters brought to the Prairies by railways killed bison, hydroelectric dams created reservoirs that flooded land upstream while impeding water flow, and highways cut through fields, wetlands, and forests. The environmental impact was essentially identical with the technology's purpose.

Later technologies posed long-term or statistical risks. They had side-effects distinct from their main purpose. The first version of the Pill caused health problems for some of the users. Pesticides killed or affected animals that were not targeted, and pesticide residues accumulated and rose to dangerous levels for humans. In Sudbury (Ontario), the nickel smelters produced emissions that turned the soil toxic and polluted lakes downwind from the smokestacks.

Now, we have to deal with what might be called second-order side-effects. The carbon dioxide released by fossil fuel combustion (as shown by isotopic studies), by the burning of (tropical) forests, and by some manufacturing processes (cement production) is not wanted *per se*. And it is not harmful in itself, at least as part of the air we breathe.

On the other hand, work completed as early as 2004 strongly suggested that the oceans had absorbed half the fossil carbon released in the atmosphere since the beginning of the Industrial Revolution, which has implications for the acidification of the ocean and the survival of marine life. Carbon dioxide in the ocean forms carbonic acid, releasing hydrogen ions into solution and moving seawater lower down the pH scale. At some point, as seawater becomes more acidic, small marine organisms may become unable to build bone. Currently, the ocean is estimated to absorb about 30 percent of newly released fossil carbon.

Similarly, while the introduction of genetically-modified crops may reduce local biodiversity in a field, the direct environmental effects of substituting a genetically-modified corn species, say, for a hybrid corn species are probably slight, even taking into account changes in the use of pesticides. Any health effects remain unproven. But the effects of the new genes escaping (through wind-borne fertilization, etc.) into the wild may prove destabilizing to existing ecological equilibriums.

Today's challenge is to regulate wisely, without stifling innovation or technological benefits, while always giving due weight to the health of the general population. The United States passed laws such as the Clean Air Act to reduce pollution. The European Union adopted the so-called "Seveso Directives" to reduce the risks of chemical accidents. In Italy, the original Seveso accident, in July 1976, led to the deaths of over 3,000 domestic animals and affected the health of hundreds of people; over 70,000 heads of cattle were killed and decontaminating the local houses as well as the soil was immensely costly. In France, an explosion at the AZF chemical plant in Toulouse in September 2001 killed 30 people, wounded 2,500, and damaged 20,000 homes.

Remediation is another challenge, taken up by many countries since the 1960s and 1970s, when the impact of pollution became impossible to deny.

Though smog is still a concern, it is less often associated with industry and domestic heating as it once was, and more often with power plants burning fossil fuels (coal) and cars. Even though relative emissions have often been reduced, the sheer rise in the number of cars or power plants has fed continued air pollution.

In many Western countries, rivers and lakes are cleaner than at any time since the Industrial Revolution; industrial waste has been curtailed and special plants treat raw sewage to reduce its toxicity. On the other hand, the increasing use of chemicals in farming leads to agricultural run-off laced with pesticides, antibiotics, and fertilizers contaminating groundwater and rivers. Around the world, it is estimated by the Millennium Ecosystem Assessment that one-third of all amphibians, one-fifth of all mammals, and one-eighth of birds are now threatened with extinction, in most cases as a result of human-made pressures.

In Sudbury, Ontario, building taller smokestacks to disperse pollutants over a greater area was one of the earliest attempt at remediation.

This only served to spread the problem to a wider area, creating acid rain that acidified lakes in the Canadian Shield. Emissions were later controlled and reduced. In the Sudbury area, city lands were nearly barren by 1965 due to the combination of logging, forest fires, and smelter emissions. As a consequence of long-term deforestation, soil eroded easily and the absence of an insulating mulch made from the leaves that normally fall in autumn fostered severe freezing of the remaining soil in winter and overheating in summer. Furthermore, the soil was so contaminated that nothing could set down roots. One solution was devised by Keith Winterhalder (1935–2005), a Laurentian University professor who determined that an application of crushed limestone could detoxify soil; grass could then be made to grow with the help of fertilizer and create a suitable medium for local trees like poplars, willows, and birches to take

FIGURE 1 ▶ The "INCO Superstack" was the world's tallest chimney when it was built in 1972 to release waste gases as far away from the surrounding city of Sudbury, Ontario, as possible. While pollution levels improved locally, the resulting plume contributed to acid rain over a much greater area. *(Picture by author, 2009.)*

root in. The "Winterhalder Method" was applied starting in 1978, allowing the city of Sudbury to re-establish much of its ground cover.

Often, answering the challenge may involve going beyond remediation. The set-up of large technological systems and the lay-out of our infrastructures have long-term consequences. Choices made over the entire twentieth century, to favour highways, urban sprawl, and the use of cars still affect us today. The cost of changing them is high and such self-reinforcing choices are sometimes described as a form of *technological lock-in*. The technologies we choose determine other technologies. Highways made it possible to build sprawling suburbs that were too spread-out to be served efficiently by public transit, thus making car ownership a necessity that led to a demand for more highways. Such a case of technological lock-in explains some of the obduracy of the global warming problem.

The carbon dioxide produced by cars and trucks is incriminated in climate change, a transformation of the global environment that could prove incalculably harmful. Four centuries ago, carbon dioxide only accounted for 280 molecules out of every million making up the air we breathe; today, carbon dioxide accounts for nearly 390 molecules out of every million, and its share is still increasing.

Basic Atmospheric CO_2 Data
(Antarctic Ice Cores and Mauna Loa Air Samples)

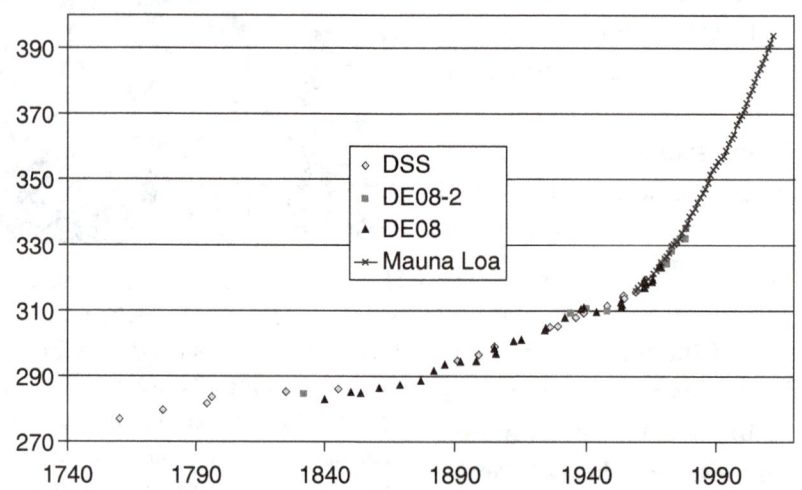

FIGURE 2 ▶ The measurements of carbon dioxide concentrations in the atmosphere taken from Antarctic ice cores (DSS, DE08, DE08-2) and atmospheric sampling atop a Hawaiian volcano cover different time periods (since the beginnings of the Industrial Revolution, in this case) and match very closely. The vertical axis has been truncated to better illustrate the overlap of the data from different sources.

The presence of other greenhouse gases in the atmosphere also contributes to global warming. The primary ones include methane, (tropospheric) ozone, a class of chemicals known as halocarbons, and nitrous oxide.

The problem is a global one and requires an international solution. However, carbon emissions resulting from the combustion of fossil fuels mainly originate in the temperate zone of the Northern hemisphere. Furthermore, even within this zone, emissions have shifted over time. Historically, North America and Europe contributed the greatest share of greenhouse gas emissions by far. As a fraction of the world's total, their share of the emissions up to the year 2000 is in fact larger than their share of emissions between 2001 and 2008. However, the share of the emissions of China, India, and Southeast Asia between 2001 and 2008 is larger than their share up to 2000. As a result, negotiations have been held up by disagreements as to who bears the greatest responsibility for historical emissions.

Furthermore, emissions per capita differ widely between countries. China's carbon dioxide emissions per capita only caught up to those of France in 2009 and French levels were still clearly below those of most other advanced economies (the United Kingdom, Japan, Germany, Canada, the United States, and Australia). International negotiations have also been hampered by poorer countries and countries with lower per capita emissions claiming that countries with higher emissions per capita have more room to back.

Both Canada and the United States signed the Kyoto Protocol in 1997, an international agreement binding major emitters to various emissions reductions by 2012 and 2020. Of the two countries, only Canada ratified it, committing to a 6 percent reduction of its emissions from 1990 levels by the year 2012. However, while the federal government had consulted the provinces beforehand, the federal-provincial Regina accord of 1997 only agreed on aiming for 1990 emission levels by 2010. The provinces felt blindsided by Canada's last-minute higher bid at Kyoto, purportedly to outdo the United States. As a result, federal-provincial cooperation was initially poor and the federal government did not pursue emissions reduction with any alacrity until the beginning of the twenty-first century. As a result, Canada's actual emissions increasingly diverged from the level the country had committed to reaching.

They were driven higher by population growth, drawing upon massive immigration totals, and by economic growth. Unlike other countries, Canada escaped relatively unscathed from the bursting of the dot-com bubble, the post-September 11 recession, and even the 2008 recession, thanks in large part to the resource boom. While the 2008–2009 recession did markedly reduce Canadian emissions, it wasn't enough to achieve the Kyoto targets and the Canadian government decided to withdraw

Canadian GHG Emissions
(CO_2-equivalent Emissions in Mt
[excluding land use, land-use change and forestry])

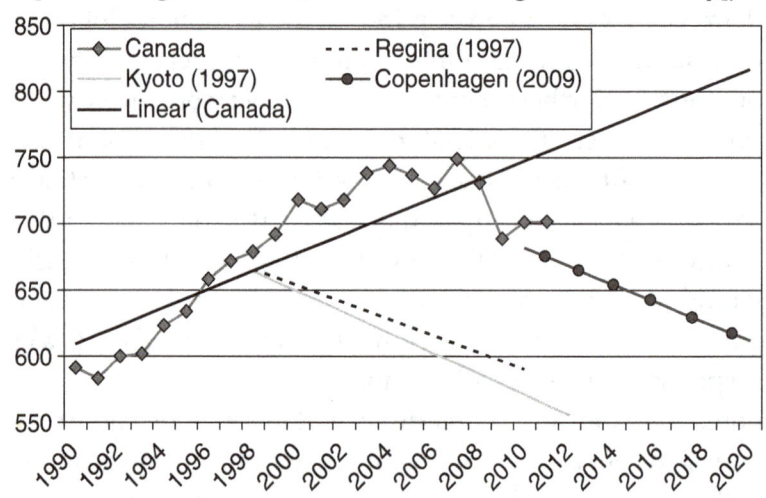

FIGURE 3 ▶ The evolution of Canadian greenhouse gas emissions since 1990 has trended upward while targets set by internal and international agreements have remained out of reach. The emissions (excluding those resulting from land use, land-use change, and forestry) are given here as the equivalent total in megatonnes of carbon dioxide. *(Data source: Canada's National Inventory Reports.)*

from the Kyoto Protocol in 2011 after committing in 2009 at the Copenhagen talks to a new target, namely a 17 percent reduction from 2005 level by 2020.

With respect to the hoped-for emissions reduction, Canada's poor performance is attributable to a conjunction of unfavourable factors. Unlike many European countries, Canada enjoys relatively high population growth. Each new resident requires additional housing and transportation, two energy-hungry sectors especially when supply must be increased. As the economy grows, so does the absolute income that Canadians can spend on energy-intensive activities. Finally, as an oil and gas producer, Canada incurs the energy cost of extraction and initial refining, even though these fuels may well be burned abroad.

In part, Canada's emissions reveal social and political preferences. In part, they also reveal technological choices.

Are such choices wholly political? US philosopher Langdon Winner has argued that some choices compel other choices once a given technology is selected and adopted. This raises the question of whether these choices are made knowingly. Are technologies not only shaped to achieve certain political goals, but also chosen to yield certain inescapable consequences? Or do modern societies simply give in to the prevailing enthusiasm and hype about a new technology while remaining willfully blind to its costs?

Going even further than Winner, in a famous essay, US technologist Bill Joy tackled the question of how to decide whether certain technologies are worth pursuing before they are fully developed. In the face of uncertainty, should utopian hopes prevail or is it possible to find an ethical basis for thinking about the proper development of future technologies? New and emerging technologies, such as robotics, nanotechnology, and full-fledged genetic engineering, share troubling properties, such as easy self-replication and a low threshold of use by individuals. Given their potential power, these properties would seem to point to a high risk of errors with severe consequences. Whether or not humanity decides to relinquish such technologies as too dangerous, the onus is squarely on the scientists and technologists involved to demonstrate responsibility and an awareness of the broader issues.

The connection between technology and politics has also been tackled by US historian Leo Marx, who analyzes the relationship between society and technology as a dynamic one. For the Enlightenment thinkers of the 18th century, science and the practical arts were valuable means needed to achieve a worthwhile end—a more just and peaceful society of equals based on the consent of the governed. However, throughout the nineteenth century, the more it seemed that democracy was achieved for good, the more the emphasis was put on improving technology. In the end, the idea of progress was reduced to that of technological improvements, which were made to stand for everything else.

As technological improvements provided striking improvements in comfort, communications, and performance, progress appeared by the dawn of the twentieth century to be an unstoppable force. Its ideals of speed, efficiency, and standardization were to be applied to all fields. The triumph of technological progress was undermined by the failures and malfunctions of certain technologies after World War II, feeding what Marx calls "postmodern pessimism." Marx distinguishes two strands in this reaction to technology-based progress. On the one hand, there is a basic philosophical skepticism that questions whether technological improvement always equates with progress, thus endorsing a more realistic vision of social progress while accepting that innovation can still be a useful means towards the end of social improvement. On the other hand, there is the view that modern societies capitulate to the power of technological systems by accepting constrained social choices.

Extensive hierarchies and management systems are enabled by technologies that facilitate communications but also tracking, surveillance, and administration. The two (management structures and communications technologies) merge together in such a tight embrace that little hope is left of technological progress leading to greater freedom or more real choices.

Whether such grim views of our collective future are justified, these analyses are intended to open up the black box of technology, raise our consciousness of the risks associated with technological innovations, and foster greater attention to the choices to be made.

BASIC DEFINITIONS OF GLOBAL WARMING

Carbon dioxide is a molecule made up of one carbon atom and two oxygen atoms (CO_2). Plants evolved to use the carbon dioxide in the atmosphere, retaining the carbon and releasing the oxygen. On the other hand, animals breathe in oxygen and breathe out carbon dioxide. The carbon incorporated in plant and animal tissues may be trapped in sediments and converted into oil, coal, and gas (*i.e.*, fossil fuels). When these are burned (for heating or in motors), the carbon combines with the oxygen in the air to produce carbon dioxide. Because the oxygen atoms taken from the atmosphere account for most of the mass (roughly 73%) in a carbon dioxide molecule, a fuel that is mainly carbon will produce about three times its mass in carbon dioxide.

Aerosols are fine particles suspended in the air. Some can be highly reflective, such as sulphates arising from the burning of sulphur-bearing fossil fuels. However, the incomplete combustion of fossil fuels also produces black carbon (soot) that absorbs sunlight and helps to heat the atmosphere.

Ozone is an oxygen molecule made up of three oxygen atoms (O_3). Its existence high in the atmosphere creates a filter that intercepts a large proportion of the ultraviolet light emitted by the Sun. Without this *ozone layer*, life on the Earth's surface would be exposed to dangerous levels of ultraviolet rays.

Water vapour is the gaseous form of liquid water. Like carbon dioxide, it is a highly effective absorber of infrared radiation in the atmosphere, but it does not accumulate in the same way as other greenhouse gases. For a given temperature, the air will be quickly saturated with water in most locations, after which small temperature fluctuations will suffice to remove the water vapour in the form of dew, rain, hail, or snow. As a result, water vapour added to the atmosphere by evaporation (from lakes, rivers, or the oceans) does not remain long in this form. The average length of its stay is usually estimated to be on the order of hours to days. Since the amount of water vapour held by a parcel of air increases along with the air's temperature, water vapour will play a larger role in the greenhouse effect as temperatures rise. However, since it is easily removed, water vapour is considered to play the role of a climate feedback, not of a climate forcing.